Psychosomatics

Psychosomatics

The Uses of Psychotherapy

Peter Shoenberg

Consultant Editor: *Ann Scott*

palgrave
macmillan

First published 2007 by
PALGRAVE MACMILLAN
Houndmills, Basingstoke, Hampshire RG21 6XS and
175 Fifth Avenue, New York, N.Y. 10010
Companies and representatives throughout the world

PALGRAVE MACMILLAN is the global academic imprint of the Palgrave Macmillan division of St. Martin's Press, LLC and of Palgrave Macmillan Ltd. Macmillan® is a registered trademark in the United States, United Kingdom and other countries. Palgrave is a registered trademark in the European Union and other countries.

ISBN–13: 978 0–333–94650–3   hardback
ISBN–10: 0–333–94650–2   hardback
ISBN–13: 978 0–333–94651–0   paperback
ISBN–10: 0–333–94651–0   paperback

This book is printed on paper suitable for recycling and made from fully managed and sustained forest sources.

A catalogue record for this book is available from the British Library.

A catalog record for this book is available from the Library of Congress.

10   9   8   7   6   5   4   3   2   1
16   15   14   13   12   11   10   09   08   07

Printed in China

In memory of Kate and David

Contents

List of Illustrations

Foreword

Ann Scott

The practices of medicine and of psychotherapy centre on professional engagement with individual experience. Sometimes the focus of attention in these practices overlaps, at other times it diverges. With psychosomatic illness, however, each practice needs the other to a marked degree. The medical practitioner needs to know what meaning his or her patient gives to their condition; how they deal with feelings and with relationships, and what their defences are; how their past continues to influence their present. The psychotherapist needs to know what is known about his or her patient's medical condition generally; what might be significant about a pattern of symptoms, and at what stage in the life-cycle; the likely prognosis and medical treatment of choice.

Peter Shoenberg's concern, in this even-handed, moving and inspiring book, is to integrate contemporary psychoanalytic psychosomatic thinking with accurate clinical information about each of the psychosomatic disorders. At the same time, he respects the diversity of psychological therapies available for these conditions and their relevance and use in specific circumstances. Shoenberg argues that psychoanalytic approaches to psychosomatic conditions have helped psychologists, psychotherapists and doctors to develop a psychosomatic imagination. This imagination – making links between *psyche* and *soma*, and allowing for attention to both doctor's and patient's emotions – has fostered a creative relationship with psychosomatic and other patients. Equally, he believes, such an imagination can only be useful if it is based on awareness of all the relevant clinical information about psychosomatic disorders. *Psychosomatics: The Uses of Psychotherapy* is even-handed in its review of the evidence for a psychological contribution to psychosomatic conditions; and moving, indeed inspiring, in its accounts of individual difficulty and the therapeutic potential of an integrated approach to treatment. At the same time, it is realistic in its recognition that some conditions will nevertheless remain with the patient, albeit with modification of symptoms.

Shoenberg's approach is rooted in many years' experience in a psychotherapy department, at University College Hospital, with a strong research base. He is well placed to contribute significantly to the contemporary and legitimate requirement that psychotherapy should demonstrate its evidence-base. Thus, much of the book is a review of clinical and research studies. In presenting such a body of knowledge, the book will serve as a guide for practitioners and students against which they can match their own clinical observations and experiences with psychosomatic patients. At the same time, his long association with the international Balint movement, with its commitment to deep understanding of the doctor–patient relationship, enables him to include the practitioner's subjectivity as well as the patient's as an object of study.

At source, therefore, is the individual experience – be this the individual patient's, or the individual practitioner's. Something of the unfinished, provisional, uncertain nature of that experience is captured in the drawing by Victor Pasmore on the cover of the book. We are presented with an array of lines, in a complex relationship with one another. In the centre is a zone of disturbance – a knot of lines. It will evoke different responses in different individuals. The knotted lines may suggest physical disturbance, psychic disturbance, or a combination of the two. How we make a therapeutic link between physical and psychic dimensions of disturbance is the project of this important book.

Preface

*In some strange way we devalue things as soon as we give
utterance to them. We believe we have dived to the uttermost
depths of the abyss, and yet when we return to the surface, the
drop of water on our pallid finger-tips no longer resembles
the sea from which it came. We think we have discovered a
hoard of wonderful treasure-trove, yet when we emerge again
into the light of day we see that all we have brought back with
us is false stones and chips of glass. But for all this, the treasure
goes on glimmering in the darkness, unchanged.*

Maeterlinck as quoted by Robert Musil in
Young Torless (1906)

A psychosomatic imagination allows for an approach to illness in
which the body and the mind can be taken into account. The poet
Samuel Taylor Coleridge spoke of his 'Psychosomatic *Ology*'
in the course of a discussion of the origins and nature of the
passions (Coleridge, 1995, p. 1444). The Romantics reacted to
the 18th-century revolution in medical thinking, which had so
many benefits, with concern that man was being turned into a
machine. Out of this concern psychosomatics was born. Two
centuries later Freud's investigations into hysteria led to a new
understanding of the unconscious and its role in mind–body
interactions in psychosomatic disorders.

Many acute psychosomatic disorders are short lived and
recover spontaneously or respond to careful medical examination and reassurance by the doctor. Likewise, some chronic
psychosomatic disorders respond to short-term psychological
approaches, the majority of which are behavioural or psychoeducational. Only a few such patients are prepared to seek out or
are referred for psychoanalytic psychotherapy.

The psychosomatic approach to illness has not always found
acceptance amongst doctors, and they have been sceptical of the
claims of the psychoanalytic approach to psychosomatic conditions partly because of its slowness in practice. Nevertheless, the
medical profession has increasingly acknowledged the roles of

stress and depression in illness and has come to value the combination of psychological and medical approaches, even if they often favour shorter term behavioural strategies.

An exception to this has been the development in Germany and Austria of psychosomatics as a medical speciality, of which psychodynamic psychotherapy is an important ingredient. Combined with this, the rapidly growing field of psycho-oncology in Europe and North America has also greatly influenced the care of cancer patients. The international Balint movement with its development in Europe of Balint groups for general practitioners has focused on the doctor–patient relationship, although the increasing emphasis on health targets in some countries has hampered this work because of the shorter times available for each consultation.

Psychoanalytic approaches to psychosomatic conditions have helped psychologists, psychotherapists and doctors to develop a psychosomatic imagination that has fostered a creative relationship with these patients. However, such an imagination can only be useful if it is based on the awareness of all the relevant clinical information about psychosomatic disorders. The history of psychoanalytic thinking in this field is full of theories that seemed initially to promise much, but which were later abandoned because they proved medically inaccurate.

It is clear that often patients with these disorders have difficulty in expressing emotions and therefore have a tendency to use their bodies for this purpose. In some cases this difficulty results from a denial of feelings; then *symbolic communication* in body language may be accessible to conventional psychoanalytic technique. However, in many other cases it is far less clear which mental mechanisms are at work and there is greater resistance to psychoanalytic interpretation. With some of these patients a difficulty in finding words for their feelings (*alexithymia*) may be the problem, and this has led to modifications to a classical psychoanalytic approach. It has also led to a reconsideration of the impact of the early maternal environment on the development of adequate affect regulation in the growing child; with this there has been a growing awareness of the significance of the early use of the body in the expression of affects in the baby and its possible links to later somatization in the adult. This new emphasis on a possible central role of affect regulation in psychosomatic psychopathology, has also led to interesting correlations with neurobiology (see Chapter 4).

There is clearly a danger in trying to find a one-theory-fits-all. In all cases the individual story of the patient is often more relevant than any generalization about psychopathology. Nearly always psychological factors are mixed up with physical factors and so cannot be considered in isolation. Transference may only develop slowly, because these patients fear becoming dependent on a single person. More inaccessible and narcissistically damaged psychosomatic patients may require endorsement and recognition of their hidden emotions in the early phases of the therapy. Only then can such patients begin to make links between their disturbed feelings and their bodily disturbances. The first three chapters in this book trace the evolution of psychoanalytic and other psychological approaches, and include a comprehensive review of contemporary psychoanalytic technique in the treatment of psychosomatic illnesses (see Chapter 3).

This is followed by a review of our current knowledge about stress and the body (Chapter 4), together with a review of the uses of psychoanalytic psychotherapy in the different psychosomatic disorders according to body system (Chapters 5–15). It will become clear that in some conditions there is far less controversy about the uses of psychotherapy (for example, in eating disorders and some somatizations) than there is with others (for example, ulcerative colitis). With certain conditions psychotherapy has a very limited place compared with other psychological approaches (for example, the importance of psychoeducational programmes in preventing heart disease). In cancer treatments psychological approaches, while clearly helping to improve quality of life, have not yet been shown to improve prognosis, and there is very little evidence for psychogenesis in the pathology of cancer (where there is a gap between medical and lay thinking). Where there has been controversy I have devoted extra space to the arguments and to the available evidence.

This book aims to provide accurate descriptions of the wide variety of psychosomatic conditions, and to give an account of the role of psychological and medical treatments (where relevant) in these disorders. It ends with a discussion of ways in which psychotherapists can help the doctors of the future to develop a psychosomatic imagination (Chapter 16). Throughout

I have tried to illustrate the discussion about the uses of psychotherapy with clinical examples drawn from my own and others' experience.

Holding both the psychoanalytic and the medical frame of reference in mind poses a dilemma for the therapist: trying to ride both these horses threatens one with the problem of therapeutic omnipotence, but riding one alone may lead to a therapeutic impasse. Experience suggests that good sharing of the care of such patients with a doctor is often the wisest course of action. However, to help a patient make a useful connection between *psyche* and *soma* takes much time and patience as many of these patients are very afraid of exploring their inner world. Such an exploration, though, may be very beneficial.

P.S.

Author's Note

There is a Glossary at the end of the text. Words appearing in the Glossary are signalled in **bold** on their first appearance in the text.

Acknowledgements

My first thanks go to Ann Scott, the consultant editor who, with Palgrave, invited me to write this book and who has been so generous and encouraging. I also wish to thank Palgrave's editorial team, Catherine Gray, Sarah Lodge, Mari Shullaw and Valery Rose who helped so much to make this book possible.

I would like to thank the late Mark Prior who made it possible for me to study medicine and the late Liz Shoenberg who encouraged me to do so and remained a continuing source of inspiration. I owe my interest in psychosomatics to the late Rosalie Taylor and John Horder. Many others opened doors for me: John Pippard and the late Desmond Pond to psychiatry, and the late Heinz Wolff to psychotherapy and to teaching, and John Lennard-Jones to gastroenterology. My students at the Royal Free and University College School of Medicine and the British Association of Psychotherapists taught me how to teach. I owe my knowledge of psychosomatics to many friends, especially Sotiris Zalidis, Gary Rodin and Graeme Taylor, and the late Regina Woidera. Vital to my learning about this subject have been my patients who taught me by their experiences.

Many have helped me to think more clearly about the issues underlying this subject. In particular I would like to thank Evgenia Boldova, Gwen Douglas, Erika Drucker, Sue Gagg, Jane and Peter Gatrell, Patrice Guex, Rosi Jafelice, Dick Joyce, Marion Kagan, Wolf Langewitz, Kevin Leddy, Susan Loden, Malcolm Pines, Paul Robinson, Gary Rodin, the late Liz Shoenberg, Donna Stewart, Graeme Taylor and John Turner, whose comments on the different chapters were very useful. Special thanks go to Jamie Arkell, Shirley Borgetti-Hiscock, Mireille Colahan, Elsa Gubert, Yoram Inspector, Susan Loden, Suzanne Macdonald, Paul Robinson and Libby Sallnow, all of whom let me publish accounts of their clinical work in this book, and to the medical students in the initial Balint group that Heather Suckling and I ran, who allowed me to publish an account of this in Chapter 16. I would also like to thank

Francisco Vega-Lopez for providing a photograph of an example of skin disorders. The members of the Psychosomatic Workshop at University College Hospital have been a source of encouragement and helped me to continue to focus my interest on this area. Above all, my endlessly hard-working and devoted secretaries made the completion of this text possible: I owe very much to Valerie Fenn, Bernice Levy-Falcon and Teena Ollington.

In writing a study of this kind I am also indebted to a wide variety of experts who have done important work in this field. I am especially indebted to Professors C. Barr Taylor, S. P. Fortmann, K. D. Brownell, T. A. Wadden, S. Phelan, W. D. Engels, M. J. Martin, N. L. Stotland and the late Professors E. H. Ackerknecht, H. Ellenberger, P. Knapp and J. P. Strang, and the late Dr D. Pines whose work I have drawn upon in writing the different chapters, and to Professors P. Guex, K. Halmi, N. H. Raskin, R. H. Rimón, R. Sapolski, D. E. Stewart and G. J. Taylor who also read and commented on some chapters. I have endeavoured to contact those who are still alive: if there are any errors in this text that require alteration, they will be amended in subsequent editions. I am grateful to the librarians of the British Medical Association, the Royal College of Physicians in London, the Royal Society of Medicine and the Tavistock and Portman Clinic who were very helpful.

I would also like to thank the Random House Group Ltd for permission to quote from *In Siberia* by Colin Thubron, published by William Heinemann, Paterson Marsh Ltd on behalf of the Winnicott Trust for permission to publish extracts from the works of Donald Winnicott, and Basic Books, a member of Perseus Books L.L.C., for permission to quote from *Conversations with Anorexics* by Hilde Bruch, and Alfred T. Kamajian and *Scientific American* for permission to copy his diagram 'Vicious Cycle of Stress' from the September 2003 issue of *Scientific American*, and Lippincott Williams and Wilkins for permission to reproduce the two photographs of the infant Monica from an article by Engel, Reichsman and Segal (1956). I would also like to thank Dr Lore Schacht for permission to quote extracts by Groddeck and Freud from her book *The Meaning of Illness* (published by the Hogarth Press), as well as *The Journal of the Balint Society* for permission to publish a modified version of my paper which appeared in 2005 in volume 33 (as Chapter 16), and the editors (the late Heinz Wolff, Anthony Bateman and David Sturgeon) of *The UCH Textbook of Psychiatry* for permission to draw upon extracts from the chapter on psychosomatic aspects of individual disorders (jointly written with the late Heinz Wolff). I would like to thank A. P. Watt Ltd, on behalf of Michael B. Yeats, for permission to quote from his poem 'Into the Twilight'.

1 Introduction

> The word 'psycho-somatic' is needed because no simple word exists which is appropriate in description of certain clinical states.
>
> (Winnicott, 1989, p. 103)

A mother's confidence and care in holding and handling her baby will convey a sense of unity of being and so facilitate an integration of mind with body: this allows a healthy development of emotional expression, so that feelings can be experienced as safe and meaningful. This book is about the ways in which such a state of affairs may be disturbed and later disrupted, causing such unity between mind and body to be challenged. It describes the mental and psychophysiological mechanisms that then result in the emergence of psychosomatic symptoms.

We know from subjective experience[1] that we have a mind and a body: although in health these are mostly felt to exist in some sort of unity and we feel we live inside our bodies, there are times when we experience them as separate entities. For example, in dissociative disorders such as **depersonalization**, the feeling of not quite belonging to one's body can result in a sense of painful unreality. In those clinical states we refer to as psychosomatic disorders, there may also be dissociation between mind and body, although it is **unconscious**. In some individuals, when their minds are too overwhelmed by emotions to handle them adequately, let alone be aware of them, their bodies produce, directly or indirectly, physical symptoms or illnesses: these physical manifestations are considered by the patient and sometimes their doctors to be the main problem. The following story illustrates this.

Case Study

A young man developed strange stabbing pains in his right cheek shortly after he had been to the dentist for a filling.

1

He attributed these unpleasant pains to the dental treatment he had received, and over the next two years he underwent numerous dental, anaesthetic and neurological treatments, all of which were to no avail. In the end he was referred to a psychotherapy clinic in our hospital where he was first seen by a medical student. He told her about how he had grown up in an unemotional family where he was picked on by his father, a policeman. At school he had been bullied by other boys for being effeminate. He realized early on that he was sexually interested in other boys, but felt intensely ashamed of this and could never bring himself to tell his parents about it. When as an adult he eventually found the courage to tell them, he was shocked and angered by their reaction. It was not long after this that he developed his atypical facial pains.

After telling the student his story he and the student were astonished to find that his pains had disappeared. They both could now see that his troubled emotions were contributing significantly to his physical symptoms. Being listened to in this way by a warm and caring person had temporarily allowed his symptoms to vanish. He was on the verge of tears but because of his tendency to suppress his feelings he could not cry. He realized how much he needed to go on talking to someone about his life and childhood if he was ever to change his symptoms, which were psychosomatic. Shortly after this he began psychotherapy.

The Romantics (for example, Coleridge and Heinroth) invented the word 'psychosomatic' to describe certain physical conditions that they felt required an emotional as well as a physical explanation. Theirs was a reaction to the prevailing scientific materialism of the early 19th-century doctors, whose discoveries had revolutionized clinical practice and the medical understanding of illness, by means of new knowledge about **morbid anatomy** (Foucault, 1973). However, it was not until the end of the 19th century that through the work of Charcot, Breuer and Freud we gained some understanding of how the mind could influence the body. It was through their discoveries about one particular psychosomatic condition, **conversion** disorder (referred to as 'conversion hysteria' at that time), and through Freud's conception of the workings of the unconscious mind that this understanding was effected. The following chapters are about psychosomatic conditions and the scope for psychotherapy in helping individuals overcome them.

Our emotions and thoughts are in a continuous interaction with our bodies. We blush with shame, we sweat and tremble with anxiety, we become sleepless, tired and fatigued easily in depression. Likewise, our hearts beat more rapidly and we feel a greater sense of physical energy when we are excited. Under certain circumstances we feel a mental detachment from our body: this is often a problem for **schizoid personalities**. Under other circumstances, for example, when experiencing chronic severe physical pain, we may feel preoccupied with our body to the point of mental exhaustion. In severe and potentially lethal physical illnesses, such preoccupation includes intense fear, as well as sadness and depressing thoughts, about the imminent threat of death.

Some physical illnesses, through their effects on the brain, produce major emotional disturbances and alterations in thinking and even consciousness. Our endocrine system, for example, can influence emotions, so that if the thyroid is over-active the increased levels of **thyroid** hormone will make one feel tense. Conversely, if the thyroid is under-active, there is likely to be depression secondary to changes in cerebral metabolism (Lishman, 1978, p. 596 and p. 607). In over-activity of the **adrenal cortex**, a patient may become depressed or manic when there are major changes in the levels of corticosteroids. The same is true when a patient needs to take a steroid as a drug for treatment of chronic bronchial asthma or for chronic rheumatoid arthritis. In another example, the memory may be severely affected by certain vitamin deficiencies, such as the deficiency of vitamin B6 in alcoholism.

In major mental illnesses such as depression or anxiety there are profound changes in body function. In a severe depression, patients often neglect to take care of themselves. They have interrupted sleep, wake early in the morning, and are tired and easily fatigued; they lack energy and **libido**. In addition, there may be constipation and loss of appetite, with consequent weight loss. In a woman, there may also be loss or alteration of menstruation. In anxiety, there are generalized signs of arousal of the **autonomic nervous system**, so that the pupils are widely dilated, accompanied by sweating and tremor of the hands. The mouth is dry and there may be nausea, vomiting and diarrhoea. There is an increased pulse rate, and palpitations may be experienced. There is difficulty in getting off to sleep and a feeling of tiredness.

As can be seen from the above examples, in both health and disease there is a vital interaction between mind and body, and we are constantly being made aware of our own and our patients' psychosomatic existence. Although psychosomatic medicine is concerned with understanding the influence of mental events and emotions on the body, we know that, in reality, this is part of a two-way process, not least because each psychosomatic condition may evoke the same anxiety and fear as other physical illnesses. Patients can feel stigmatised by a diagnosis of a psychosomatic illness, feeling in effect that they are being told that they are making up or imagining their symptoms when, in reality, nothing could be further from the truth. Also, if such a diagnosis leads to them being referred to specialists in psychological treatments, they may feel rejected or abandoned by their doctor.

Many psychosomatic conditions are not purely psychosomatic: a backache started by poor physical posture, and which has interacted with changes in the structure of the vertebral column from arthritis, leading to local and possibly referred pain, may be affected by a pre-existing depression or anxiety, making the whole condition worse. So new symptoms of pain may be produced by this added emotional disturbance. These may lead to fear, resignation and helplessness, and possibly lead to **secondary gain** (the development of a sick role/illness behaviour) with a complex interaction between the patient, the carers and the environment.

There are also **unconscious** factors (Winnicott, 1989) that maintain a psychosomatic symptom, which make a patient resistant to acknowledging the role of his emotions in producing or exacerbating his symptoms. Such resistance has to be respected by a psychotherapist at the outset of therapy, where there may be the additional fear of dependence on a single person (i.e., the psychotherapist). Winnicott (1989) and Balint (1964) both observed that these patients often acquire a vast array of specialists who take care of them in different ways, so developing multiple dependencies. These dependencies may reflect the significant **splitting** in the unconscious of the patient, and protect him from becoming too dependent on one person alone.

There are a number of psychobiological systems in which brain and body interact, including the central nervous system, the autonomic nervous system, the endocrine systems and the immune system. With each system there are not only the effects of the brain on the body but also complex feedback loops, giving the brain information about the state of each internal organ and tissue and the effects of its regulation on them (see Chapter 4). These psychobiological systems are influenced by our emotional state, which is, in turn, influenced by unconscious as well as conscious factors.

Freud saw in the physical deficits of conversion disorder (formerly called 'conversion hysteria') how each physical symptom might be understood as a symbolic representation, in physical language, of an underlying unresolved unconscious conflict. This conflict was in danger of causing painful emotions which the patient had to deny, **repress** and then convert into the symbolic form as a physical symptom that mimicked a voluntary sensory or motor nervous system deficit. The resolution of the conflict was a compromise which allowed the painful emotions not to be felt.

Case Study

A daughter dealing with the fear of her unresolved hostility towards her mother, who had recently died and whom she had previously looked after when the mother had a paralysed leg caused by a stroke, in her grief developed weakness in the same limb as the mother, instead of facing the pain of her ambivalent feelings towards the dead mother.

Freud realized that such conflicts belonged mainly to childhood, when he discovered that many of his patients had been sexually abused in childhood[2] which, at the time, had aroused fear, guilt, excitement and humiliation, but which had subsequently been **repressed** and forgotten. These conflicts had been reawoken by a new conflict in the present that had provoked memories from the past, causing the conversion symptom to occur. We still see conversion disorder in neurological and medical clinics and in patients suffering from post-traumatic stress disorders, such as those who have been in war zones (see Chapter 5, 'Somatization').

Freud, in making these links between unconscious conflicts and body language in conversion disorder, led his medical colleagues, especially the German physician George Groddeck (Groddeck, 1977), to speculate that other stress-related physical conditions had symbolic meaning rendering them responsive to a combination of psychoanalysis and medicine. Later, the American psychoanalyst and physician Flanders Dunbar argued that the vulnerability of personality in a patient with a certain physical condition might contribute to the cause of the condition by means of psychological mechanisms other than conversion. This led to the development of the Chicago School of Psychoanalysis, whose members argued that specific personalities were associated with specific psychosomatic illnesses (Alexander, French and Pollock, 1968) (see Chapter 2, 'Historical Outline').

We no longer regard the personality as so specific for a particular disease but consider that in some psychosomatic conditions certain psychological precipitants have interacted with various non-specific vulnerabilities in a personality to produce illness. This is because emotional processing and regulation by the brain are affected, leading to changes in the body which then precipitate or even contribute to the cause of an illness or change in function (see Chapter 3, 'The Scope for Psychotherapy in Psychosomatic Disorders').

Definition of Psychosomatic Illness

A psychosomatic illness can be defined as any physical illness in which psychological factors have played a significant role in its precipitation and maintenance and, in certain cases, in its causation as well. In practice, the psychological factors are rarely the sole or even the dominant ones, except in the case of eating disorders, conversion disorder, hypochondriasis and body dysmorphic disorder. Psychological factors are often only one of a group of many other factors, including genetic, immune and environmental factors (e.g., infections) and, as yet unknown, physical factors leading to the onset and maintenance of a condition. Whilst psychological factors, such as bereavement, may act as a precipitant to the illness, they cannot in themselves be considered to be the cause.

Types of Psychosomatic Illness

The commonest psychosomatic illnesses are the functional disturbances of the body in which disordered physiology has led to physical symptoms: here there is no structural pathology (i.e., no damage to the tissues of the body). These are often called *somatizations* or the *somatoform disorders*. They account for up to 30 per cent of all medical outpatient attendances. Some fit into clear diagnostic classifications, such as conversion disorder (formerly called conversion hysteria), somatization disorder, body dysmorphic disorder (formerly called dysmorphophobia), hypochondriasis, irritable bowel syndrome, pruritus (itching), chronic fatigue syndrome, dysmenorrhoea and tension headache. However, many other somatizations elude precise classification and may be fleeting in duration and not so distinct in their presentation. I have considered many of the diagnostic groups of somatization in Chapter 5. Wherever they represent a functional disorder of a particular bodily system, I have considered them under the relevant chapter heading relating to that part of the body (i.e., Chapters 8–14).

Less common but more life-threatening are eating disorders where the outcome is weight restriction, culminating in the rare anorexia nervosa or the commoner bulimia nervosa. In these conditions there are significant risks to health and well-being; with anorexia nervosa there is also a high risk of suicide (higher than for any other psychiatric condition). Here there is significant weight loss produced by self-starvation caused by a morbid fear of being fat. In bulimia nervosa, the patient resorts to compulsive bingeing and vomiting and, although there may be no significant weight loss, the patient may be in danger of significant metabolic disorders. In psychogenic obesity the patient has put on a significant amount of weight, endangering health and life-expectancy as well as causing embarrassment about appearance to the extent of not engaging in normal social activities. These disorders are considered in Chapters 6 and 7.

Less well understood are the structural disorders in which stress has in some way interacted with vulnerabilities in the individual's personality so as to cause brain–body interactions that damage tissues in the body: these tissues may themselves already be vulnerable for other reasons (e.g., genetic). Here there is both a structural (tissue change) and a functional (physiological change) pathology. The different psychosomatic hypotheses about these conditions remain controversial: physicians and psychotherapists have traditionally been at odds about the relative significance of psychological factors in these conditions and the potential relevance of personality vulnerability in causing them. This is because they have a multifactorial aetiology (i.e., causation) which may include genetic, immune and environmental physical factors as well as psychological factors; the relative significance of any one of these factors may vary from individual to individual (e.g., in inflammatory bowel disease; see Chapter 8) or according to different stages of the life-cycle (e.g., in chronic bronchial asthma; see Chapter 11).

The psychological factors themselves are complex and still mostly unknown; they involve a chain of interactions between externally stressful life situations (such as a loss or the threat of a loss, i.e., a life-event), with an emotional vulnerability in a physically susceptible individual. The consequent emotional disturbance, possibly a dysregulation of emotions (Taylor, 1987), causes changes in the brain–body regulatory systems, e.g., autonomic, neuro–endocrine and neuro-immune (see Chapter 4). These systems can affect a vulnerable target organ at a cellular or metabolic level, e.g., the colonic **mucosal cell** in ulcerative colitis, or the bronchial mucosal and smooth muscle cells in bronchial asthma, to produce physical symptoms (abdominal pains, with altered bowel movements and sometimes rectal bleeding in ulcerative colitis, and **bronchospasm** with breathlessness and wheezing in bronchial asthma, respectively).

The degree to which psychological factors have an influence in these conditions is also very variable as, for example, with ulcerative colitis and asthma. This has led to misunderstandings by some doctors about the role of psychosomatic factors. So far, in only one structural disorder have psychological factors been scientifically proven to be a cause of structural pathology: this is in post-traumatic stress disorder where there is good evidence that, if the stressful situation is sufficiently prolonged, lasting damage to the hippocampus in the brain ensues (Sapolsky, 2003).

Nevertheless, in those conditions that have been most extensively researched, there does seem to be clear evidence of a significant role for stress and life-events as triggers of physical pathology in particular organs or bodily systems, such as in eczema, neurodermatitis, urticaria, chronic peptic ulceration, inflammatory bowel disease (ulcerative colitis and Crohn's disease), bronchial asthma, coronary artery disease and essential hypertension. The evidence for psychogenicity and the role of various psychological treatments is reviewed in Chapters 8–14 (i.e., under the relevant bodily system).

Often, doctors' unwillingness to consider the psychological factors in potentially psychosomatic structural illnesses leads to a collusion with their patients' futile and sometimes self-destructive search for a purely physical solution. The management of psychosomatic patients requires careful cooperation between the general practitioner, the medical specialist and the psychotherapist. In this way a patient can receive adequate physical as well as psychological treatment; both are needed in the effective management of these conditions

When we explore the possible significance of psychological events (life-events) in the genesis of any psychosomatic disorder, we must try to distinguish between those events that may have precipitated an illness and those which are likely to be causal. Life-events research (Miller, 1989) helps to make such distinctions which may be difficult to discern from retrospective case material gleaned from psychotherapy.

Psychosomatics has a rich history which is considered specifically in Chapter 2. This is followed by a summary of contemporary psychoanalytic views about the management and treatment of psychosomatic disorders (see Chapter 3).[3] This chapter may require cross-reference to the chapters on individual psychosomatic disorders, as well as to the chapter on stress and the body (Chapter 4) which discusses how psychologically stressful life events interact with the brain to produce psychobiological changes in the body. There has been so much misunderstanding about the role of psychological factors in cancer that I have devoted a separate chapter to this (Chapter 15).

In each of these chapters on individual psychosomatic disorders I describe their natural history, their clinical presentation, their aetiology, including the theories and evidence for a psychological contribution to their causation, as well as reviewing the efficacy of psychological and physical treatments.

Psychosomatic medicine is an exciting and rewarding part of medicine and psychotherapy because it offers the possibility of bringing the mind and the body together in ways that can help certain patients recover from distressing and disabling conditions. Much of the work of psychotherapists threatens them with too great an emphasis on the mind, just as the physician's work can present him or her with too great an emphasis on the body. Psychotherapy and medicine need to find ways to integrate the *psyche* with the *soma* and to work together if they are to achieve a greater understanding and treatment of psychosomatic conditions. To achieve this, it is necessary that doctors and psychotherapists adopt *a psychosomatic* approach to all illness. This book is about the uses of psychotherapy in psychosomatic disorders and how a psychotherapeutic imagination can inform a psychosomatic approach to illness.

We need to help future generations of doctors develop an interest in this subject and find a psychosomatic approach to all their patients. I describe some ways that may be achieved in Chapter 16.

Further Reading

Taylor, G.J. (1987) *Psychosomatic Medicine and Contemporary Psychoanalysis* (Madison: International Universities Press).

Winnicott, D. W. (1989) 'Psycho-somatic illness in its positive and negative aspects', in *Psycho-analytic Explorations*, ed. C. Winnicott, R. Shepherd and M. Davies (London: Karnac) pp. 103–15.

2 Historical Outline of Psychosomatic Medicine

> *Anger, for example, contracts and good feelings dilate the heart; every feeling governs an organ; if the soul is simultaneously on fire, it consumes the body; confidence is very important for treatment, joy is always good.*
>
> Hippocrates (1839)

The history of psychosomatic medicine is a history of the struggle of doctors to understand the role of emotions in illness. In the 20th century we have witnessed important breakthroughs in our knowledge about the physical causes of illness, accompanied by a tendency to solve medical problems by creating ever more specialities (Ackerknecht, 1982).[1] Such specialization has limited the scope for treating the patient as a whole person. The 19th-century discoveries about the unconscious, which helped to understand and treat the hysteric, gave 20th-century doctors a new way of listening to psychosomatic patients which has enabled doctors to localize their patients' pain in their memories and **phantasies** as well as their pathological anatomy (Pontalis, 1981).

Early Approaches to Healing

Before the Greek and Roman civilizations, medicine was based on supernatural beliefs. There were three theories about the causation of illness:

1 *The theory of mystical causation*: illness was seen as the result of a transgressive act or experience (e.g., the breaking of a taboo).
2 *the theory of animistic causation*: illness was seen as being caused by a supernatural being.

11

3   *the theory of magical causation*: illness was regarded as being caused by a malicious human who was using a secret to make someone sick (Porter, 1997).

Such approaches are still used by priest-healers or shamans in traditional societies. Here is a contemporary description of Siberian shamans:

> Even the sceptical Russians were moved by their trances at the sick-bed: the reverberation of their drums as they danced in the fire-lit tent, the fantastical jangle of their ornaments, the weird ecstasy of their chanting. When they invoked their animal spirit-helpers, they trilled or screamed with unearthly similitude. Then they entered a shadow land. They flew through the 26-odd levels of the Tuvan nether-life, summoning the help of friendly demons, fighting off the hostile, and plunging – if they dared – into zones strewn with the corpses of shamans who had failed, until they reached the sunless basement of Erlik, god of the dead. Sometimes they returned carrying the patient's soul in their hands, and reinserted it through the mouth.   (Thubron, 2000, p. 100)

The Concept of Passions: The Greco-Roman Era to the Middle Ages

Greco-Roman medicine was the first system based on a somatic point of view, independent of the supernatural and dependent on natural philosophy (Porter, 1997). In the Hippocratic text 'On the Sacred Disease' (410 BC), on epilepsy, is written

> Men regard its nature and cause as divine from ignorance and wonder and this notion is kept up by their inability to comprehend it.

Hippocrates (*c*.500–400 BC) believed that health was a state of equilibrium of four humours and that illness was caused by an upset of this equilibrium. Healers had to preserve or restore a balance of the bodily fluids ('chymoi') or humours. Yellow bile, phlegm and black bile were associated with illness. The other humour was blood. The four humours correlated with the four primary qualities: hot, dry, cold and wet, and these in turn correlated with the four ages of man: infancy, youth, adulthood and old age; the four elements: air, fire, earth and water; and the four temperaments: choleric, sanguine, phlegmatic and melancholic (Porter, 1997).

Hippocrates argued that every feeling could affect an organ. Plato (429–347 BC) wrote in his book *Charmenides*:

> For the greatest failure in the treatment of disease is that there are physicians for the body and physicians for the mind when the body and mind cannot be separated. But the Greek doctors overlook that fact and that is why so many diseases elude them.   (Plato, 1919, p. 5)

The physician Galen (AD 129–216?) believed that the passions produced by the vital soul were one of six 'non-natural' causes of physical illness. The other five causes were:

1 air;
2 food and drink;
3 work, exercise and rest;
4 sleep and waking;
5 excretion/retention and repletion/starvation.
   (Paré, 1628)

In the Middle Ages, Galen's views about the passions dominated thinking about the relationship between mind and body. Treatments included occupational therapy and entertainments to improve the mood of the patient (Ackerknecht, 1982).

According to Fernel (1592), the passions were divided into *metus* (fear), *mestitia* (sadness), *ira* (anger), *gaudium* (joy), *agonia* (anxiety) and *verecundia* (shame). Each passion was thought to cause alterations in body temperature: anger heated excessively, whilst fear and sadness cooled the body; joy produced a moderate heat. Such changes in temperature were considered to influence the dilatation and constriction of the heart and other body organs. Paré believed that there were also natural causes of disease, which resided in the body's physiology and in the mixture and temperature of the four primary elements (Starobinski, 1980).

The famous physician Maimonides (1135–1204) was one of the first doctors to use the word 'emotion' instead of the word 'passion' (Maimonides, 1963), arguing that emotions could produce bodily change. For conditions in which the emotions were involved, psychological treatments took precedence over physical treatment: for the treatment of bronchial asthma, he recommended the use of perfumes and music and telling the patient enjoyable stories to make them feel more energetic (Ackerknecht, 1982, p. 18)

The Role of the Imagination

During the Renaissance, the famous physicians Cornelius Agrippa (1486–1535), Paracelsus (1493–1541) and Johann Weyer (1515–88) saw how the imagination might produce a certain illness. Weyer wrote a revolutionary text challenging the ideas of the Dominican brothers Johann Sprenger and Heinrich Kraemer, whose text *Malleus Maleficarum* (1487–9) advocated the extermination of witches (Zilboorg, 1967). Weyer argued that witchcraft was caused by mental unbalance that was the result of disturbed imagination. This challenged the prevailing religious view that these conditions were caused by witchcraft.

Psychological approaches to certain conditions were increasingly recommended. Robert Burton (1577–1640), who wrote *The Anatomy of Melancholy*, advised that, after prayer and medication, sorrow could be removed by discussing one's troubles with the physician (Burton, 1931). If sorrow was removed, the passions would be rectified. However, Falconer (1783) argued that apoplexy (a **seizure** caused by a stroke) and fever could be caused by rage. Some of these theories were muddled and inaccurate and often the interventions recommended were inappropriate or even dangerous – for example, Falconer wrote that confidence could prevent the **plague** and that, whilst depression might induce **scurvy**, joy would protect against it (Ackerknecht, 1982, p. 19).

The 18th and 19th Centuries: the Concept of Man as a Machine

In the early 19th century, France became an international centre of medicine (Schneider, 1964) with its discoveries in pathological anatomy and the new physical diagnoses of diseases. Diseases were now classified by organic pathology rather than merely by their individual physical symptoms. These developments were based on the earlier revolutionary discoveries about human anatomy made by the Flemish physician Vesalius (1514–64) whose findings conflicted with the fantastical ideas about the human body of Galenic medicine. Nineteenth-century French medicine was organized into a scientifically based clinical discipline in which each symptom and sign of the patient's illness was related to an underlying disturbance of structure and/or function in an organ or system of organs in the body (Morgagni, 1761). Bichat (1771–1802) and Corvisart (1755–1821) developed a new language of the physical signs of illness (Foucault, 1973). The 16th and 17th century discoveries about human physiology and anatomy, e.g., the circulation of the blood (Harvey, 1676), were used to understand how people became physically ill: this generated a totally new approach to the patient. It involved systematically questioning the patient and then carefully examining him with the help of new instruments like the stethoscope (Laënnec, 1819). These new clinical skills allowed physical diseases to be accurately localized. A new relationship developed between doctor and patient in which the doctor's question changed from 'What is the matter?' to 'Where does it hurt?' (Foucault, 1973).

The discoveries by Morgagni (1682–1771) about organic pathology were refined by Bichat, resulting in the idea that physical illnesses were located in the body's tissues. Later, Virchow (1821–1902) located these illnesses in the cell.

However, the cost of these changes in medical thinking was that doctors increasingly regarded man as a mere machine (La Metrie, 1709–1751). While Volz (1806–82) wrote 'The sick person has become a thing', there were clinicians such as Pinel (1745–1826) who promoted a much more humane approach to the insane and who considered some of the cardiovascular and digestive illnesses to have a neurotic basis. Laënnec (1781–1826) came to similar conclusions about asthma, cancer and pulmonary tuberculosis (Ackerknecht, 1982). Trousseau (1801–67) recommended that doctors should study the patient's personality in chronic illnesses. He himself suffered with asthma and wrote a remarkable account of his own experiences. He described how an attack of asthma occurred in his dusty grain loft in the presence of his coachman, but not because of the dust, but instead because of his suspicions about this man's honesty. The attack occurred as the servant was measuring the oats out in front of Trousseau, who feared he had been previously stealing them (Trousseau, 1861, p. 516).

19th-Century Medical Practice in England: The Emergence of the General Practitioner and Social Medicine

In 19th-century England, doctors were divided into three categories: surgeons (formerly described as the barber surgeons), physicians, and a growing group of pharmacists, called apothecaries or apothecary-surgeons. Physicians had to hold a university degree and were allowed by law to give both medical advice and to prescribe medicine. Apothecaries, by contrast, were originally forbidden to give medical advice and could only prescribe to their patient but it was often the apothecaries who treated the poorest members of the community. Most doctors could expect to deal with mental illness, especially if they worked with rich clients. Poorer clients were more likely to come with contagious fevers caused by **scarlet fever, typhoid** and typhus (Cule, 1980; Loudon, 1986).

The formal recognition of the apothecary's status, giving them the right both to prescribe medicine and to give advice to patients, came about as a result of important Acts of Parliament in 1815, 1830 and 1834. This paved the way for the emergence of a new type of doctor, who could not only learn about and tackle the diseases resulting from poverty, poor hygiene and social deprivation, but also consider at first hand the psychological factors in physical illness, so allowing him to treat the patient as a whole person. These doctors were the forerunners of today's general practitioners. The idea of social provision of medical care did not exist in either North America or Europe, except in the Prussian duchy of Nassau (Pollak, 1963).

The Romantic Movement and the Development of the Word 'Psychosomatic' and the Psychotherapies

The adjective 'psychosomatic' was coined by Johan Heinroth, a professor of psychiatry at Leipzig University, a leader of the spiritualistic or psychic school of psychiatry in Germany (Margetts, 1950). Heinroth used the word to account for the origin of insomnia (Heinroth, 1818). The word was also used by the English poet Samuel Taylor Coleridge who also saw the need for such a term (Bate, 1968). It was, however, not until 1922 that Felix Deutsch introduced the term 'psychosomatic medicine' (Lipsitt, 2001).

This concept, which followed the Romantic ideal, promoted the idea of man as an individual who could not be reduced to a machine. In a letter to his friend Charles Lloyd in 1796, Coleridge wrote:

I know a great many Physicians. They are shallow Animals: Having always employed their minds about Body and Gut, they imagine that in the whole system of things there is nothing but Gut and Body. (Quoted by Nemiah in Taylor, 1987)

The Romantic movement saw man's imagination as an important factor in his predicament, which included his physical illnesses. The psychiatrist Daniel Hack Tuke (1827–95) (whose great-grandfather, William Tuke, had founded the York Retreat, pioneering the humane treatment of mentally ill patients), wrote the book *On the Influence of the Mind on the Body* (1872).

Physiologists such as the surgeon Brodie also made important psychophysiological observations on dyspepsia (1837). In America, Beaumont (1785–1853) reported direct observations on a man with a gastric fistula (a passage caused by a gunshot wound from the skin of the abdominal wall to the inside of the stomach), demonstrating the influence of the emotions on the gastric mucosa. He found that the stomach emptied more slowly and that acid secretion was reduced when his patient was frightened. When his patient was angry, his stomach was more mobile and produced increased amounts of acid. During the 19th century, Bichat also made the discovery of the autonomic nervous system as a separate nervous system from the **peripheral nervous system**. This led to the important psychophysiological discoveries by Stilling (1811) and Bernard (1822) about the response of the body's organs and blood vessels to psychological changes mediated by this system of nerves and, eventually, to Cannon's observations on the 'fight or flight' autonomic responses of the body (1919) to dangerous situations (see Chapter 4, 'The Effects of Stress').

Some psychological theories of physical illness were unfortunately misconceived as, for example, in explanations of the causation of typhus, **cholera** and the **general paralysis of the insane** (Ackerknecht, 1981) and were disproved by important discoveries in bacteriology, such as those of Pasteur.

The Discovery and Uses of Hypnosis and its Effects on Mind–Body Interaction

In France, Charcot (1825–1893), Bernheim (1840–1919) and Liébault (1823–1904) and, in England, Elliotson (1791–1868), introduced hypnosis as a way of treating certain conditions, especially hysteria (Ellenberger, 1970). During the 19th century, hysteria was defined as a syndrome in which there were physical symptoms which did not correspond with an underlying neurological disturbance. These doctors were unpopular with their colleagues who considered this new psychological approach to hysteria the province of charlatans.

With hypnosis, it became possible to alter the physical symptoms of the hysteric, either by removing them or by transferring them from one part of the body to another during the hypnotic trance. Elliotson showed that, under the influence of hypnosis, a patient could have surgery without experiencing physical pain. These discoveries provided dramatic evidence of the influence of the mind on the body. Liébault founded a hospital in Nancy, where he used hypnosis to treat other physical disorders, using **suggestion** to make symptoms disappear. Dubois (1848–1918) used reassurance to treat hypochondriasis (Ellenberger, 1970). Bonjour, in 1895, found that when his patients were under hypnosis they revealed painful thoughts they were too shy to discuss in a waking state (Ellenberger, 1970).

Psychological Theories of Hysteria: The Idea that the Hysterical Symptom has a Symbolic Meaning

Although Charcot found hysteria responded to psychological treatment, he still believed it was caused by a brain disorder. Two of his followers, the psychologist Janet (1859–1947) and the neurologist Freud (1856–1939), argued for a psychological mechanism causing hysteria. Whilst Janet proposed that the hysteric suffered from **subconsciously fixed ideas**, which needed to be brought to consciousness by hypnotism, Freud found that hypnosis had no lasting effects. Together with Breuer (1842–1925), he found that when he allowed his hysterical patients to talk to him, they brought up painful and emotionally-charged reminiscences which, when abreacted (by catharsis), relieved them of the physical symptoms caused by their hysteria.

In 1896 Freud and Breuer published *Studies in Hysteria*, in which they proposed that the hysteric's physical symptoms resulted from painful memories of unresolved mental conflicts that were repressed in the unconscious mind. These memories were of abusive experiences in childhood. He later believed these to have been mainly phantasies of abuse rather than memories of actual abuse. Subsequently, in puberty or adult life, these same conflicts were reawakened by an external conflict, usually having to do with sexuality. The result of this reawakening led to the dramatic representation of the conflict by converting the original repressed affect into a symbolically meaningful somatic symptom resulting in hysteria.

Freud's new form of psychoanalytic treatment allowed his patients to talk using the **free association** of ideas and so to arrive at the painful memories evoked by childhood traumas. Freud's understanding about the unconscious mind suggested that the forces of the instincts were organized in a **dynamic** system in which there was a conflict of one instinct with another.

Freud and Psychoanalysis

Freud's approach led to a theory of the mind that argued that experiences that had not been resolved in the conscious mind were repressed and retained. This approach led to a way of uncovering the unconscious by means of psychoanalysis in which the analyst's interpretations of the patient's free associations, dreams and parapraxes helped produce psychic change.

Freud's later appreciation of the significance of the relationship between the patient and the analyst led him to believe that aspects of this relationship, which he called the **transference** phenomena, were crucial for helping the analyst and patient to understand the patient's early life and previous significant relationships. The ability of the therapist to interpret these transferences (the projections onto the analyst's person of the significant figures from the patient's past) allowed therapist and patient to understand and thus reconstruct the important emotional conflicts of childhood and then to work through them.

Freud argued that the psychic energy of the repressed experiences of childhood was derived from the unconscious driving force, the libido, or the energy of the sex drive. This libido could be in conflict with the prevailing moral laws of society and could when repressed lead to symptoms, as in the conversion symptoms of the hysteric, which had symbolic meaning. Alternatively, the repression of the libido could trigger the diffuse anxiety of the anxiety neurotic, where bodily symptoms had no symbolic meaning (the actual neuroses) (Freud, 1898).

In his later structural model of the mind, he argued that the id represented the unconscious instinctual forces of the individual, that the ego represented the conscious and unconscious parts of the personality responsible for self-awareness and mastery of the environment, and that the superego conformed to the obligation and rules of the parents and, later, society. Different neuroses resulted from arrests in emotional development, which he called **fixations**, at any one of three crucial phases: (1) the oral phase, connected with the infant's feeding from the mother's breast; (2) the anal phase, connected with the child's learning that excretion could be pleasurable and the discovery of mastery of bowel and bladder function; and (3) the Oedipal phase, in which largely unconscious conflicts centred on possessing the parent of the opposite sex and eliminating that of the same sex. This structural theory paved the way for a deeper understanding of the conflicts in the individual between ego and id and between superego and ego as, for example, in depression.

His work on melancholia, which linked depression to **object loss** and grief, gave psychiatrists a new understanding of the depressive patient's attacks on himself, helping understanding of how these self-attacks were a way of working through an actual or symbolic loss of an object that had once been ambivalently loved but lost (Freud, 1917 [1915]). These discoveries also proved helpful in the eventual understanding of the psychopathology of hypochondriasis (Luban-Plozza et al., 1992).

This model of unconscious conflict, symbolically expressed in conversion hysteria in which a physical symptom had meaning, had significant consequences for thinking about psychosomatics. It led Freud's followers to look at other physical disorders in which emotional factors might be relevant and which might also be interpreted symbolically. Freud's model stressed the role of the individual's relationships to others in childhood and in adult life and also the effects of psychological conflicts and the loss of relationships on the individual's psychological state. This role of loss and life-events would later prove to be crucial for understanding the precipitation of psychosomatic disorders, particularly in the work of the psychoanalyst and physician Engel on the precipitation of episodes of ulcerative colitis (Engel, 1955). Freud's conception of transference and countertransference paved the way for understanding the role of the doctor–patient relationship in determining a patient's physical health (Balint, 1964).

Early Theories of Psychotherapy and Psychosomatics: The Symbolic Meaning of Physical Symptoms

Although Freud differentiated between the symbolic significance of the physical symptoms of the hysteric and the non-symbolic meaning of the physical symptoms of anxiety, his understanding of the symbolic meaning of the hysteric symptoms appealed to followers like Groddeck (1866–1934) and Ferenczi (1873–1933). In 1913, Groddeck, an established physician in Germany, was reading Freud's *Psychopathology of Everyday Life* as well as *The Interpretation of Dreams*. Shortly after this he began a long correspondence with Freud, leading to their lifelong friendship (Schacht in Groddeck, 1977). Groddeck wrote:

> The distinction between body and mind is only verbal and not essential, but body and mind are one unit that contains an It, a force which lives us while we believe we are living. (Groddeck, 1977)

Groddeck's conception of 'the It' as a force underlying all illness was broader than Freud's conception of the Id. The It was seen as an instinctual force in the neurotic's illness as well as a more general life-force. Groddeck argued that all illnesses had a meaning (Groddeck, [1925] 1977). He wrote in his 1925 paper 'The Meaning of Illness' about the unconscious forces at work that might lead someone to fracture their femur by falling. He argued that the person sought to be helpless and to gain attention from and security in adults: illness not only signalled a return to the helplessness of childhood but was also a symbol of an individual's death. All this could be interpreted for the patient and such interpretations might form the basis of psychotherapy for organic illness. However, Groddeck failed to differentiate between the unconscious factors in such self-inflicted injuries and the unconscious factors in less self-determined physical illnesses. Freud wrote to Groddeck on 5 June 1917:

> Your experience does not take you any further than the realisation that the psychological factor is of an imaginably great importance also in the origin of organic disease. Yet does it cause these illnesses by itself, does this invalidate the distinction between mental and somatic in any way? It seems to me as wilful completely to spiritualise nature as radically to despiritualise it. Let's leave it its extraordinary variety which reaches from the inanimate to the organic and living, from the physical life to the spiritual. Certainly the unconscious is the proper mediator between the somatic and the mental, perhaps the long sought 'missing link'. Yet because we have seen this at last, should we no longer see anything else? (Freud, quoted in Groddeck, 1977)

The psychiatrist Kretchmer, famed for his studies of the way in which body build might be related to personality and mental illness in an individual, also tackled psychosomatic problems with psychotherapy as did other early psychoanalysts such as Felix Deutsch, Ernst Simmel and Sandor Ferenczi (Ackerknecht, 1982).

Whilst Freud believed that conversion could not occur before the Oedipus complex had taken place, Abraham (1927), Fenichel (1945) and Ferenczi (1955) argued that unresolved **pregenital conflicts** could influence organs to cause what were described as 'organ neuroses'.

The psychoanalyst Flanders Dunbar argued that unique personality types might be associated with given diseases (Dunbar, 1943). The Chicago Psychoanalytic school of Alexander, French and Pollock took this one step further to argue that in seven psychosomatic conditions (bronchial asthma, eczema, ulcerative colitis, peptic ulcer, rheumatoid arthritis, thyrotoxicosis and essential hypertension) a specific personality type with underlying non-hysterical unconscious conflicts was associated with each of the seven conditions (Alexander, French and Pollock, 1968). However, their conclusions were not substantiated by subsequent clinical observations.

Felix Deutsch (Deutsch, 1959) argued that conversion and symbolization determined the choice of organ in psychosomatic illness. However, he argued that in these illnesses there was an additional physiological regression and that constitutional factors were important in causing the illness to take place. His main theory of psychosomatic psychopathology was that symbolization was the mechanism for overcoming real or threatened object loss by a process of retrojection. The lost object was symbolically represented by a body part, cathected with aggressive and libidinous energy, so changing its function (Taylor, 1987).

However, as Taylor points out, as early as 1939 Glover had argued that psychosomatic disorders had no psychic content and so could not be thought about in the same way as psychoneuroses (Glover, 1939). Glover felt that in the psychosomatic disorder there was an underlying narcissistic character structure. Others (Reiser, 1975, 1978; Hunter, 1979; Weiner, 1982) also argued that bodily events became only *secondarily* linked to phantasy and affect the patient with a psychosomatic disorder, and that symbolisation played no role in initiating these conditions. By contrast, Garma (1953) and Sperling (1978) continued to argue for symbolic meaning in all psychosomatic diseases.

In the 1960s, Marty and de M'Uzan in Paris proposed that a single personality difficulty might be associated with the development of psychosomatic illness, namely 'la pensée opératoire', characterized by a lack of fantasy life and difficulty in free associating, with a utilitarian style of thinking (Marty and de M'Uzan, 1963). In Boston in the 1970s, Nemiah and Sifneos came to similar conclusions, finding that patients with psychosomatic disorders had difficulty in finding words for their feelings as a result of an *'alexithymic personality'*, which rendered these patients unresponsive to a classical psychoanalytic approach in psychodynamic psychotherapy (Nemiah and Sifneos, 1970). This personality type could be reliably assessed by psychological testing (Taylor and Bagby, 1988; Taylor, Bagby and Parker, 1992; Taylor, Bagby and Luminet, 2000).

Conclusions

The early psychoanalytic pioneers ushered in a new era of psychosomatic medicine, prompting the next generation of psychoanalysts and psychosomatists to consider new ways in which psychotherapy might help the psychosomatic patient. This new psychological approach allowed the doctor to do more than localize, identify and treat physical illness; it involved listening and relating to the patient and relied on an appreciation of the patient's unconscious emotions and conflicts. This provided doctors with a way of developing a psychosomatic approach to patients.

Much more recent discoveries about the immune system and its regulation by the brain (Ader and Cohen, 1975) as well as the discoveries about the neurochemistry of the brain centres for emotion (Sapolski, 2003), have enabled us to understand how stress causes the brain to bring about change in the body. Also, the recognition of the link between depression and certain illnesses such as **myocardial infarction** has helped find new ways of improving the prognosis for these conditions (Stansfield and Fuhrer, 2002).

This new specialization of psychosomatic medicine would be divided between psychotherapists, with their new techniques for listening to the patient, and GPs with an interest in psychosomatics who were also influenced by psychoanalysis (by the work of Michael Balint in England and Alexander Mitscherlich in Germany). Mainstream psychiatry has continued to focus on the psychological reactions of the patient's medical illness and has developed a sub-speciality, liaison-consultation psychiatry (Lipowski, 1977), as has clinical psychology, which has developed its own specialty of health psychology.

In certain centres, these different professionals collaborated to develop the specialization of psychosomatic medicine in the hospital setting (Stephanos, 1989) as well as in general practice. In the USA, the publication of Dunbar's 'Psychosomatic Diagnosis' (Dunbar, 1943), together with the foundation by Alexander of the Chicago Institute of Psychoanalysis, established psychosomatics and its new journal, *The Journal of Psychosomatic Medicine*, first published in 1939. In Germany, France and other European countries, psychosomatic inpatient and outpatient treatment units, run by specialists in internal medicine and psychotherapy, were developed after World War II (see Chapter 3). In 1953 in the USA the new journal *Psychosomatics* appeared; in England, *The Journal of Psychosomatic Research* was first published in 1956, and in Europe a new journal, *Psychotherapy and Psychosomatics,* was started. Although the recent vogue for managed care in the provision of health services in the UK and the USA has encouraged a new separation of mental health professionals from the general medical hospitals and funding for American psychosomatic research has dwindled (Brown, 2000), the psychosomatic movement has remained a powerful force in encouraging a psychosomatic approach to all patients.

Further Reading

Ackerknecht, E. H. (1982) 'The history of psychosomatic medicine', *Psychological Medicine*, 12: 17–24.

Ellenberger, H. (1970) *The Discovery of the Unconscious*, Chapters 2, 3 and 4 (New York: Basic Books).

Groddeck, G. (1988) *Selected Psychoanalytic Writings: The Meaning of Illness*, ed. L. Schacht (London: Karnac).
Porter, R. (1997) *The Greatest Benefit to Mankind* (London: Harper Collins).

3 The Scope for Psychotherapy with Psychosomatic Patients: Psychotherapeutic Technique

As such a variety of psychosomatic conditions have multi-factorial causation, the same mental mechanism is unlikely to be involved in each of the different disorders. It follows that one psychological approach cannot work for all conditions. The fact that there are also physical, as well as psychological, causal factors in many disorders means that a purely psychological approach is not sufficient.

Each condition has a range of severity and chronicity and this has implications: at one extreme of somatization a mild and acute psychosomatic symptom may respond to simple reassurance and never recur. At the other extreme, a psychosomatic symptom that is chronic, severe and disabling with secondary gain, leading to multiple consultations, may require a more complex rehabilitative approach involving psychological and physical techniques. For instance, at one extreme of psychosomatic structural disorder a patient may cope perfectly adequately when given medication, support and follow-up from their GP. Conversely, where there is major tissue damage, disability and systemic complications, such patients will require not only treatment by their GP but often also regular inpatient admissions to specialist units. In such cases, psychotherapy may be contra-indicated. Some patients with a psychosomatic disorder may have a psychotic potential that will also present a contra-indication for therapy.

Between these two extremes are patients with chronic and sometimes recurrent psychosomatic symptoms (either as a result of a somatization or as a result of structural pathology) that may respond to both short- and long-term psychodynamic interventions in addition to any relevant physical treatments. Many patients ask for or are only offered psychotropic medication (e.g., antidepressants) or else short-term cognitive behavioural psychological approaches by their GP. In some conditions such treatments may result in major improvements in the symptoms as well as the quality of life (e.g., bulimia nervosa, chronic fatigue syndrome and some forms of hypochondriasis). For others, including some somatizations, anorexia nervosa and some psychosomatic structural disorders (e.g., ulcerative colitis and asthma), a psychoanalytic approach can be very helpful.

In such cases, psychosomatic patients are highly ambivalent and often hesitant about embarking on psychotherapy,[1] fearing the psychological implications of such a commitment, both in terms of how their physical symptom might be regarded of as well as fearing the possibility of becoming too dependent on a therapist. Referral to the psychotherapist is often a last resort on the part of the general practitioner, or comes at the end of a long sequence of consultations with physicians and surgeons and a host of futile investigations and treatments. Often the patient arrives rather passively, feeling already rejected by their referring doctor with whom they may have had a significant long-term relationship.

Such an approach must take into account the special feature of *resistance*. Winnicott commented on this resistance in his paper on psychosomatic disorders (1989). He argued that appreciating this resistance was central to understanding the fear psychosomatic patients had of linking *psyche* to *soma* and of making a dependency on the single figure of the psychoanalyst/psychotherapist. He observed that they might, as with hypochondriasis and chronic pain syndromes, have multiple caregivers who represented what he called a 'scatter of therapeutic agents' as a consequence of a need to have many dependencies caused by multiple splits in their ego.

In this chapter, I want to explore how these difficulties affect the psychotherapy assessment of the psychosomatic patient and also how they affect the process of psychotherapy. I will examine the current theories of underlying personality difficulty and the controversies about psychoanalytic technique to help with these problems. I believe that no single theoretical approach can do justice to the enormous variety of personalities and conditions involved. Some somatizations, including conversion disorder, respond to a conventional psychoanalytic psychotherapeutic approach in which it is helpful to explore the symbolic meaning of the symptom. Others may require modifications to allow the therapist to make better empathic contact with the patient and so establish a good **working alliance**: an example is the use of a self-psychological approach in the psychoanalytic psychotherapy of adult anorexic patients (see Chapter 6). Clearly, psychosomatic patients have varying degrees of difficulty in expressing their emotions. Some may have alexithymic qualities (a difficulty in finding words for their feelings) but others may be hiding emotions by resorting to massive denial.

In all these disorders the therapist must take into account the patient's own experience of poor physical health and the ways in which this has affected the quality of their life (e.g., in chronic fatigue syndrome or somatoform pain disorder; see Chapter 5). A therapist is bound to worry about the physical consequences of a given condition (e.g., the local and systemic complications of ulcerative colitis, anorexia nervosa or bronchial asthma; see Chapters 8, 6 and 11 respectively), especially when these are life-threatening. The possibility that there may be an alternative diagnosis should be a concern with certain somatizations such as hypochondriasis and conversion disorder: it is vital that a therapist is satisfied that a patient has been adequately medically investigated before taking them into treatment.

Some patients are in search of an omnipotent solution. Those with multiple sclerosis, cancer or degenerative disorders (e.g., Parkinson's disease) may come to a psychotherapist with unrealistic hopes of psychotherapy's chances of improving their prognosis: work with such patients may help them make a better psychological adjustment to a deteriorating situation of increasing disability, pain and the threat of loss of life (see Chapter 15, 'Psychosomatic Approaches to Cancer').

Winnicott said that he liked to work together with a physician who was 'a scientist on holiday from science' (1989), by which perhaps he meant a doctor capable of imaginatively understanding psychotherapy, who would not intrude on the therapy. It is always important to be able to work alongside a physician or

GP who is caring and careful as well as unintrusive with regard to the psychotherapy. In practice, a therapist rarely has such a choice but they should try to establish a good working relationship with the patient's main doctor so that care of such patients can be shared. By the same token a therapist should not try to interfere with the physical treatment of their patient: medication may be an essential component of the effective management of the patient's condition.

Psychotherapy Assessment

> *In other words, my body is not a hero.*
>
> Roland Barthes (1977)

Most patients, as Barthes' comment implies, would rather regard their body than their mind as lacking courage. Referral for psychological help requires tact and sensitivity. One gastroenterologist, suspecting a case of irritable bowel syndrome after taking a careful medical history and thoroughly examining his patient, explains that he plans to run a few tests but that he does not expect these to show any significant physical pathology. When the patient returns to see him after completed tests do indeed prove to be negative, he then explains with the help of diagrams how their abdominal pains and irregular bowel action, while still very real, had been produced by disturbed physiological processes which cause irregular bowel movements and painful spasms; finally he introduces the idea that stress might have caused this disturbed physiology and suggests making a referral to a psychotherapist (Lennard-Jones, personal communication).

Case Study

In Chapter 13 on headache I describe a young woman, Elysa, with tension headache that persisted throughout the day, only disappearing when she fell asleep. She was referred to me by a rheumatologist. She had a three-year history of a severe band-like frontal headache. Her GP, who had a special interest in psychosomatic disorders, had spent a good deal of time trying to understand these headaches which he suspected had no organic basis and had a psychological cause. His efforts were unrewarded as the patient turned to another GP in the practice, who referred her to a consultant neurologist. The neurologist fully investigated her for a neurological disorder but with no positive finding. He referred her to a consultant rheumatologist who, after some further investigations, found some minimal evidence of an immune disorder, namely Systemic Lupus Erythematosus (for discussion of SLE, see Chapter 12). He now referred her to a consultant immunologist, who could not confirm this diagnosis. The consultant rheumatologist then referred her to me for psychological help.

Elysa was a rather tense, intelligent young woman. Although she was preoccupied with the headache, she seemed curiously unaffected by it. Each day she carried out demanding scientific research. She was still living with her mother. Her background pointed to a variety of possible psychological factors for her headache. Her mother had been a heavy drinker during her early childhood. When she was 12 years old her parents had separated. At 16, Elysa had developed **agoraphobia**. She was helped by behaviour therapy for this. She was studying at a private tutorial college where she became very attached to a male teacher with whom she fell in love. Some time soon after this her younger sister had a psychotic breakdown. She was deeply affected by this frightening illness. Her feelings for her teacher deepened but she was disappointed when she found out that he was a homosexual and could not reciprocate her love. Soon after this she developed her frontal headache.

The telling of this story, while revealing much about her past life, did not allow her to share any great emotion with me or relieve her of her headache. In fact she remained deeply suspicious that there was a physical cause for her headaches which had yet to be discovered. She complained to me that her headache was no better and that she did not trust my approach. She felt abandoned by her doctor.

At the fourth assessment she told me that not only was the headache worse but that she had now developed nausea over the last 48 hours. I now wondered whether the headaches were psychogenic and was concerned that there might be raised intracranial tension. I examined her optic fundi (the visible part of the optic nerve at the back of the eye) to see whether there was any evidence for this and convinced myself that she indeed had blurred margins to her optic discs (a sign of raised intracranial pressure). I referred her to the casualty department, where the doctor agreed with my findings and made an urgent referral of this patient to the consultant neurologist. However, he could find no evidence of raised intracranial tension and decided that my patient was depressed and started her on a course of antidepressants. He sent her back to the rheumatologist who now referred her back to me. As there was no evidence for clinical depression, I stopped the antidepressants and continued with this lengthy psychotherapy assessment. Finally, Elysa decided to have psychotherapy. This therapy enabled her to express her emotions and to cry about the recent events of her past and, eventually, her headache remitted.

This story illustrates how a psychotherapy assessment of a psychosomatic patient may require a series of interviews in order to help the therapist and the patient arrive at some sense of the patient's motivation. It also illustrates how the possibility of an underlying, as yet undiagnosed, physical pathology continues as a real and persistent anxiety for the therapist. The progress of this patient through so many doctors is typical, as Balint (1964) first noted. Other psychotherapy assessments may be shorter and clearer as this second case history illustrates.

Case Study

A few patients with ulcerative colitis spontaneously come forward for psychoanalytic psychotherapy. Caroline, who had a mild proctocolitis, is described in Chapter 8 (on gastrointestinal disorders). She was referred to me by her gastroenterologist and her social worker, who were concerned about her emotional state. Her proctocolitis meant that her ulcerative colitis was largely restricted to the rectum. She told me she was anxious about taking the contraceptive pill and also anxious that her colitis might at some stage cause a development of a cancer of the large bowel, a rare complication of colitis. She was worried that the episodes of diarrhoea were making her afraid to be in the company of other people. Her gastroenterologist had reassured her that she was unlikely to develop cancer but she remained worried about this possibility. Also her attacks of colitis were beginning to interfere with her work in film production.

Her symptoms had begun whilst preparing for 'O' level exams when she had been worried that the other girls in the class might do better than her. She told me about her parents' difficult marriage and how she and her brother tended to act as go-betweens in their rows. She was living at home with her parents and currently without a partner. She said that she had had a few short-lived friendships with men. During each of them her bowel symptoms had cleared up. This led us into a brief discussion about how her colitis might be linked to her feelings. What impressed me most in my interview with her was how sad this young lady looked. I commented on this towards the end of our interview. She seemed surprised and even disconcerted by my comment and appeared to dwell on it. We arranged to meet for a second assessment a week later.

When she returned she told me that I had made her very unhappy by my comment that she had seemed sad. For her this implied that she might be depressed. The thought that she might be considered depressed had lingered in her mind and had upset her for some days until the evening before an important occasion, a wedding. That evening she had felt an acute need to open her bowels. She had passed large amounts of loose stools over a period of about 20 minutes. After this the diarrhoea had stopped and she noticed that she had stopped feeling so worried and depressed, as she felt the physical relief.

After our discussion she revealed to me that all along she had been thinking, quite independently of her physician and her social worker, that she would like to have psychotherapy. A few months before seeing me she had met a man at a dinner party. He also suffered with colitis and had told her how helpful psychotherapy was for him. She decided to have the psychotherapy which was to help her with her personal life as well as with her colitis which, although it became less frequent, never went away completely. This is not an uncommon physical outcome for patients having psychotherapy with mild colitis.

This story illustrates how, like many other psychosomatic patients, Caroline was afraid that aspects of her physical condition might be viewed psychologically. It is also worth noting that, unlike the first patient, she was independently motivated to have psychotherapy. More severe and extensive ulcerative colitis may present for psychotherapy as an emergency but be far less rewarding to work with (see below and also the case of Janet in Chapter 8 on gastrointestinal disorders). Such severe colitis may be associated with greater personality difficulties for which it is better to plan a therapy that will be more supportive than interpretive (Karush et al., 1977).

As Winnicott notes, most patients with psychosomatic disorders are very afraid of psychotherapy and find the commitment threatening.

Case Study

As one hypochondriac put it to me (see the Case Study on hypochondria in Chapter 5), she was terrified of becoming dependent on one person alone. She had a wide scatter of therapeutic agents (Winnicott, 1964) that included two GPs, a homeopath, an osteopath, a gastroenterologist (who treated her with antidepressants for her irritable bowel syndrome), a gynaecologist, a breast surgeon and an exercise therapist. I knew from the start that she would find making transference very difficult. Also, she had come to me because she wanted to see a medically qualified therapist. However, she was in touch with the depression that lay behind her severe hypochondriasis which had to do with her profound grief over the recent deaths in succession of a brother and her mother.

For some patients with psychosomatic disorders it may be worth considering offering them a trial of psychotherapy:

Case Study

The middle-aged patient, Maria, with chronic irritable bowel syndrome (described in Chapter 8 on gastrointestinal Disorders), which had recurred after the loss of a close friend, was convinced that she needed help for depression but not for her bowel symptoms. She felt these required further physical investigations. Initially I was unsure about her capacity to use a psychodynamic approach and we agreed to meet for a ten-session trial of psychotherapy, before deciding to make a commitment on either side to taking the therapy further. After ten sessions we both decided that it would be a good idea for us to continue but it was at least two more months before this patient was able to make a link between her emotions and her bowel symptoms.

Psychoanalytic Psychotherapeutic Techniques

> *It was a 'red letter' day for me when the patient rang me up by mistake when intending to ring her butcher.*
> D. W. Winnicott, 'Psychosomatic Illness in its Positive and Negative Aspects', *Psychoanalytic Explorations* (1989)

Originally psychoanalysts like Ferenczi and the physician Groddeck looked for hysterical mechanisms in psychosomatic illness (see Chapter 2). This approach was replaced by Alexander and colleagues' concern to identify core underlying conflicts in seven given psychosomatic conditions (bronchial asthma, eczema, ulcerative colitis, essential hypertension, thyrotoxicosis, peptic ulcer and rheumatoid arthritis) (Alexander, French and Pollock, 1968; see Chapter 2). They argued that they were able to identify a core conflict at an early interview and to focus the analysis on this aspect of the person using classical technique. But eventually their approach was found to be ineffective and their concept of psychosomatic specificity for given psychosomatic conditions proved to be unreliable. Subsequent attempts to unify psychoanalytic theory about the personality underlying psychosomatic disorders have led to much controversy and debate.

The Concept of Pregenital Conversion as a Cause for Psychosomatic Disorders

Freud (1910) believed that conversion did not occur prior to the Oedipus complex, but Abraham (1927), Fenichel (1945) and Ferenczi (1955) proposed that unresolved **pregenital conflicts** could influence various organs of the body. This led to the concept of organ neuroses: for example, Fenichel (1945) attributed disturbed respiratory function in asthma to a conflict between intrinsic physiological need and the unconscious wish towards an introjected but ambivalently regarded love object incorporated through the respiratory tract. Felix Deutsch (1927) also felt that there were pregenital determinants to conversion that determined the choice of organ in a psychosomatic illness (see also Chapter 2).

Melitta Sperling (1973, 1978) concluded that such pregenital conflicts were *converted* into symptoms which became symbolic psychosomatic expressions, just as sexual conflicts and phantasies were responsible for the symptoms of conversion disorder. She described a patient whose colon had assumed the role of a sexual organ that symbolically expressed pregenital fears and phantasies through ulcerative colitis. She claimed this psychodynamic constellation was present in every case of ulcerative colitis that she treated. She also believed that the choice of psychosomatic disease depended to a large degree on the quality of the original mother–child relationship. In her view the mother's preoccupation with certain organs and organ functions resulted in an early acquisition of a disposition to respond with a disturbance of these specific organs and functions when faced with a traumatic situation.

Felix Deutsch (1959) did not accept symbolization as the sole explanation for the choice of disease, combining the idea of conversion with the idea of physiological regression when there was object loss. Mushatt (1954), Sperling (1978) and Mintz (1989) agreed with this view. In addition, Hogan and Sperling argued that a medical psychotherapist should retain the role of primary physician in treating patients with structural psychosomatic disorders, i.e., while analysing them (Hogan, 1995). Adopting such a dual role poses major technical problems, even if it avoids splitting carers, for medication by the psychotherapist of a psychotherapy patient is beset with boundary issues and changes the psychoanalytic frame.

My experience of patients using denial and bodily symptoms as a symbolic representation of an unconscious conflict has largely been in working with patients with somatizations where in some cases the underlying difficulties are amenable to symbolic interpretation:

Case Study

Some months after Maria (described in Chapter 8 on gastrointestinal disorders) had seen a link between her irritable bowel symptoms and her tendency to get depressed, she reported a dream in which she was coming to see me but had lost control of her bowels. She was in a great state of distress and rushed into my consulting room where she found her mother seated in the patient's chair. She sat down on another chair and a hypnotist proceeded to cure her by removing all her unhappy memories. In her associations she spoke for the first time of her mother's depression and her preoccupation with her (the mother's) anal fistula (an abnormal very narrow passage between her bowel wall and the skin on her trunk). Her mother, with her own bowel habit preoccupation, also worried about her children's bowel habits: when they were small children she used to make them consume large quantities of the laxative cascara which they both hated. Now it seemed possible for us to understand her mother's vulnerability and how possibly Maria's preoccupation with her bowel control and her constipation might have developed when she left home to marry. Separations were a major problem for this person whose insecurity in childhood was heightened by many early experiences of separation from her parents during evacuations during the London Blitz. It was through this gradual understanding of the psychological origins and significance of her constipation and abdominal pains that she was able to loose these symptoms.

Not all somatizations are amenable to symbolic interpretation (see the section on psychodynamic treatments in Chapter 5, 'Somatization'). It is clear that in structural psychosomatic disorders the physical symptom (possibly produced by a given vulnerability in the personality) is unlikely to have a primary symbolic meaning. However, it will have a secondary symbolic significance. Here is an example:

Case Study

Caroline (already described here and later in Chapter 8) had a mild form of ulcerative colitis. By now in her therapy she had left home and fallen in love with a man she later married. One day she reported a dream in which she was at a dance. All the men were in evening dress and had floppy legs. One of them came up to her and asked her for a dance; it might have been her partner or me. In her associations for this dream she recalled that the previous night she had felt hurt that her partner had wanted to discuss the need for her to take out a medical insurance policy, in case her colitis became worse. However as was her wont she had hidden her feelings from her partner. Then she remembered how as a younger woman she had enjoyed helping out at a dance where there were teenagers in wheelchairs. I interpreted how much in reality she felt stigmatized by the physical handicap of her colitis, perhaps especially in relation to her partner and me. In her dream she had been able to turn tables on us, for we were the physically handicapped ones with our floppy legs.

For her the colitis was a significant stigma. But this was a secondary symbolic meaning. There was *nothing* in the reconstructive work of this therapy to suggest that there was a primary symbolic meaning connected with events in childhood to do with bowel control or an anal fixation as with the patient with irritable bowel syndrome. However, like this other patient, Caroline was insecurely attached and major separations in and out of the therapy led to rectal bleeding with diarrhoea.

The Concept of Alexithymia

In 1934 Meng described patients with psychosomatic disturbance as suffering with organ psychosis, indicating that he considered the ego disturbance in these patients to be much more severe than previously realized. In 1939 Glover had already emphasized that these disorders had 'no psychic content' and described the narcissistic constitution and character of these patients. He argued that transference neurosis did not happen. Several psychoanalysts (Reiser, 1975, 1978; Hunter, 1979; Weiner, 1982) criticized the theory of pregenital conversion arguing that bodily events only became secondarily linked with phantasies and affects so that symbolization uncovered in psychoanalysis actually might have played no part in initiating the disease process. Later Bruch was to argue that anorexic patients are more like narcissistic or borderline patients with a deficient sense of self and she advised against interpreting the symbolic meaning of the patient's refusal of food.

In 1963 two French psychoanalysts, Marty and de M'Uzan, noted a group of personality characteristics common to many psychosomatic patients. They noticed that they lacked phantasies and that their associations were often tethered to everyday reality and a recital of the activities of the day. They spoke initially of *la pensée opératoire*. Later Marty and DeBray (1989) changed this to the concept of *la vie opératoire*.[2]

Two American psychoanalysts, Nemiah and Sifneos (1970; Nemiah, 1973) found similar personality characteristics. Sifneos called these personalities alexithymic, by which he meant that they had an incapacity to find words for their feelings. He noted the following characteristics:

1 often they gave an endless description of their physical symptoms;
2 they also complained of tension, irritability, frustration, pain, a feeling of a void, restlessness, agitation and nervousness;
3 there was an absence of phantasy and an elaborate description of trivial environmental detail (like *la pensée opératoire*);
4 there was marked difficulty in finding appropriate words to describe feelings;
5 crying was rare but when it happened it seemed not to be related to the appropriate feelings;
6 dreaming was rare;

7   the affect was inappropriate;

8   activity: it was noted that these patients had a tendency to
act impulsively and that action was a predominant way of
life for them;

9   interpersonal relations: these were poor or else over-
dependent or avoidant in style;

10   countertransference: the therapists often found themselves feeling bored.

Hogan, believing in the role of pregenital conversion in
symptom formation in inflammatory bowel disease, argues that
alexithymia is an overgeneralization which might lead the
therapist and the patient to **denying** or avoiding looking at
latent subjective mental content that might in fact be available
(Hogan, 1995). It is clear that many patients with psychosomatic
symptoms are not alexithymic and that alexithymia does not
necessarily lead to psychosomatic illness. Proponents of this
concept have argued that in a psychosomatic patient only a part
of their personality may function at an alexithymic level (Taylor,
1987). Here is an illustration of a patient who might be considered to be alexithymic:

Case Study

Sheila was a student who developed Crohn's disease (see
Chapter 8) during her final year of accountancy studies. Her
parents split up during her adolescence. She came to see me
because her father, with whom she lived, wanted her to see a
psychotherapist. The father, whom she much admired, was a
powerful hospital administrator with whose wishes she felt
she must always comply. He was also a man who drank
heavily, was depressed and tended to work too hard. Her
mother had remarried and was living in another country. In
the year before seeing me she had noticed that whenever she
felt stressed she developed bouts of diarrhoea. Two months
before coming to see me she had had a severe attack of
diarrhoea with rectal bleeding and abdominal pains; Crohn's
disease was diagnosed. Also, during the year before she saw
me, she had developed a tendency to being depressed. She was
under some psychological pressure as she was preparing for

her final exams. However, because of her illness she had only been able to take one paper that summer, postponing the rest until the following summer. She felt that finishing her exams would imply that she had grown up. It had also been a very stressful year because during this time she had fallen in love for the first time with a boy called Richard. She felt that he was able to draw her out of herself. She became jealous when he got interested in another girl and then seemed to lose interest in her and had not seen her for some weeks. In addition to all this Sheila's only brother, with whom she was very close, had developed multiple sclerosis the previous year and everyone in the family was worried about this.

She was a shy, withdrawn, sensitive and intelligent young woman. She seemed to affect a cool manner, speaking quietly and sometimes monotonously, which made me feel sleepy at times. In the initial consultation she smiled briefly when I told her that I thought we were both in a difficult situation as she seemed to have come to me rather like a package sent by her father. She said, however, that she had been thinking that she would like to come and see what therapy was all about. She wondered if the stress she was under could have caused her Crohn's disease, so we agreed to meet for a few sessions of psychotherapy as a trial.

Our first session concerned her relationship with the boyfriend and her fear of being rejected by him. I tried to link this to my sense of her general fear of being rejected by her family and to the comment she had made about her father being a distant person. She agreed with this. In the next session she told me she had always been shy, particularly after being sent to a boarding school at the age of 13. There she had made two friends but they had subsequently begun to tease her, which had only increased her shyness. When her parents split up she felt angry with her father who later had a nervous breakdown. She could remember crying only once during this time but never again. She told me that as a small child she used to cry a lot and that this used to anger her mother. She said that meeting her boyfriend had made her feel happy for the first time in her life. She seemed keen at this point to commit herself to therapy and so we planned to embark on this on a twice-weekly basis.

In the next session she told me how difficult it was to be spontaneous, especially when she was with a group of people. She told me how, the previous weekend, she had been to another town to stay with her best friend. When they had joined a group of her friend's friends, she found herself trying too hard to please them. She told me how hard she had tried to please her father and how very hurt she had been when her father had dismissed her relationship with her new boyfriend, refusing to allow him to stay in the house. As Sheila could never get angry with her father directly, she decided to stop speaking to him as a way of dealing with her anger. She felt she tended to conform to others' wishes too easily and ended the session by saying to me, 'I suppose I'm really still tied to my mother's apron strings.' I wondered if this might be an important theme to pursue and talk about in the next session.

However, she missed the next session and telephoned me afterwards to tell me, rather casually, that she had had to be admitted to hospital. I was most concerned to hear this. When she came to the next session she began to talk about her relationship with her mother and concluded again that she had always been shy. I was very worried about her physical condition. I asked her about this and about her trip to hospital and how she felt now. She replied rather casually, 'Oh, I'm OK now but I did get very dehydrated. I lost weight and couldn't take any of the medicines they wanted to give me. I began to bleed from my back passage. My father got me admitted to his hospital for a week, where I was put on a high dose of steroids. My father always puts pressure on me to get a job and I always worry about what he wants.' I said, 'Do you worry about that here too?' She said, 'Maybe'. She then added, 'I think I was stressed by trying to fit in with that group of friends that weekend. I felt if I didn't try I would be judged to be lazy and people would have felt there was nothing inside me. I can't seem to get to my own emotions.' I said, 'Sometimes what people call nothingness is really a form of crying and sadness inside', and the session came to an end.

She did not come to the next session. I was worried that she might again be physically ill, only this time she did not telephone me. I decided to telephone her. She told me she had gone to visit an aunt in Devon. She said she would like another session but her voice sounded more diffident. When she came to the session she told me she was finding it difficult to connect with me in the sessions. She told me also that she had worried when her friends did not get on. She returned to the subject of her trip to the other town and how upset she had been when her ex-boyfriend had annoyed her two girlfriends. Both of them had telephoned her afterwards to complain about him. She felt the only way she could deal with all this was to get away from everyone and to stay with the aunt, who she knew would spoil her. We planned another session but Sheila never returned to see me. Instead she wrote me a polite and friendly letter to end the therapy.

Sheila's conflicts seemed to be centred on a tension between a wish to try something out, perhaps her new social life, possibly her psychotherapy, and her intense fear of being disapproved of and let down by important figures, especially her father. At this point in the therapy she had a recurrence of Crohn's disease, after which she withdrew from the therapy. Clearly the strong forces that Winnicott describes prevented the development of a therapeutic relationship. By her own admission, she was someone who had enormous difficulty in finding words for her feelings and who was both physically and emotionally vulnerable. As well as being provoked by stress, her physical illness provided a screen for her unverbalized emotion.

McDougall (1980) emphasizes the non-symbolic role of many psychosomatic conditions and argues that in these conditions physical symptoms reveal neither a neurotic nor a psychotic story. In her view, these patients need to preserve their illness not only as a reassurance about their body limits but also as proof of their psychic survival. This is very true for the asthmatic patient described in Chapter 11. McDougall's view is close to Winnicott's in that this might be a positive aspect of the psychosomatic symptom in connecting the body to the mind as opposed to experiencing the depersonalization that a schizoid individual is more prone to. She argues that psychosomatic patients maintain a camouflage of pseudonormality (also used by Jackson, personal communication) which helps them to avoid thinking about the inner pain and conflict caused by threats to significant relationships. If the mother, in childhood, has failed to shield the infant from traumatic overstimulation, the baby is left with poorly defined body limits. There is a foreclosure (as opposed to **negating**, denying or **disavowal** that occur in a neurosis), of certain perceptions, thoughts and phantasies. Body signals of anxiety have not been dealt with in ways that give meaning to early experience, and psychic pain cannot be communicated; consequently the defences of primitive splitting and **projective identification** predominate. Later in life psychic pain and mental conflicts are likely to be discharged psychosomatically or psychotically. McDougall discovered that behind the pseudonormality of the patient there is often an anti-analysand (one who resists analysis) as Winnicott also argued. Winnicott wrote

> One wants to be able to say that the *psyche* and the *soma* (that is to say, the person and the body together are that person) do not start off as a unit. They form a unit if all goes well in the development of that individual; but this is an achievement. We can by no means take for granted that in every case the baby's *psyche* and *soma* will come to work as a unit with the child living in the body and the body functioning according to the child's enjoyment of his or her body ...
> ... There are some mothers, or people who care for children, who make good contact with the baby as a person but who seem to be unable to know what the baby's body is feeling like or needing; and, similarly, there are others who are naturally good at physical care but who seem ignorant of the fact that there is a human being becoming lodged in the body they are bathing and cleaning up. When those who care for a baby or a small child have this kind of difficulty of their own, then the child they care for cannot become integrated into a unit.
> In that case the basis for a psychosomatic split is laid down.
> (D. W. Winnicott, 'Physiotherapy and Human Relations', in *Psycho-Analytic Explorations*, 1989, p. 566)

Winnicott recognized from his work with schizoid and borderline patients how much they longed for a sense of 'aliveness'. In his paper 'Primitive Emotional Development' (1945), he argued that babies initially experienced unintegrated states in which various anxieties were tolerable only because of successful 'holding' of the baby in the mind of the mother. This 'holding' permitted a later integration of the self. Later in life these *unintegrated* states might be safely returned to in moments of relaxation in the healthy adult but not in the schizoid individual. For the latter, experiencing an unintegrated state might lead to the fear of breakdown (Winnicott, 1989). Breakdown was defended against by the individual using self-holding (against the fear of falling for ever) and depersonalization (protecting against psychosomatic disunity).

Complementing a mother's 'holding' of a baby was her physical handling of it. These two processes (holding and handling) in the mother–baby relationship led to the *psyche*'s 'indwelling' in the *soma* in the early months of the baby's life. Then *psyche* could be experienced as a part of the body, with a sense of continuity of being. Winnicott spelt this out in his last paper on psychosomatics, 'On the Basis for Self in the Body' (1989). A false localization of the mind in the head might result from a failure of this indwelling, with a splitting off of mind from body. This defence, combined with an overvaluation of mentalization (at the expense of the sense of personal aliveness), is seen in the schizoid personality and is described in Winnicott's paper 'The Mind in its Relation to the Psyche-Soma' (1949). Such patients feel painfully out of touch with their bodies. For them a minor physical illness, such as an attack of 'flu, may be experienced as a relief as it brings about a sort of temporary psychosomatic unity.

In psychosomatic illnesses emotions which are too threatening are no longer experienced as feelings but are registered as somatic experiences in physical symptoms. While the link between psyche and soma in the schizoid person might appear to be almost missing, in the psychosomatic patient the bodily symptom provides a sort of linkage in which the emotions are not all registered at a mental level (Shoenberg, 2001).

Taylor argues that the mother's capacity to receive the feelings of the child and appreciate their expression gradually enables the child to tolerate them and leads to adequate affect regulation. If there has been an incapacity to receive and appreciate the feelings of the child, the child will fail to develop a capacity to adequately identify, verbalize and modulate feelings (i.e., alexithymia). As Taylor and others argue, the unmentalized emotions can contribute potentially to the development of psychosomatic disorders as well as certain psychiatric disorders (Taylor, 1997).

Taylor argues that these patients manifest an **ego deficit** derived from an early relationship with a depressed or alexithymic mother which hampered the normal development of emotional regulation. A **'good-enough' mother** enables her child to gradually learn to handle disagreeable affects so that they can be recognized and tolerated. When this process fails, the child continues to somatize emotions in adult life. Also Krystal (1997) notes that under conditions of intense psychological trauma during childhood, such as sexual abuse, a major **regression** might occur, leading to the same situation of alexithymia and a resomatization of affects (see the discussion of this in Chapter 5).

These ideas are based on Schur's discovery of regression in the expressive aspects of emotions in psychosomatic patients (Schur, 1955). Krystal writes that in the newborn there are affect precursors of states of contentment and of distress (Krystal, 1988) which are expressed through the body. Out of these basic reaction patterns evolve all the adult type affects. Pleasurable affects develop from contentment and painful emergency affects from distress. As these affect components mature and differentiate, the cognitive aspects of the affect begin to take on a meaning and a story. When the individual can pay more attention to the cognitive aspects as opposed to the physiological aspects of an emotion then he or she can observe this emotion and become reflectively self-aware. According to Krystal this allows the optimal utilization of affects as signals to the self (Krystal, 1988). Taylor and Krystal argue that such personalities require a radically different approach, at least in the initial phases of therapy, to help them get in touch with feelings by means of a form of emotional coaching. This enables them to identify certain feelings underlying their psychosomatic symptom by connecting them with images and words, and so begin to express them (see discussion of this in Chapter 5).

Clearly more disturbed personalities, some of whom are alexithymic, who develop psychosomatic illness may require technical modification, in particular in the early stages of psycho-therapy. I agree with what appears to be Winnicott's position of 'wait and see', taking the psychosomatic patient's hesitancy into account (see Winnicott's decription of an asthmatic child in Chapter 12) so as to allow the patient to gradually become more involved in the psychotherapy and for their dependency on the therapist to become clear: this means being cautious about making transference interpretations early in the therapy. I am less certain that emotional coaching has a place in long-term psycho-therapy of psychosomatic disorders: it is clearly helpful in short-term interventions such as Guthrie's brief psychotherapy with patients with irritable bowel syndrome (see Chapters 5 and 8) and Zalidis' approach to hyperventilation (see Chapter 11).

Inpatient Psychosomatic Treatment for More Severely Ill Psychosomatic Patients

In 1988, there were around 5,000 hospital beds in the former Federal Republic of Germany specifically for inpatient treat-ment of psychoneurotic and psychosomatic patients (Woidera, personal communication). After the reunification of Germany, a further 760 beds became available from within the former German Democratic Republic. This treatment of more severely ill psychosomatic patients had its origins in the Federal Republic of Germany's provision of health insurance schemes committed to providing psychotherapy.

In Germany doctors can train to be dually qualified in internal medicine and psychotherapy so as to become psychosomatic specialists (this is a unique situation even though in other countries such as France there are also psychosomatic hospitals). A number of university chairs in psychosomatics were estab-lished in the early 1960s and now all medical schools are required by law to teach medical students about psychosomatic medicine (Petzold, personal communication). In Germany during the post-war period, psychosomatic medicine was pioneered by two physicians, von Uexküll, who for many years edited the German textbook *Psychosomatic Medicine*, and Mitscherlich.

In Giessen, at the Justus Liebig University, where a psychoso-matic inpatient unit was established, headed by a psychoanalyst who was also a specialist in internal medicine, the orientation was initially to individual psychoanalytic psychotherapy. The psychosomatic patient was encouraged to develop **idealizing transferences** to the doctor and nurses (Stephanos, 1989). Family and group therapeutic approaches were later introduced in this unit (Woidera, personal communication). Such original ways of treating very ill psychosomatic patients with severe personality difficulties has been helpful for patients with difficulty in identifying and verbalizing their feelings. Though this innovation has not significantly caught on in other countries (with the exception of Austria), these units and the academic recognition of the discipline of psychosomatic medicine have influenced generations of internal medicine specialists in Germany to consider taking a psychosomatic approach to their patients.

Psychosomatic Incidents in Psychotherapy

Case Study

A man with a strong family history of coronary artery disease came to see me because of anxiety about the recent failure of his business and about his physical health. He was well-built with an anxious, restless manner and a tendency to be always on the go. He was grieving for his mother who had died a year before of a heart attack. He seemed to try to deal with his sadness by pushing himself harder and harder at work and by strenuous physical exercise in a city gym. As a child he had been fairly happy until the age of eleven, when his father fell in love with another woman and left his mother. Up until this break-up of the marriage he had had a close and warm relationship with his father. The separation of his parents had been a great disillusionment for him. Later in life he was aware of his constant search for father figures.

Some years before seeing me, the patient's father had died, also of a coronary. His younger brother suffered from **angina pectoris**. He rightly feared that he was at a greater than normal risk of developing coronary artery disease (see Chapter 10, 'Cardiovascular Disorders'). My hope was that psychotherapy might help him to overcome his tendency to compensate for his current and past depressive anxieties by physical overactivity, which clearly was of no help to him as a coronary-prone individual.

Early in the therapy, shortly before the first break in the treatment, he told me about a dream. In it he was driving his car towards the entrance of a motorway. He overtook a small car driven by a man wearing a blue shirt, who ignored him. My patient drove on, now entering the motorway. Soon he saw flashing lights by the side of the road. He ignored these lights and his car went into a spin, at which point he awoke from his dream.

In his associations to this dream, he thought that the other driver's shirt was the same colour as ones I often wore. It seemed to me that, perhaps like his father who had taken no notice of him and abandoned him in childhood, it was I who was now failing to prevent him from continuing onto the motorway. Here, in his dream, my patient in his car seemed to be using his body to protect himself against the depressive anxieties of a separation. I interpreted this to him, linking his forthcoming separation from me to the earlier loss of his father in his childhood. He smiled at me quizzically.

When I returned from holiday, he telephoned me to cancel his first session. He said he would not be coming, because during the holiday he had pulled a muscle in his neck whilst exercising. He had an appointment with his physiotherapist, which clashed with his appointment time with me. When he came to the next session I tried to interpret to him that, as his dream had seemed to predict, something had indeed happened to his body by way of an accident whilst I was away and seemingly ignoring him. I had not been able to protect him.

Such psychosomatic incidents during the course of psychotherapy are not uncommon. Here is another example of a psychosomatic symptom developing in the transference around the time of a holiday break:

Case Study

Maria's irritable bowel symptoms (described here and in Chapter 8) were linked to the significant attention that her depressed mother paid to her bowel functions, forcing her and her sister to use laxatives. This was to become a source of conflict over her bowel and emotional control, which was later expressed as an adult in the development of irritable bowel symptoms when she left home to marry.

After some years of working together, Maria completely recovered from her irritable bowel. Then, I had had to take a long period of leave lasting some months. Shortly after telling her about this she developed a feeling of tension in her chest with pain radiating down her right arm. She went to her GP who could not find anything physically wrong with her. However she was afraid that there might be something more seriously wrong, such as a tumour. She felt her pain had been made worse by my telling her about my going away and she linked it to her sense that, apart from her husband and myself, there was no one in her life left to help her (her parents and an aunt had died some years before). I was worried that there might be medical as well as psychological reasons for the pain and encouraged her to get a specialist opinion. She went to a chest physician, who did a chest X-ray that proved to be normal. However, she was still frightened by her symptoms. In the following session she told me of a dream about going on holiday in France. She then reported quarrelling with her husband because he decided not to pursue the psychotherapy she so much wanted him to receive. I said that she seemed to be trying to resolve all her difficulties in her relationship to her husband before I went away.

She now sought help from an osteopath for the pain. She then cancelled the next session with me. When she came the next time she told me it had been my fault that she had got the pain because I caused her so much distress by going away. She again cancelled the next session but by the time we came to the last session before I went away her pains had completely disappeared. I believe that her pains were a somatic representation of her anger and anxiety about such a long forthcoming separation, particularly in the light of the fact that as a child she had been evacuated from London to escape the Blitz on 11 occasions and on each occasion had been separated from her parents.

Also in any psychotherapy, transient hysterical conversion symptoms as well as other somatizations can occur as a result of events in the transference. Here is an example:

Case Study

One patient, whom I saw for once-weekly psychoanalytic psychotherapy, presented initially with a prolonged grief reaction following the death of her father. She was a physiotherapist in her early twenties who had had a close but ambivalent relationship with the father. After his death she could not deal with this loss. She knew there had been difficulties in the relationship which stemmed from childhood experiences to do with the earlier more significant loss of her mother when she was five. After this bereavement she had no opportunity to share her sadness with her family and formed an over-intense attachment to the father. This was spoilt by his second marriage to a woman with whom she was to have a poor relationship. Later, when she fell in love and married her partner, a nurse, her father was not able to accept him. The young couple had a child, aged one. Therapy with this patient initially proceeded well during which time she told me much about her past. She told me about her difficulties in her relationship with her husband, of whom she was very easily jealous.

At this point in the therapy I took a holiday of two weeks. When I returned I was concerned to hear from her husband that she wanted to see me urgently: she felt she needed to be admitted to hospital. When I saw her she told me that she had been frightened of harming her baby while I was away. She was sure that she and her baby should be protected from this ever happening by her being hospitalized and so separated from the baby. However, during the session she soon calmed down. She told me how, on the day and at the time when we would have met in the first week when I had been away, she had suddenly found herself unable to swallow. This difficulty in swallowing had gone on for a number of minutes before she had driven over to the casualty department of the hospital where her husband was working. He was called to reassure her and the episode of choking disappeared. We were both struck by the fact that it had happened precisely at the moment when the session would have occurred and it had not recurred after that time. This choking sounded like an episode of hysterical dysphagia or *globus hystericus*.

It was clear to me that her hope in the attack was for some sort of understanding. In staking her claim for understanding from her husband, there was self-punishment built into her symptom formation so that with him her despair was translated into the exaggerated attack of choking, whereas with myself this despair was communicated as her depression. I was able to see how there had been a hysterical element in her behaviour which had escaped me until now and which gave the account of her worries about harming the baby an exaggerated quality. This account had more to do with a demand for my attention in the transference as her missing parent, either father or mother. I never admitted her to hospital.

Many months later she told me that she had, indeed, exaggerated her feelings about hurting the baby and, in fact, had only slapped the baby very lightly on the occasion when I was away. The transformation of her symptoms from depression transferentially manifested to myself, as her therapist, to the conversion symptoms she showed her husband, as a nurse, emphasizes how a somatization might catch a therapist quite unaware as an enactment of a transference issue during a separation.

Psychosomatic incidents do not always occur in such an obvious way. How should we deal with other minor physical symptoms that crop up in the course of therapy, such as mild headaches or musculoskeletal tension states like backache or recurrent infections (see the clinical example of Jenny in Chapter 16)? Once major physical pathology has been excluded by the doctor, it is always worth considering what may be being communicated by this symptom that we have not yet taken up in the therapy.

If more worrying symptoms occur, like runs of irregular heartbeat with chest pains, it is of the utmost importance to encourage the patient to get a medical opinion as soon as possible. Here is an example:

Case Study

My patient had first developed a continuous bilateral severe dull headache and was diagnosed as suffering from severe essential hypertension (see Chapter 10), for which she was given antihypertensive medication. Then in a session just after a weekend, she reported developing palpitations and chest pains on two nights in succession. I stopped the session and encouraged her to go straight to the casualty department where coronary artery insufficiency was diagnosed and investigations were set in train. She dieted and was put on a cholesterol lowering agent and lost two stone in weight over the next three months. Her blood pressure returned to normal and her palpitations disappeared.

In the end we are always preoccupied with how well patients are able to take care of themselves. So many have had experiences of mothers who could not do this for themselves or their children; a fundamental aspect of psychotherapeutic work lies in helping the patient to recognize and to overcome this deep-seated problem.

Conclusion

Each psychotherapist is alone with many strands, psychic and somatic, to identify in the psychosomatic patient. One cannot be dogmatic about which approach is best; but the more severely disturbed psychosomatic patients do require patience and skill to reach them empathically before they can begin to recognize the difficulties in their internal world that have led to their psychosomatic symptoms. Although a psychotherapist may see only a few patients who come for help for a psychosomatic disorder, he or she is likely to encounter many psychosomatic incidents during the course of their work. Recognizing and thinking about these is relevant to the process of any psychotherapy where certain conflicts and emotions are communicated through the body and not verbalized (Shoenberg, 2002).

Further Reading

Taylor, G. J. (1987) *Psychosomatic Medicine and Contemporary Psychoanalysis* (Madison: International Universities Press).

Winnicott, D. W. (1964, 1989) 'Psycho-somatic illness in its positive and negative aspects'. In *Psycho-Analytic Explorations*, ed. C. Winnicott, R. Shepherd and M. Davies (London: Karnac), pp. 103–15.

4 The Effects of Stress

Stress: Its Effects on the Body

> *The physical changes that accompany certain emotions are a means to an end; they prepare the body to fight or flee. Thus rage, for example, brings with it an adjustment of the autonomic functions to external activity demands. The emotion prepares the body to cope at lightning speed with any emergencies that may arise. It is, so to speak, the mobilisation order that brings to the ready the means to fight or flee.*
>
> Walter Cannon (1939)

To appreciate the mental mechanisms in psychosomatic disorders, it is helpful to understand what is meant by the word 'stress' and how 'stress' affects the brain and subsequently the rest of the body.

The physiologist Cannon argued that man is always in a state of readiness for events that might appear as emergencies. When these events occur, this readiness can be converted into adaptive physiological changes (mediated by the sympathetic component of the autonomic nervous system). In mammals, stress might be an actual threat from a predator, which means that the threatened mammal must fight with or else flee from it. Hence the concept of the 'fight or flight' response. In primates, the stress response can be invoked not only by a concrete event but also by a symbolic one, as well as by the anticipation or threat of such an event. Stress may be exacerbated when there is no outlet for frustration, no sense of control, no social support and no sense that anything better might follow.

Where there is a possibility of escape or of control of the stressful situation, then the physiological stress response decreases. Repeated challenges, without such hope, result in chronic stress and a chronic state of vigilance in the individual, leading to anxiety. Alternatively the chronic stress, if insurmountable, can give rise to feelings of helplessness, and this, if over-generalized, might lead to depression.

Anxiety and the Brain: The Limbic System[1]

Anxiety affects a part of the brain known as the limbic system. The limbic system is made up of a number of nuclei (nerve centres which contain collections of nerve cells), situated in the forebrain and the midbrain (at the base of the brain). These nuclei connect with the **hypothalamus** and with the **brainstem reticular activating system,** in which the autonomic nuclei that control the autonomic nervous system are situated. The nuclei also connect with two parts of the cerebral cortex involved in the regulation of autonomic nervous outflow. These are:

1 The insular cortex, which mediates stress-induced cardio-vascular responses, for example heart arrhythmias.
2 The medial prefrontal cortex and infralimbic cortex, which mediate **visceral** sensory responses such as control of heart rate, blood pressure and gastric tone regulation.

In stress, the main structures that are affected in the limbic system are the amygdala. These are two symmetrically arranged nuclei made up of grey matter in the shape of almonds, hence their name. The amygdala are involved in the perception of and the response to fear-evoking stimuli and play a central role in aggression. In order to carry out their role in sensing a threat, the amygdala receive input from nerves in the outermost layers of the cerebral cortex, where thinking takes place. Included in this input is information from the parts of the cortex that process sensory information (the sensorimotor cortex), including the specialized areas that can recognize individuals' faces, and also the **frontal cortex** which deals with abstract associations (e.g., associating the sight of a gun with a hijacked plane and an anthrax-tainted envelope; see Figure 4.1).

Sensory information, in addition, may bypass the cerebral cortex on its way to the amygdala. In this way a subliminal pre-conscious menace might activate the amygdala (e.g. via the

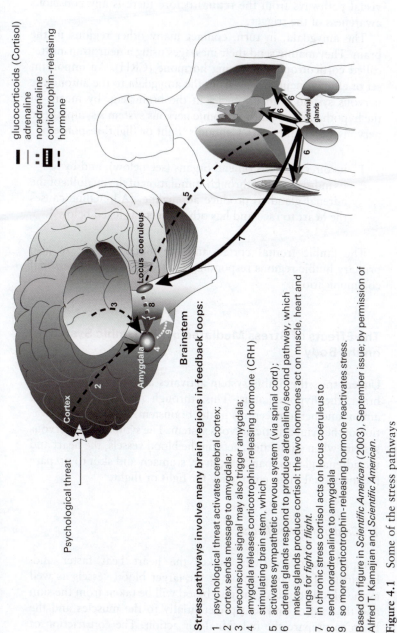

glucocorticoids (Cortisol)
adrenaline
noradrenaline
corticotrophin-releasing hormone

Stress pathways involve many brain regions in feedback loops:

1. psychological threat activates cerebral cortex;
2. cortex sends message to amygdala;
3. preconscious signal may also trigger amygdala;
4. amygdala releases corticotrophin-releasing hormone (CRH) stimulating brain stem, which
5. activates sympathetic nervous system (via spinal cord);
6. adrenal glands respond to produce adrenaline/second pathway, which makes glands produce cortisol: the two hormones act on muscle, heart and lungs for *fight* or *flight*.
7. in chronic stress cortisol acts on locus coeruleus to
8. send noradrenaline to amygdala
9. so more corticotrophin-releasing hormone reactivates stress.

Based on figure in *Scientific American* (2003), September issue; by permission of Alfred T. Kamajian and *Scientific American*.

Figure 4.1 Some of the stress pathways

visual pathways from the retina) before there is any conscious awareness of the trigger.

The amygdala, in turn, contact many other regions in the brain. They mainly send their messages using a neurotransmitter called **corticotrophin releasing hormone** (CRH). An important set of efferent neurones go from the amygdala to the autonomic nervous system with its nuclei in the brainstem, by means of the hypothalamus. The autonomic nervous system's sympathetic nervous system mediates Cannon's 'fight or flight' response by

1   its direct actions on end organs (see below); and by
2   its indirect action through stimulation of the medulla of the adrenal gland to produce adrenaline. (Adrenaline causes the heart to race and has other effects as listed below.)

The limbic frontal cortex and the hippocampus are also primary limbic regions responding to stress (Sapolsky, personal communication).

The Effects of Stress Mediated by the Limbic System on the Body

Under stress the limbic system activates another nucleus in the brain, the hypothalamus. This, through its own centres and autonomic nervous centres in the brainstem, leads to an activation of the sympathetic nervous system. The sympathetic nervous system, when stimulated, acts on the blood vessels, the heart and the adrenal glands, pancreas, liver, stomach and skin to prepare the individual in an emergency for fight or flight.

1   Cardiovascular Effects

Sympathetic overactivity makes the heart beat faster and, by virtue of its constriction of the larger blood vessels as well as the blood vessels of the gut, blood will be taken from the skin and the viscera and sent preferentially to the muscles and the brain to prepare the individual for action. The constriction of the larger blood vessels and the increased heart rate also lead to a rise in blood pressure.

2 Gastrointestinal Effects

In the gastrointestinal system, mouth salivation is restrained or stopped. Movement of the stomach and secretion of gastric juices and the peristaltic movements of the intestine are also all inhibited. The result of this is that digestion is either slowed down or halted. This mobilizes resources for the expenditure of energy. The colon and bladder also do not empty so easily and constipation may result. If there has been a rapid onset of the sympathetic effects, there may be a brief compensatory outflow of parasympathetic impulses from the autonomic nervous system giving rise to defecation and urination.

3 Endocrine Effects

The increased sympathetic outflow activates directly the **adrenal medulla** in the adrenal gland to cause an increase in secretion of the hormone adrenaline. Adrenaline:

(a) has additional **vasoconstricting** effects on the larger blood vessels and acts to accelerate the heart rate;

(b) causes **glycogen** in the liver to be converted into sugar which can be released into the bloodstream. The rise in blood sugar can meet the increased requirements for energy expenditure demanded by the brain and muscles;

(c) stimulates the thyroid gland to produce more thyroxine. The effect of greater thyroxine is to increase general oxidation in the body which will be needed with greater muscle activity;

(d) inhibits the release of **insulin** from the insulin-producing beta cells of the pancreas. The lowering of blood insulin enhances the levels of sugar in the blood. In this way increased sugar and oxygen are made more available and this leads to more energy being available for the muscles, again to prepare them for fight or flight.

4 Respiratory Effects

Profound changes in respiration may also take place but do not follow a set pattern. Gasps, catching of breath, panting or laboured breathing may occur. The bronchioles in the lungs also dilate under the influence of the sympathetic stimulation so that there is increased exchange of oxygen and carbon dioxide in the lungs, allowing more oxygen into the blood for energy requirements. The red corpuscles in the **spleen** are released from storage and this allows the oxygen-carrying capacity of the blood to be increased.

5 Dermatological Effects

The sweat glands under the skin are stimulated so as to secrete large amounts of fluid that have been set free by the increased physical activity. The muscles at the bases of the hair follicles contract so that the hairs are erect and goose pimples form.

Additional Neuroendocrine Changes in Stress: Leading to Release of Glucocorticoids by the Adrenal Cortex (see Figure 4.1)

The increased activity in the limbic system stimulates the hypo-thalamus to produce corticotrophin-releasing hormone (CRH) and this stimulates the pituitary gland to produce a hormone known as adrenocorticotrophic hormone (ACTH). ACTH, in turn, causes the release of glucocorticoids (cortisol) from the adrenal cortex of the adrenal glands. Higher levels of cortisol:

1 help to mobilize muscle energy and to increase cardiovascular tone;
2 cortisol increases the breakdown of proteins and the production of glycogen and glucose in the liver, resulting in an increase in blood glucose. Glucocorticoids have an anti-insulin action in the peripheral tissues and this has an additional effect on the lowering of the blood sugar;
3 also stimulate vascular activity necessary for an adequate fight/flight response to adrenalin;

4 in the gastrointestinal system increase the secretion of gastric acid and pepsin.

Case Study

At five in the morning a refugee and his young family heard the dreaded ring on the front doorbell. He knew that, as he had failed to get asylum, he and his family were about to be taken to a detention centre from where they would be deported from the country. His wife and child began screaming. He felt quite helpless in the face of this awful threat: his knees and legs began to shake; he broke out into a profuse sweat, became pale and began to feel very faint. His breathing became rapid and shallow. His heart began to race and he felt palpitations. He felt nauseous and wanted to pass urine and to defecate.

Lasting Effects of Stress on the Brain: Changes in the Amygdala and the Hippocampus

Other efferent (outgoing) fibres from the amygdala send information back to the **frontal cortex**. This enables the frontal cortex to make judgements about the threat and to initiate new behaviours. In addition, the amygdala send information through efferent fibres to the **sensory cortex**. The amygdala have been found to be involved in implicit memory (Le Doux, 1996). This form of memory includes procedural memories about learned skills, such as learning to ride a bike, and memories to do with fearfulness (i.e., affectively loaded). Implicit memory in the amygdala is established when certain sets of nerve cells communicate with one another repeatedly, causing the communication across particular nerve synapses to be strengthened by a process known as long-term potentiation. As well as the long-term potentiation, additional neural connections are sprouted at these junctions as a result of increased amounts of nerve cell communication in the amygdala (by expansion of the dendritic branch patterns forming new synapses). The additional neural connections and increased communication of nerve synapses enhances the implicit memory. This may explain why sensations are so vivid in the victims of trauma where the post-traumatic stress disorder has led to the creation of strong sensory memories in the implicit memory stored in the amygdala.

In very severe stress leading to post-traumatic stress disorder, another region of the brain may be actually harmed. This region is also in the limbic system and is called the hippocampus and is responsible for conscious or explicit declarative memory. Severe stress enhances implicit memory in the amygdala whilst causing atrophy of the nerve cells in the hippocampus. The outcome of this may be free-floating anxiety occurring in situations where the amygdala have responded to pre-conscious information without conscious awareness of memory as a result of the earlier stress-induced hippocampal damage from the initiating trauma that produced the severe stress.

It is possible that these changes in the hippocampus are brought about by excessive amounts of cortisol produced under stress by the activation of the adrenal cortex within the adrenal gland. Cortisol activates a brain region called the *locus coeruleus*, which sends a powerful activating projection back to the amygdala using a neurotransmitter called noradrenaline. At the same time, with severe stress the increased cortisol directly disrupts memory formation in the hippocampus by causing **neural atrophy** and the loss of neuronal branches and the prevention of growth of new nerve cells (by contrast exercise and environmental enrichment will stimulate neurogenesis in the hippocampus).

It is worth noting that depression over many years causes a decrease of 10–20 per cent in volume of the hippocampus, resulting in impairment and deterioration of memory formation. High cortisol levels make the amygdala more electrophysiologically excitable, both at the level of individual synapses which become more excitable and at the level of the dendritic branch patterns expanding to form new synapses (Sapolski, personal communication).

Post-Traumatic Stress Disorder

In post-traumatic stress disorder (PTSD) there is a different response of the brain to that seen in moderate stress. In PTSD the cortisol levels may actually be lower than normal, even decades after the event, whilst the corticotrophin-releasing hormone in the cerebrospinal fluid has actually been increased. It seems that there is an increased sensitivity to the corticotrophin-releasing hormone that causes a negative feedback on the secretion of cortisol via the neuroendocrine **hypothalamic pituitary adrenal system**. Positron-emission tomography and functional magnetic resonance show that reactivity of the amygdala and another part of the limbic system, the anterior paralimbic region, to trauma-related stimuli is increased. They also show a decreased reactivity of the **anterior cingulate gyrus** and the **orbitofrontal** cortical areas.

Patients who have chronic PTSD have:

1   increased circulating levels of noradrenaline;
2   increased reactivity of the **alpha 2 adrenaline receptors**;
3   increased thyroid hormone levels;
4   increased hippocampal atrophy.

Neuroimmune Responses to Stress

The immune system protects us from infection by means of chemicals called antibodies, which are proteins called immuno-globulins with highly specific structures designed to recognize and deal with foreign (i.e., non-self) matter, and by a cellular response (from **T-lymphocytes**, macrophages and natural killer cells, made in the spleen, the **thymus**, the bone marrow and the lymph glands) to infectious agents.

This system protects us from infections and other foreign invasions of the body by means of:

(a)   humeral responses with antibodies circulating in the blood (these are made by cells called **B-lymphocytes**, made in the lymphoid tissues such as the tonsils). These antibodies combine with and neutralize infectious agents (e.g., bacteria) and other foreign invaders of the body.

(b)   the cellular response to infection and foreign invasion of the body is provided by T-lymphocytes which have antibody on their surface and by natural killer cells and macrophages. The T-lymphocytes are produced in the

thymus gland. Both the B- and the T-lymphocytes origi-
nate in the bone marrow and the spleen.

Direct neuroimmune links

The thymus and spleen are innervated by the sympathetic
nervous system (a component of the autonomic nervous system)
with its nerve terminals close to the T-lymphocytes. The neural
modulation of immune activity involves the areas of the brain
involved with emotion and cognition, namely the limbic forebrain and the cortical regions, where corticotrophin-releasing
hormone is produced under stress. Indeed if CRF is administered
directly into the cerebral ventricles (where the cerebrospinal fluid
that bathes the brain is produced), not only is there an increased
emotional reactivity but there is also activation of the sympathetic nervous system leading to a reduction of natural killer cells
in the spleen, as shown by Stein and colleagues (1985).

Indirect neuroendocrine effects of stress on the immune system

It is known that the hormones ACTH (adrenocorticotrophic
hormone), TSH (thyroid stimulating hormone) and cortisol
(all of which are proteins called **neuropeptides**) also have a
modulating effect on the immune system. In stressful situations,
such as bereavement or depression, cortisol levels are elevated:
this has a suppressant effect on cellular immunity.

It has been found that in carers of relatives with Alzheimer's
disease, this chronically stressful situation for the carer leads to
significant delays in wound healing. Likewise it has been found
that certain chronic infections such as genital herpes, known to
be susceptible to immune dysregulation, tends to recur when
immunity is suppressed by stress.

This implication of the mind and brain in control of immune
functions was first demonstrated by a crucial experiment by
Ader and Cohen (1975). They showed that it was possible to
condition mice to saccharine, by giving them a saccharine
solution which acted as a conditioned stimulus, together with
an immunosuppressant drug called cyclophosphamide, which
acted as an unconditioned stimulus, causing an inhibition of
antibody production. When these behaviourally conditioned
mice were later exposed to saccharine alone (which is not an

immunosuppressant stimulus), their antibody production was nevertheless still inhibited. These were antibodies to sheep red blood cells.

Stein and colleagues (1985) showed that lesions to the hypothalamus modified immune processes and anaphylactic responses (a form of immune response) across all species of animals. They speculated that the hypothalamus transmits signals to the immune system via its control of the neuroendocrine production of cortisol and autonomic activity modulating immune physiology.

Changes in Immunity in Depression

Clinical evidence from various studies has found that the most consistent changes in immune functioning occur in clinical depression. It is also known that in many types of cancer there are significant changes in immune function. It was argued that by improving depression in patients with cancer it might be possible to improve their immune function and so improve their chances of survival. Spiegel and his colleagues (Spiegel and Classen, 2000) originally thought that psychosocial interventions in women with breast cancer not only improved their quality of life, but also possibly improved their survival. These original studies showed that patients with metastatic breast cancer who attended group therapy lived longer than those with metastatic breast cancer who did not attend groups.

However, more recent studies, which have tried to replicate Spiegel's original work with group therapy for breast cancer, have only been able to confirm that it is the quality of life that has been improved by the group therapy without any corresponding improvement in the prognosis of patients (see Chapter 15). Clearly an improved quality of life makes for greater patient compliance with a treatment regime but there is no demonstrable change in immune function (Sapolski, personal communication).

The neuroimmune system is extremely complex. It is clear that acute and chronic stress have an effect on the immune system via both the autonomic nervous system and the neuroendocrine outlets described above which, in turn, have an impact on the formation and activity of the immune cells that are produced by the thymus, the lymph nodes and the bone marrow and spleen, as well as the immune cells circulating in the blood.

This system, in addition, has **important feedback pathways** by direct action on the brainstem as well as **cytokine** receptors in the brain and, indirectly by means of afferent fibres carried up through the parasympathetic vagal nerve to the brainstem. Three cytokines, interleukins 1 and 6 and tumour necrosis factor alpha, have effects on higher cortical function, the limbic centres and the pituitary gland, although it is not understood how cytokines are able to affect the brain, given their inability to cross the **blood–brain** barrier. (It is possible their access is via the **circumventricular organs** around the **Circle of Willis** and another site where cerebrospinal fluid is generated (Sapolski, personal communication).) These feedback loops from the immune factors to the brain help regulate the overall control of production of immune factors via the brain in the neuroimmune regulatory system.

Stress and the Onset of Disease[2]

General Adaptation Syndrome

After Cannon's discoveries about the fight/flight response, Selye (1936) described a physiological response pattern to a variety of stressors, which he called the general adaptation syndrome (GAS). This was linked to endocrine changes mediated by the same pathways described above. He argued that, whilst these changes were initially adaptive, they might also precipitate the onset of diseases, especially when stress was prolonged or intense.

Life-Events

In 1950 Wolff wrote of diseases that might be the consequence of a failure to adapt to stressful life-events, leading to more specific responses of the body. In 1958 Hinkle and Wolff conducted a large study known as the Cornell Medical Project, in which they explored the relationship between life-events and physical illnesses in telephone employees over a 20-year period. They found that episodes of illness occurred in 25 per cent of their subjects. As the number of life-events occurring increased, they found more organ systems involved, with a consequent increase in the number of diseases. They also noticed that the episodes of illness occurred in clusters when individuals were having major interpersonal difficulties or else were experiencing their life situations as threatening or unsatisfactory.

Holmes and Rahe (1967) developed a Social Readjustment Rating Scale in which 43 common life situations were weighted according to their various degrees of significance for an average individual. They were able to show that people were more vulnerable to disease when experiencing many life changes. They also showed that this relationship between life events and disease was not a simple linear one. Factors modifying or mediating the relationship included the individual's cognitive appraisal of their life situation, their conscious coping responses and unconscious ego defence mechanisms and the availability of social support systems.

Object Loss as the Significant Psychodynamic Factor in Life-Events (Engel)

Grief that has no vent in tears makes other organs weep.
Henry Maudsley (1868)

In 1967, Engel, a pioneer physician and psychoanalyst, and his colleague Schmale wrote of the relationship between object loss and the onset of diseases in those individuals who were not able to cope psychologically with a loss and based this on studies of patients with the inflammatory bowel disease, ulcerative colitis (see Chapter 8). He noted how often the patients with ulcerative colitis were intensely dependent on a key mother figure. Their disease onset or exacerbation corresponded with a threat to disrupt or an actual disruption of the key relationship. This led to the development of feelings of helplessness and hopelessness in the sufferer. Threats of loss might include a change in the health of the key figure, or a change for the worse in the key person's behaviour. In 1958, his colleague, Schmale, studied 42 medically hospitalized patients between 18 and 45. In 41 there was evidence that they had suffered an actual or threatened symbolic loss, as well as feeling helpless and hopeless as a result. Later Engel wrote very movingly about his own mourning and anniversary reactions after the death of his twin brother (Engel, 1975).

In Britain, Bennett in 1970 studied victims of a flood in Bristol. He showed that following the flood there was an increase in morbidity and a 50 per cent increase in mortality in those victims whose homes had been flooded compared with those whose homes were spared. Object loss is a common antecedent to the onset or exacerbation of many physical diseases, including:

- ulcerative colitis (Paull and Hislop, 1974; Fava and Pavan, 1976/1977);
- diabetes mellitus (Hinkle and Wolf, 1952);
- bronchial asthma (Jessner et al., 1955);
- multiple sclerosis (Mei-Tal, Meyerowitz & Engel, 1970).

A study of a cohort of 904 close relatives of the 371 who died in the Aberfan mine disaster in Wales showed that the mortality rate was seven times higher in the bereaved group than the non-bereaved group during the first year of bereavement. The rates were higher during the second and third years as well but were not statistically significant. Young, Benjamin and Wallis found, in their study in 1963, that during the first six months after the death of a spouse the mortality rate was higher for married men of the same ages. The main cause of death was coronary thrombosis and other heart disease. A criticism of these studies has been that many were not controlled well for changes in lifestyle following loss, such as increased drinking or failure to take antihypertensive medication.

Effects of Stressful Situations (Especially Separation) on Emotional Development and the Body in Childhood: States of Helplessness (Spitz)

In 1945 and 1946 the psychoanalyst Spitz described a syndrome which he called 'hospitalism' in institutionalized infants. From their third month these infants showed an increased susceptibility to infection and other diseases and had a high mortality.

Those who survived were underweight and developmentally retarded and were subject to the bodily state of 'marasmus'.[3] In 1946 Spitz and Wolf described a series of 123 infants placed in a nursery during the second half of their first year of life. The infants developed what was termed 'anaclitic' depression. They appeared depressed and showed a low resistance to intercurrent infections. Some developed eczema or insomnia but their disturbance was reversible if they were reunited with their mothers within three to four months.

In 1952 Robertson and Bowlby described the phases of protest, despair and detachment as the infant's sequence of responses to separation from the mother. Fairly similar changes have been shown in non-human primate infants.

In 1956, Engel and Reichsman studied an infant called Monica whose mother had found it difficult to relate warmly to her (see Figure 4.2). This was because the mother was depressed and had conflicting feelings about feeding her via a gastric fistula (a passage to the stomach from outside the body), that was created surgically to temporarily manage an oesophageal atresia (i.e., absence of the normal passage between mouth and stomach), which was a birth defect. During Monica's second year of life, she developed an anaclitic depression with severe marasmus, but also became emotionally attached to one of the nurses and a doctor in the hospital where she was staying. It was noticed that in their presence she became animated and smiled. When she was in the presence of a stranger she showed what they termed a 'conservation-withdrawal response'. In this, she would be motionless with her head and eyes averted and her limbs falling with gravity. There were very interesting corresponding changes in the secretion of her gastric juices, which increased in the presence of the familiar figure (see Figure 4.2 and the section on peptic ulcer in Chapter 8).

Giving-up/Given-up Complex and Conservation-Withdrawal Response (Engel and Schmale)

In 1967 Engel and Schmale postulated that persons entered what they described as the 'giving-up/given-up complex' when

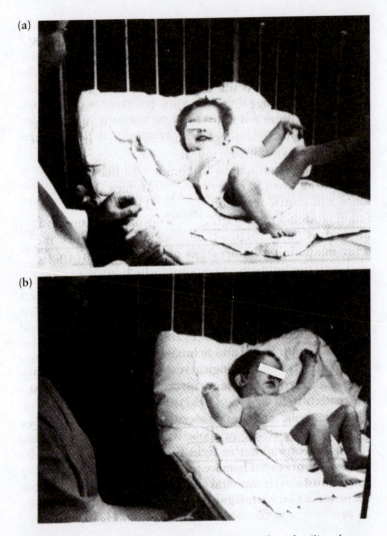

Figure 4.2 (a) Monica: she relates actively with a familiar doctor. (b) In the presence of a stranger she shows a conservation-withdrawal response: she lies motionless, head and eyes averted. (From Engel, Reichsman and Segal, 1956).

faced with object loss. This was caused by a failure of their psychological defences and coping devices which had previously assured them gratification and came with the awareness of their inability to re-achieve this gratification. The given-up stage marked a finality of the loss of gratification, as no sources of supply appeared available. In 1972 these analysts argued that, in contrast to Cannon's original 'fight or flight' response, this giving-up/given-up complex corresponded to a biological defence system called the 'conservation-withdrawal response'. In this state there was a predominance of parasympathetic activity as opposed to the predominance of sympathetic activity in the 'fight or flight' response. This predominance of parasympathetic activity was characterized by the relative immobility, quiescence and unresponsiveness to environmental input of the individual. It was accompanied by anabolic metabolic changes that put the body into a state of rest and restitution to help it to survive. However, if prolonged, it rendered the organism less resistant to a variety of pathogenic factors and this state was accompanied by the **affects** of helplessness and hopelessness (see Figure 4.2, illustration of Monica).

Physiological Effects of Loss and the Concept of Maternal Regulators

In the significant paper 'On the Nature and Consequences of Early Loss', Hofer (1996) reviewed the psychological effects of early loss. It has been found that after twenty-four hours of **maternal separation** 17–40 day-old rats showed a vigorous cortisone or ACTH response to sudden isolation, which included the loss of tactile interaction with the mother. It was proposed that the mother regulated her infant's cortisone and ACTH level by her touch and by the milk delivery (Sucheki et al., 1995). This and other studies have led to the argument that early maternal regulators of physiology and behaviour in the infant influence the subsequent regulation of the growing child's physiology in response to external stimuli. Separation, in particular, seems to influence growth in premature babies in incubators. Premature bereavement led to a failure of the normal smooth modulation and coordination of affect, behaviour and physiological function.

Conclusion

Nowadays we understand stress to affect the onset of an illness, rather than necessarily being its cause. Life-events have been identified as the measurable component of stress and it seems that the psychodynamic component of the stressful event is the threat of or the actual loss of an object (symbolic or real). This includes the loss of a close relationship and also the loss of self-esteem; thus a person may become ill when suffering from a narcissistic injury.

Acute psychological stress

This has multiple effects on the brain and the body. Its effects are transmitted chiefly via nuclei in the forebrain and midbrain which make up the limbic system in which the amygdala, hippocampus and hypothalamus are key nuclei instrumental in processing, remembering and handling the effects of stress.

1 These nuclei control the sympathetic outflow from the hypothalamus, which is responsible for the bodily effects of the fight or flight response to an acute emergency. These are:

(a) raised heart rate, raised blood pressure, with diversion of blood from the skin and digestive system to the muscles and brain, so as to prepare for action;

(b) increased secretion of adrenaline by the adrenal medulla;

(c) increased levels of blood glucose by the release of liver glycogen and a diminished secretion of insulin so as to provide more energy for the muscles;

(d) increased sweating and piloerection so as to deal with the effects of increased muscle activity;

(e) If the stress is prolonged it can, in addition to autonomic changes, initiate changes in the endocrine and immune systems which may lead to the emergence of disease if the necessary constitutional and/or environmental factors are also present;

2 Also under stress, the brain, especially the amygdala, produces an increased amount of corticotrophin releasing hormone (CRH). This causes increased ACTH (adrenacorticotrophic hormone), released by the pituitary gland, resulting in increased secretion of cortisol by the adrenal cortex. The increased cortisol leads to:

(a) elevations of blood glucose enhancing the energy production in the muscles and brain;

(b) depression of the immune response, which in turn leads to a lowered resistance to infection.

3 The immune system is regulated by the brain in various ways including via the sympathetic nervous system and the effects of increased cortisol. The immune system has feedback loops through the direct effects of immune substances (e.g., cytokines) on the brain and through indirect parasympathetic action on the brainstem. Thus stress (both acute and chronic, as a result of), its neuroimmune and its neuroendocrine action on the immune system, lowers resistance to some illnesses, in particular infections, and can also delay healing.

Chronic psychological stress

Psychoanalysts have argued that chronic stress may lead to states of hopelessness and helplessness, (also a much used idea in cognitive behavioural thinking about stress and depression) which are the opposite of the vigilant reactions of the fight or flight response to an acutely stressful situation. These states result in the person experiencing the 'giving-up/given-up complex' (Engel and Schmale). This complex leads to a state of conservation-withdrawal which may be adaptive initially but which may lead to pathology if prolonged. It has been postulated that in this depressive state there is an increase in parasympathetic activity of the autonomic nervous system leading to a period of rest and restitution with an increase in anabolic activity leading to energy conservation.

Both acute and chronic stress may result in actual direct brain damage through the effects of increased levels of cortisol. These inhibit brain-derived neurotrophic factor and impair long-term potentiation in the hippocampus of the limbic system where declarative memory is formed whilst, paradoxically, there is an enhancement of implicit memory in the amygdala (as a result of opposite effects on brain-derived neurotrophic factor and long-term potentiation of nerve signals).

Further Reading

Engel, G. L. and Reichsman, F. (1956) 'Spontaneous and experimentally induced depressions in an infant with a gastric fistula: a contribution to the problem of depression', *Journal of the American Psychoanalytic Association*, 4: 428–52.

Engel, G. L. and Schmale, A. H. (1967) 'Psychoanalytic theory of somatic disorder: conversion, specificity and the disease onset situation', *Journal of the American Psychoanalytic Association*, 15: 344–65.

Engel, G. L. and Schmale, A. H. (1972) 'Conservation-withdrawal: a primary regulatory process for organismic homeostasis', in *Physiology, Emotion and Psychosomatic Illness*, Ciba Foundation Symposium 8 (Amsterdam: Elsevier).

Hofer, M. (1996) 'On the nature and consequence of early loss', *Psychosomatic Medicine*, 58: 570–81.

Sapolsky, R. (2003) 'Taming stress', in *Scientific American* (September 2003).

Taylor, G. J. (1987) *Psychosomatic Medicine and Contemporary Psychoanalysis* (Madison: International Universities Press), pp. 39–73.

5 Somatization: The Somatoform Disorders

My mind may not remember but my body keeps the score.
Patient quoted in Saxe et al. (1994)

Somatizers are patients with chronic physical complaints caused by disturbances of body function not explained by organic pathology. Often they consume a great deal of doctors' time, and are offered reassurance, antidepressant medication or short-term psychological treatments aimed at symptom relief, rather than psychodynamic understanding or psychotherapy. The psychoanalyst Stekel introduced the term 'somatization' to describe the process whereby a deep-seated neurosis is expressed by means of conversion in a physical disorder (Stekel, 1925). In fact, a variety of psychodynamic mechanisms may operate in these functional disorders, even though patients with conversion disorder are still seen. Nowadays these disorders are also called somatoform disorders.

In general practice, the commonest symptoms of somatization are prolonged fatigue, musculoskeletal aches and pains and functional gastrointestinal symptoms. In this setting, somatization is often accompanied by depression and/or anxiety (Escobar et al., 1987; Cloninger et al., 1984; Katon et al., 1991). Often milder forms of this condition occur in general practice may represent adjustment reactions to stressful situations (Katon et al., 1991) which disappear after a short time with or without any medical intervention.

Case Study

A man with anxiety about repeated episodes of palpitations, which began shortly after his mother's death from a heart attack, consulted a second doctor after receiving grief counselling from his family GP. A thorough physical examination and reassurance that there was nothing wrong with his heart or his cardiovascular system were sufficient to allow the palpitations to disappear completely.

The palpitations were a somatization, caused by anxiety, related to his grief. This man now decided to have psychotherapy for his grief which he could now see was producing his symptoms.

Psychotherapists see only a few patients with somatoform disorders but somatizations may occur during the course of psychotherapy (Shoenberg, 2002) (see the section on psychosomatic incidents in psychotherapy in Chapter 3). Somatoform disorders have been classified by the two diagnostic systems, the North American DSM-IV-TR and ICD-10, into a number of apparently discrete conditions that still may not represent the full spectrum of clinical presentations. The two systems differ in a number of ways, and the ICD-10 includes a form of somatization called neurasthenia, also known as chronic fatigue syndrome (see Chapter 12, 'Musculoskeletal Disorders'). In this book I will follow the DSM-IV-TR system but it is important to realize that the boundaries between the diagnostic entities are fluid.

Conversion Disorder

In conversion disorder, formerly referred to as hysterical conversion, the voluntary motor and/or sensory functions are affected, suggesting an underlying neurological, or possibly other, general medical condition. Conversion symptoms can occur at any age and are more common in children than adults, and commoner in women than men. In a population of 250,000, one can expect 10 to 25 new cases per year (Akagi and House, 2001), which contradicts the view that conversion is on the wane. It has been estimated that 5–16 per cent of all liaison-psychiatric consultations in a general medical hospital setting reveal conversion disorder symptoms (Hollifield, 2005).

Conversion disorder is usually preceded by psychological conflict or other stressful situations, and begins abruptly.

1 The motor symptoms or deficits may include difficulty with balance, coordination, paralysis or else a localized

weakness of a limb, difficulty in swallowing, or the sensation of a lump in the throat.
2 The sensory symptoms or deficits may include a loss of
touch or a pain sensation or else an alteration in one of the
special sensations of sight, hearing, smell or taste.
3 Pseudoseizure commonly occurs, often in patients with a
pre-existing tendency to epilepsy.
4 Pain may also occur.

On physical examination, it becomes clear that the neurological symptom cannot be explained by neuroanatomy, but has
followed the individual's idea of a neurological deficit. Hence the
'glove and stocking' distribution of the hysterical sensory loss in
the upper and lower limbs does not correspond with any actual
neurological damage to the central or peripheral sensory nervous
system. The weaknesses or paralyses (i.e., the motor deficits) also
do not correspond with either an upper or a lower motor neurone
lesion in the nervous system. The pseudoseizures, which mimic
epilepsy but are like atypical fits, are not accompanied by
tongue-biting or loss of sphincter control of the bladder or the
bowels and there is no true loss of consciousness.

Case Study

A 19-year-old, with an alteration to a previous pattern of her
epileptic fits, was admitted to a neurology ward. Originally
these had been true epileptic fits (*grand mal* fits in childhood). More recently she had developed a new form of fit. She
appeared suddenly to lose consciousness and become lifeless
or else move her limbs in a violent fashion. Sometimes, during
an attack, she would put her hands up to her throat as if
to strangle herself. The physical examination was normal.
On the ward her fits increased in frequency. She was moved
into a room where she was given oxygen whenever she had
a fit. Her dose of anticonvulsants was increased. One day,
during a ward round, she had a fit in front of the consultant
neurologist who surprised her by speaking to her. He asked
her what she wanted. She opened her eyes and pointed to the
oxygen cylinder and asked for oxygen.

This conversation between the consultant and the patient changed the diagnosis from one of atypical epilepsy to one of hysterical pseudoseizures. It changed the approach to this patient. Her attacks diminished in frequency and she began to talk about herself, telling the doctor about her fears of leaving home and getting married. She also spoke about experiences in her early adolescence, when she had been close to a male cousin who suffered from bronchial asthma. She had witnessed him dying of suffocation during an asthmatic attack when for some reason he had deliberately not taken his bronchodilators with him on a walk. (Shoenberg, 1975)

This case not only shows aspects of the presentation of a pseudoseizure but also how, in talking with a patient, there may be the potential for discovering that the symptom has meaning. As such, it represents for the physician a form of communication about an underlying emotional disturbance in the patient. Breuer and Freud, in their first psychoanalytic essay of 1893, 'A Preliminary Communication', argued that hysterics suffer mainly from their reminiscences. This conclusion resulted from their work with hysterical patients who, under hypnosis, revealed trapped memories and feelings associated with them that had not yet been worked through.

Freud's concept of hysterical conversion only evolved slowly. It began with his introduction of the term in 1894, describing what he felt was a mental mechanism in the patient for rendering an incompatible idea safe by transforming the underlying feelings produced by the idea into 'something somatic' (Freud, 1894). The term 'conversion' had already been used as long ago as 1795 by the English physician John Ferriar (Mace, 1992). However Freud was the first to use it as a psychological explanation for the physical symptoms of the hysteric.

His argument was that the hysteric's symptoms were the symbolic expression of a conflict in the patient's unconscious mind, produced by experiences in childhood. These experiences, in Freud's original formulation, were connected to sexual abuse by an older figure of the opposite sex. The excitement, guilt and anxiety aroused by the experience had been repressed and split off. Now, in a situation where sexual anxieties were re-aroused, the patient expressed those feelings through the conversion symptom in symbolic form. Self-punishment was built into the symptom, as well as the possibility of secondary gain, allowing the patient to enjoy a sick role, thus gaining attention and also withdrawing from the conflict itself. The self-inflicted punishment of the symptom dealt with the original guilt aroused by the childhood conflicts. Later Freud came to realize that it was unlikely that actual sexual abuse had taken place but rather that his patients suffered from their phantasies of a sexually abusive situation. Many contemporary clinicians have argued that this is only true in some cases, and that in others there is strong evidence that real sexual abuse has taken place. Szasz (1962) regarded the conversion symptom as a communication alone while others regarded it as the expression of dependency needs (Nemiah, 1967).

Sometimes other somatoform disorders occur together with conversion disorder. A recent important study published by Crimslisk et al. (1998), that examined patients with unexplained motor symptoms who had consecutive admissions to the National Hospital for Nervous Diseases in London over a two-year period, found the mean duration of the presenting hysterical symptoms was 18 months. These patients did not turn out to have other pathologies. Only a small proportion of patients had a typical hysterical personality. A wide range of other personalities was also seen (see also Chodoff and Lyons, 1958). Children with this disorder seem to have less psychopathology than adults (Garralda, 1992). Although symptoms of an acute conversion disorder may remit spontaneously, there may be an underlying depression that needs urgent attention.

Although many of the conversion disorder patients seen nowadays by psychiatrists are treated by hypnosis or by cognitive behavioural therapy, (at the National Hospital for Nervous Diseases in the UK a short term inpatient programme of cognitive behavioural therapy, combined with occupational therapy and physiotherapy is offered to patients with chronic conversion disorder), a few are referred for psychoanalytic psychotherapy, as the following case history illustrates:

Case Study

Jenny, a 50-year old married woman, was referred for psychotherapy from an eye hospital. She had a two-year history of difficulty in vision, affecting the peripheral part of her visual field, of sudden onset and of a progressive nature and without any physiological and pathological explanation. One day she had noticed grey spots in the periphery of her visual field. This difficulty progressed and she found herself eventually unable to get about without using a white stick. Her husband had recently started a casual relationship with a younger woman. She was seen in once-weekly psychoanalytic psychotherapy for six months.

She had had a difficult and lonely childhood and had been raised substantially as an only child and was often in conflict with her parents. She had developed psychogenic tics at 14 and received psychotherapy. Early in her psychotherapy as an adult she mentioned that she had been sexually abused by a maternal uncle. The abuse had occurred between the ages of nine and 12 at holiday times, when the family visited him. This had cast a shadow on her relationship with her father during her adolescence, because she was afraid of any physical contact with him. At 21 she was caught up in a terrorist attack on an embassy. Although not injured herself, she saw a man on fire. She subsequently became severely depressed and withdrawn. She had been hospitalized and diagnosed with post-traumatic stress disorder and was treated with electro-convulsive therapy. During this illness, she spoke of the sexual abuse and, in a subsequent family therapy session, she discussed the problems of her childhood for the first time with her parents. Two years later she married, and later had two children. When her parents both died of heart disease she was grief-stricken. She became pregnant again but terminated this pregnancy.

In therapy, she acknowledged ongoing stresses within her family; particularly her husband's infidelity as well as the fact that she knew her husband could be dishonest in other ways. She had a feeling that neither she nor her husband had the capacity to contain the anxiety of the other. Her eye symptoms improved quite dramatically. She no longer used the white stick to come to her sessions. She acknowledged that the symptoms were a crutch and a way of looking for help and acknowledging her emotional upset without having to deal with it. It embarrassed her to view her symptoms in this way. She now linked her eye symptoms to her father.

As the therapy came to an end, she spoke about her husband's anxiety that the therapy was ending and her fear that he might now have a breakdown. The marital crisis had originally worsened the relationship between her parents and her husband. They had wanted her to leave him for good. She said that she now realized that she had had to turn a 'blind eye' to his previous misbehaviour. The couple were now attending a marital counsellor, which had been 'a real eye-opener'. She spoke of starting 'to look' at their finances. Now she had more say in their relationship. She acknowledged that her eye symptoms were an alternative expression of her conflict with her husband.

Jenny's **primary gain** from her visual difficulties was that they expressed in bodily metaphor, something which could not be acknowledged consciously and expressed openly, i.e., her wish not to see certain very unacceptable facts which aroused anxiety: her uncle's sexual abuse of her, the devastating experience of seeing a man on fire in the terrorist attack, and finally her husband's instability and dishonesty and sexual unfaithfulness, which threatened her and her family with the break-up of the marriage. There was also self-inflicted punishment in the symptom, which dealt with the original guilt aroused by her participation in the sexual abuse by her uncle. These symptoms gave rise to secondary gain, thereby allowing her to be cared for and claim disability allowance. As long as the meaning of her conversion symptom was hidden from her, she was protected from her unconscious conflicts. She expressed a degree of emotional indifference (which is nowadays rare) to the eye symptoms, but it was not clear as they improved how much any hidden depression emerged. However, she was now prepared to confront issues in her marriage which before her psychotherapy she had wished to avoid.

Somatization Disorder

This is a rare condition, with a lifetime prevalence rate varying from 0.2–2.0 per cent among women and less than 0.2 per cent in men (Hollifield, 2005).[1] It is also called Briquet's syndrome, after the 19th-century physician who argued that the disorder was related to the brain, rather than the physical pathology of the female genitalia, and proposed that unfavourable environmental events acted on the affective part of the brain in predisposed individuals (Mai and Merskey, 1980).

In this condition, multiple recurring clinically significant somatic complaints occur that are not fully explained by any known general medical condition. It begins before the age of 30 and occurs over a period of many years. There is a history of at least one sexual reproductive symptom other than pain, and a history of at least one neurological symptom (based on conversion hysteria) other than pain. None of these unexplained symptoms are intentionally feigned. The course of this condition is often chronic and fluctuating and it rarely remits completely. Patients with it form clinging relationships to their psychiatrists and other care givers, whom they may unconsciously try to divide.

If they are referred to psychiatrists, it is often with despair on the part of the referrer, reflected in such epithets as 'heart-sink patient'. Such patients resent the implication that stress or emotional factors might underlie their somatization, and therefore are likely to form an ambivalent relationship with the psychiatrist. A major complication of the disorder is that such patients may abuse medication, as well as becoming dependent on a variety of unsuitable medications. They may also seek out inappropriate surgical treatment for their difficulties, e.g., the removal of the colon for chronic constipation.

A few somatizers have gross functional impairment. In a British sample of patients with somatization disorder, 10 per cent were found to be confined to wheelchairs (Bass and Murphy, 1991). In a US survey it was found that patients with somatization disorder might spend an average of seven days in bed each month (Smith et al., 1986), leading to further disability.

Mai, referring to 31 controlled studies of cognitive behavioural therapy (CBT) carried out before 2000, argues that the first line of treatment in Somatization disorder should be CBT

(Mai, 2004). In this approach the therapist sets treatment goals in which the number and frequency of sessions and the need for homework are stated clearly. For their homework, patients read certain relevant literature, keep a diary to record their feelings and thoughts and bring these topics back to treatment sessions for discussion. The therapist's emphasis is on structuring the patient's social and physical environment to promote appropriate behaviour.

Individual psychoanalytic psychotherapy is unlikely to help these patients and may even be contraindicated. Such patients may respond better to group analytic psychotherapy (Valko, 1976). In a group, patients learn to confront each other with the relationships between stressful life-events and their somatic symptoms, and this may lessen the demands made on other health carer providers.

Undifferentiated Somatoform Disorder

This is a less severe form of somatization disorder, in which there are one or more physical complaints, for example, fatigue, loss of appetite, gastrointestinal symptoms or urinary complaints, that cannot be explained by a known general medical condition or the direct effects of a substance. The symptoms cause significant distress or impairment in social occupation or in other important areas of functioning. The disturbance has lasted for at least six months; it cannot be accounted for by other mental disturbances and is not feigned. The prevalence for this subsyndromal disorder is 100 times higher than for somatization disorder (Hollifield, 2005).

Somatoform Pain Disorder

The essential feature of this disorder is that pain is the predominant focus of the presentation and is sufficiently severe to make the patient seek help. Psychological factors play a significant role in the onset, severity, exacerbation and maintenance of the symptom, although most pain is multifactorial in origin. Some prefer to refer to this as chronic pain to avoid an assumption that it is entirely psychogenic (Rodin, personal communication). This is a common disorder, which can begin at any age. Lifetime prevalence is approximately 12 per cent (Hollifield, 2005). This disorder includes chronic pelvic pain, atypical facial pain, proctalgia fugax and certain forms of psychogenic headache and low back pain. Our understanding of the psychodynamics of pain may throw light on the dynamics of other somatizations.

Pain is clearly a subjective experience. Certain diseases have characteristic pain patterns, for example, the crushing chest pain of a myocardial infarction. Pain can exist in the absence of any peripheral stimulus and arise from central nervous system factors which must include psychological ones. Neuroanatomic and physiological theories of the perception of pain have proposed what is called the 'Gate Theory' of pain as a concept of pain control. This theory argues that pain impulses are transmitted by differing-sized nerve fibres at different speeds. The activation of some of these fibres inhibits the firing of other fibres, creating a gate, which influences the intensity of stimuli transmitted to higher central nervous system structures (Melzack and Wall, 1996). The Specificity Theory argues that the intensity of the pain signal transmitted is roughly proportional to the amount of tissue damage occurring peripherally.

The psychoanalyst Engel (1959) proposed that psychological meanings of pain are linked to childhood experiences with the parents. Pain may be associated with discomfort such as a wet nappy or hunger; the resultant crying causes the mother to come to the child and resolve the problem by providing closeness and affection as well. In this way, pain comes to mean the expectation of care and affection. Where there has been little affection to meet the child's needs, the child comes to see pain as a way of getting more parental attention.

Pain may be associated with guilt and expected punishment. Punishment in childhood may have evoked guilt. Children who have been physically abused by their parents often develop rigid and punishing super egos, unconsciously incorporating the feeling that they deserve the punishment, growing up feeling easily guilty and in need of punishment (see clinical example of body language at the end of this chapter). Engel argued that pain might also be considered an affect that was once represented mentally and is now projected from the mind, so as to be experienced as arising in some part of the body. Such unconscious determinants of psychogenic pain clearly have relevance for understanding other somatizations, especially hypochondriasis. It is interesting that nostalgia, which originally meant 'our pain', referred to a somatization known to Swiss soldiers serving in the Napoleonic army in the 18th century who developed this condition when homesick (Palmer, 1945).

Types of Somatoform Pain Disorder

1. Chronic Pelvic Pain (see Chapter 14, 'Psychosomatic Aspects of Gynaecology')

2. Atypical Facial Pain
A wide variety of complaints in the facial area may be seen by dentists, physicians and oral surgeons (Feinmann, Harris and Cawley, 1984). A population questionnaire data in the USA indicated a prevalence rate of 12 per cent for temporomandibular-related pain (Dworkin et al., 1990). Patients complain of pain over the mandible or maxillary area or else within the oral cavity. Symptoms may include a painful tongue and sensitive teeth. The pain may be unilateral or bilateral, dull, sharp, burning or nagging. Often the pain has begun after a minor dental procedure but then persisted and changed in character over time. Symptoms persist over many years and can be disabling and may result in many treatments, including removal of teeth, nerve blocks and other operations. It is important to exclude organic pathology. Where there is a clear psychogenic cause, nearly always depression is associated with the symptom complex. Some patients referred for psychoanalytic psychotherapy with associated personality problems respond well to the treatment. An example is given in Chapter 1.

3. Proctalgia Fugax
This syndrome often occurs in young men, describing severe spasmodic pain deep in the rectum, vaguely localized somewhere above the anal ring and lasting only a few minutes or less.

It usually occurs at night and often wakes the patient from a sound sleep. No physical cause is discovered for the pain.

4. Tension Headache (see Chapter 13, 'Headache')

5. Chronic Recurrent Low Backache (see Chapter 12, 'Musculoskeletal Disorders')

6. Pain as a Symptom of Conversion Disorder

Pain may be a common symptom of conversion disorder and can be described in exaggerated and bizarre terms. For example a man, whose father had died of a myocardial infarction, developed an acute chest pain, thereby identifying with his father in an unconscious attempt to deny the loss and so avoid having to mourn him. The pain led to the fear of having a heart attack and dying like his father (Wolff and Shoenberg, 1990, p. 482).

In Couvade Syndrome, a husband may identify with his wife and develop abdominal pain and other gastrointestinal symptoms while she is pregnant and going into labour (Enoch and Trethowan, 1979).

7. Pain with Organic Causation: Psychological Aspects

Many patients' reaction to organically caused pain is quite appropriate to the severity and duration of the pain. However, a pain that is chronic or relapsing may lead to the use of the pain for secondary gain in personal or work relationships. The adoption of such a sick role leads to more pain and disability.

Some patients may use pain as a form of communication, for example, a patient with a prolapsed disc pain may go to see a doctor really wanting to talk about some other problem of a more personal nature but using the condition as an excuse for seeking help (Wolff and Shoenberg, 1990).

Treatment

Pain clinics have been developed with multidisciplinary teams of pain specialists including anaesthetists, physiotherapists, health psychologists and psychotherapists and alternative medicine specialists to help people to manage their pain, often approaching the problem psychologically as well as physically. Patients with chronic psychogenic pain may do better in group therapy than in individual psychotherapy.

Case Study

One such group, based in a pain clinic, aimed to listen to the patients' stories and to help them reflect on their difficulties. More frequently than not, the stories initially focused on the symptom of physical pain but gradually became stories about relationships, or the lack of them. As the group proceeded, patients became much more aware of their difficulties about being able to take in help that was being offered to them: they began to communicate better with their doctors, and became less anxious and less keen to pursue further investigations and treatments. (Borgetti-Hiscock, personal communication).

Body Dysmorphic Disorder (formerly Dysmorphophobia)

Patients with this disorder have the firm conviction that their bodies or parts of their bodies are ugly or misshapen in some way. They repeatedly seek out medical help to remedy the situation. The complaint is usually one of believing themselves to be ugly, for example having the wrong-shaped nose, and it is the cosmetic surgeon from whom help is sought. The term dysmorphophobia was originally coined by Morselli in 1886 but it is misleading as the problem is an obsession rather than a phobia and the obsession is with the body. Most commonly it is about parts of the face, especially the nose, but the complaint may be about the hair, the breasts or the genitalia as well.

A study by Connelly and Gipson (1978) indicated that approximately 2 per cent of patients going to a plastic surgeon have body dysmorphic disorder. Community prevalence is between 1.0 and 2.2 per cent and cosmetic surgery and dermatology clinics prevalence is between 6 and 15 per cent (Hollifield, 2005).

A few patients are psychotic and usually have schizophrenia or, occasionally, **bipolar disorder**. There may also be an association with paranoid disorders. Patients with this disorder must be distinguished from those with anorexia, who have an unreasonable fear of being fat and, thus, feel dissatisfied with their body shape and size. They must also be distinguished from people with gender identity disorder who are seeking operations for sex change. This condition usually begins in adolescence but may not be diagnosed for many years.

One particular condition worthy of note is bromosis, where patients seek repeated medical help, complaining of emitting an offensive odour. They frequently change their clothes and use deodorants excessively. Such patients are commonly male, single and comparatively young and may have an underlying depression, schizophrenia or even temporal lobe epilepsy.

Hypochondriasis

Pilowsky defined hypochondriasis as 'a concern with health or disease in oneself which is present for the major part of the time. The preoccupation must be unjustified by the amount of organic pathology and does not respond more than temporarily to clear reassurance given after a thorough examination of the patient' (Pilowsky, 1970).

Hypochondria literally means 'beneath the ribs' and it originally referred to the anatomical area where the spleen is situated. This organ was thought to be the site of origin for hypochondriasis, formerly supposed to be the cause of melancholy and the 'vapours' (1652; *The Shorter Oxford English Dictionary*, 1984). In the 17th and 18th centuries, the diagnosis became so popular in England that the syndrome was known as 'the English malady'. The famous 17th-century physician Sydenham regarded hysteria as a female disease and hypochondriasis as a male disease (Fischer-Homberger, 1983). In fact, hypochondriasis occurs as commonly in men as in women. The condition should last more than six months to qualify as hypochondriasis. There is a 1.1–4.5 per cent prevalence of hypochondriasis in the community. About 10 per cent of people have hypochondriacal fears and beliefs. Medical speciality clinics, such as those for gastroenterology and neurology, have a higher rate of hypochondriasis (Hollifield, 2005). Transient hypochondriasis is common in the primary care setting. It can begin at any age but, most commonly begins in early adult life.

Case Study

A young woman, seen for psychoanalytic psychotherapy, presented with multiple physical complaints, including a fear that she had cancer of the throat and cancer of the breast, not demonstrated by specialist consultations, and also a fear of bowel cancer because of abnormal bowel movements; these had not been confirmed by many investigations and specialist consultations. She had been suffering with these complaints for over a year, following an attack of appendicitis leading to peritonitis that followed the deaths, in close succession, of a much loved brother and her mother, with whom she had had a very ambivalent relationship since childhood.

She had grown up in an émigré family, where the father was an embittered veteran of the anti-fascist movement in Italy. He had subsequently joined the British navy during the war and been interned in a Japanese prisoner-of-war camp. He had a poor relationship with her older brother. She and her brother grew up in an atmosphere where there was anxiety that the father, who had had heart attacks, might have a stroke as a result of getting angry. So expressions of anger were discouraged in this family. She had always tried to be pleasing as a child. From the ages of five to ten, she and her brother were sent away during the summer holidays to stay with a very cruel and mocking relative. Eventually she and her brother protested so much that they were no longer sent away.

When she was 18 and about to go to university, her father had a stroke (after becoming enraged at the execution of a political detainee in a fascist state) and she was obliged to stay at home rather than live away whilst at university. As a result of this she developed an eating disorder.

In psychotherapy she revealed that her relationship with her mother had always felt detached and distant: as a child it was only when she was ill that the mother had given her close attention. Psychotherapy involved the therapist tolerating a variety of dependencies on medical and alternative healthcare professionals (a 'scatter of therapeutic agents', Winnicott, 1964). Eventually her hypochondriacal symptoms, that recurred many times during the therapy, diminished as she got in touch with the anger and hurt of her childhood and could see their connection with her current experiences of separation and loss. (*See also* Chapter 3)

Freud (1914) distinguished conversion disorders from hypochondriasis. He suggested that hypochondriasis resulted from a withdrawal of libido from the objects of the external world and its concentration on internal organs. Wahl suggested that the somatic symptoms served as a way of expiating guilt (Wahl, 1963) and pointed to the personal symbolic meaning of the physical symptoms. Rosenfeld (1965) argued that a temporary hypochondriasis was caused by **infantile psychotic anxieties** and that chronic hypochondriasis was a defence against confusional states, often of a psychotic nature. Mushatt (1975) regarded hypochondriasis as a response to loss. Broden and Myers considered hypochondriacal symptoms to be related to unconscious phantasies of being beaten or tortured (1981).

Common Approaches to the Management of Somatizations

> *Misomedian*: But you think, perhaps, I'm a Mad-man, to send for a Physician, when I know before-hand that he can do me no good: Truly, Doctor, I am not far from it: But first of all, are you in haste, pray?
>
> *Philoperio*: Not in great haste, Sir.
>
> *Misomedian*: I am glad of that; for most of your Profession always either are, or at least pretend to be, in a great hurry. But tho' you are at leisure, Can you hear a Man talk for half an Hour together, and, perhaps, not always to the purpose, without interrupting him? For I have a great deal to say to you, several Questions to ask you, and know I shall be very tedious; but if you can bear with me, I'll consider your Trouble, and pay you for your Time, and Patience both. Can you stay an Hour?
>
> *Philoperio*: Yes, Sir, or longer, if there be occasion.
>
> *Misomedian*: Then, pray Sir, sit down ...
>
> De Mandeville, *A Treatise on the Hypochondriack* (1711)

Many somatizations are short-lived, needing no specific treatment at all other than possible reassurance after a careful physical examination that has excluded all physical pathology. Some disorders such as somatoform pain disorder are best helped by specialist treatment centres such as the pain clinics described above. Guthrie (1991) has shown how important it may be for a psychotherapist to work alongside gastroenterologists in a gastroenterology clinic, when seeing patients with irritable bowel syndrome. This allows patients to consider a psychological approach in a setting that is acceptable to them.

Some patients, for example certain hypochondriacs with depression, may in fact respond better to treatment with anti-depressants than to a dynamic psychotherapy. A study by Pilowsky and Barrow (1990) compared the use of the anti-depressant amitriptyline and the use of **psychodynamic psychotherapy**, and combined treatment with amitriptyline and psychodynamic psychotherapy, in a randomized controlled trial of patients with psychogenic pain in a pain clinic. They found that the antidepressants reduced pain and led to increased levels of activity in chronic pain patients, whereas psychodynamic psychotherapy led to an increase in activity, but also to an increase in pain.

Non-psychodynamically oriented short-term psychological therapies are also commonly used in certain somatizing conditions to alleviate symptoms. Cognitive behavioural therapy has been found helpful with patients with chronic fatigue (Sharpe et al., 1996; Wessely et al., 1989; see also Chapter 12, 'Musculoskeletal Disorders') and with chronic pain syndromes (Pearce, 1983; Farquar et al., 1990; Dworkin et al., 1994). Kirmayer and colleagues emphasize the importance of under-standing and appreciating the bodily quality and cultural meaning of the somatizer's symptoms (Kirmayer et al., 2004).

Guthrie argues that at one extreme of the spectrum of somatizations are patients with a history of severe emotional deprivation who find it difficult to make and sustain mature relationships (Guthrie and Creed, 1996). Their relationships are chaotic, fragile or symbiotic and often their partners are likely to become their carers. The physical symptoms are used by the patient to express and defend themselves against intolerable emotion. Any attempt to change this type of relationship is resisted by the patient. At the other extreme are individuals who have had sufficient emotional care in childhood and have later developed somatic symptoms after significant life-events. These more secure patients are able to form healthy and supportive relationships and can use a psychodynamic approach as they have a degree of psychological mindedness.

Psychodynamic Approaches to Management[2]

Taylor (2003) argues that, apart from conversion disorder in which there is a symbolic meaning to the somatic symptom, interpretable in a classical psychoanalytic psychotherapy, somatoform disorders are often associated with alexithymia. Others have argued that there may be an overlapping psychopathology for these two conditions (e.g., Rangell, 1959; Engel, 1968). Alexithymia is a term introduced by Nemiah and Sifneos (1970) to describe the difficulty that certain patients have in recognizing and acknowledging their underlying emotional states. The term 'alexithymia' literally means a difficulty in finding words for feelings. These patients have a limited phantasy life and a limited capacity to recall dreams (see Chapter 3). Often they speak in an unemotional way about charged emotional events. They find it difficult to use the technique of free association in analysis. Their thinking has been described as *operational* by Marty and de M'Uzan (1963). Krystal (1988) argues that somatizers are similar to the victims of massive trauma, who develop post-traumatic stress disorder. He found that many patients with post-traumatic stress disorder also manifested alexithymic characteristics. It is often the case that there is a history of abuse or other traumatic experience in childhood in somatizers. Krystal argues that the psychic trauma in somatizations and in post-traumatic stress disorder has caused a dissociation of feelings as well as a regression in the patient's capacity to handle emotions, which were experienced primarily in the body rather than consciously perceived in the mind.

Kellner (1985, 1987 and 1990) attributes the majority of **functional somatic symptoms** to physiological changes accompanying emotions. He argues that the symptoms of most somatoform disorders reinforced these emotions. Tyrer (1973) argues that a person is not always able to recognize the provoking emotional stimulus of a morbid emotion and so might not know that the stimulus arises from an internal psychological source.

This failure of recognition of this source means that the bodily feelings of the symptom are not understood, and are looked upon by the patient as primary phenomena, with a denial of the psychological aspects of their condition. Loewenstein (1990) and other authors found a greatly elevated prevalence of somatizations in adult survivors of incest. Morrison (1989) found a significantly higher rate of childhood sexual abuse amongst female somatizers and depressives. Craig and his colleagues (1993) showed that acute somatization was associated with a history of early parental neglect, indifference and childhood abuse. Barsky and colleagues (1994) compared a group of patients with hypochondriasis with a group of non-hypochondriacal patients attending a general medical outpatient clinic. The hypochondriacal group also reported significantly more traumatic sexual contact and victimization by physical violence with major parental upheaval before the age of seventeen.

These connections found between somatization, dissociation, alexithymia and trauma have led Nemiah (1991) and Saxe and his colleagues (1994) to argue that dissociation acts as a defence against emotionally distressing memories of childhood trauma. They see somatizations as a direct manifestation of emotions and sensations associated with traumatic events. Krystal (1978, 1988) argues that intense emotions caused by psychic trauma, interfere with the cognitive processing of experience. He writes that a patient subjected to psychological trauma returns to an earlier developmental phase where emotions were expressed entirely through bodily experience by means of a 'resomatization'. He argues that these emotions have not yet been mentally elaborated as distinct entities. Rodin describes a psychodynamic approach to hypochondriasis based on **self-psychology** in his review of somatization (Rodin, 1991).

Such views have led Taylor (1997) to try a different psychodynamic approach to the treatment of somatizations in alexithymic patients. He recommends an initial form of emotional coaching rather than a more conventional interpretive approach. This allows the patient to identify the underlying feelings that have caused their somatizations and link them to images and words, and so to begin to express them. Taylor describes his approach in his article on the analysis of a man with spasmodic torticollis (Taylor, 1993). In a more recent article on somatization, he distinguishes between the use of this approach in the alexithymic somatizing patient and the more classical approach to somatizers with conversion symptoms who respond to symbolic interpretation (Taylor, 2003). With the former type of patient he argues that the therapist is dealing with unsymbolized rather than repressed emotions. The aim of his psychotherapy is to strengthen connections between non-verbal emotional representations and words so that the patient may become more aware of their emotional needs and feelings (Bucci and Miller, 1993). By contrast, conversion symptoms may require a more conventional psychoanalytical psychother- apy aimed at identifying and resolving unconscious conflict. Although conflict might be present in both conversion and the other somatoform disorders, in the latter it provokes chronic states of emotional arousal rather than being expressed sym- bolically in the body (Taylor, 2003). My own experience has been that this distinction is often not so clear.

Some patients who are somatizers have enormous second- ary gain and low levels of psychological mindedness and do poorly with any psychological approach (e.g., patients with somatization disorder or severe hypochondriasis). Clearly others respond better to behavioural or cognitive approaches or else psychopharmacological treatments. There are many patients who are psychologically-minded enough to begin a trial of psychoanalytic psychotherapy and may respond to a more conventional interpretive approach if given sufficient time and support. Early attempts to take up issues relating to trans- ference may have negative results and, in certain cases (for example, the case history of hypochondriasis in this chapter and Chapter 3), it may be very important to tolerate the 'scatter of therapeutic agents' which represents the patient's initial need for multiple dependencies (Winnicott, 1989).

Some somatizations may signify important identifications with major illnesses in significant persons from the past or else in the body of a patient from childhood ('body memories').

Case Study

A patient developed nocturnal shock like sensations in her head during the course of a very unhappy marriage to an unfaithful husband, when he was yet again unfaithful to her. She decided, as a result of these strange and disturbing symptoms, that she could no longer put up with the poor relationship that she was in that was now making her feel physically ill.

Originally she had been unable to leave her husband until the development of this complaint which woke her in the night. The shock-like sensations were often preceded by nightmares. Sleep studies, performed by medical specialists, suggested she was developing a form of breathing difficulty in the night, causing changes in her blood gases, which resulted in migrainous headaches. A further opinion from a neurologist was that these were a somatization rather than organically based. She recalled that as a small child, she had suffered with frightening nightmares, possibly night terrors, from which she woke screaming, after a much-loved nanny had been forced by her mother to leave the house. Her mother herself had also suffered from bad headaches. She had a poor relationship with both her parents but especially with the mother who neglected her as a small child. In early childhood she was sent away to boarding school. After this separation from home, she developed bad migrainous headaches herself. Now she was caught in a conflict about whether to stay with her husband or to leave him and she developed these symptoms in her head that were in many ways very similar to her night terrors and the migraines of her childhood.

She had difficulties in expressing anger in general, especially towards her husband. It was only after the development of the shock-like sensations that she began to get directly angry with him and then decided to leave him. This led to a complete remission from these frightening symptoms and a capacity to express her feelings more directly. It was not possible to arrive at a meaningful reconstruction of her physical disturbance until this somatization was on its way out: the somatization represented past conflicts to do with separation and loss and her identification with the head-aches she had experienced in childhood, like her mother's, when she was sent away to school. They were also a form of self-punishment.

A psychodynamic understanding, even if it does not lead to psychodynamic treatment, can be extremely helpful in establishing a good working relationship between the doctor and the patient, allowing for effective support and care in the future, which may also involve a degree of physical rehabilitation where there is chronic disability.

Further Reading

Crimlisk, H. L., Bhatia, K., Cope, H., David, A., Marsden, C. D. and Ron, M. A. (1998) 'Slater revisited: 6-year-follow-up study of patients with medically unexplained motor symptoms', *British Medical Journal*, **316**: 582–86.

Engel, G. L. (1959) ' "Psychogenic" pain and the pain-prone patient', *American Journal of Medicine*, **26**: 899–918.

Guthrie, E. and Creed, F. (1996) 'Treatment methods and their effectiveness', in *Liaison Psychiatry*, ed. E. Guthrie and F. Creed (Glasgow: The Royal College of Psychiatrists), pp. 238–74.

Krystal, H. (1988) *Integration and Self-Healing: Affect, Trauma and Alexithymia* (Hillsdale, NJ: Analytic Press).

6 Anorexia Nervosa and Bulimia Nervosa

Anorexia Nervosa

> *I still have not been able to alter my attitude and approach to food and eating; I feel it is a struggle with which I alone must cope ... Closely tied with problems of mealtimes are my fabrications or value judgements of types of food and the imposition of 'oughts' as to the amount I 'should' eat ... In trying to cope with the task of eating a balanced diet I have found myself most dependent on, and in rebellion against, my parents, most especially my mother ... I feel a failure and have a need to be in control ... and I struggle with the problem of dependence and independence ... Outwardly I readily acknowledge that I am thin, tired, physically unattractive, and that I should gain some weight; but when it comes down to practical tasks, emotional reactions usually predominate.*
>
> Letter from a young anorexic to Hilde Bruch, quoted in *Conversations with Anorexics* (Bruch, 1988)

The term 'anorexia nervosa' was introduced by Gull (1873) and Lasègue (1873) who assumed that this was a condition in which the appetite disappeared. It was not until 1895 that Gilles de la Tourette recognized the ravenous and frightening nature of the hunger his patients experienced. By the 1940s this denial of hunger was connected with the fear of becoming fat.

Patients with anorexia nervosa continually engage in patterns of behaviour that maintain or increase a marked weight loss (DSM-IV-TR requires less than 85 per cent of healthy weight; the ICD-10 criterion of a Body Mass Index of less than 17.5 is commonly used, measured by dividing the weight (in kg) of an individual by the height in metres squared). This is an uncommon disorder with a prevalence of about 1 in 1,000 (Jones et al., 2001). Sufferers try to get rid of their food intake and decrease excessively intake of high carbohydrate or fat-containing foods. Some engage in rigorous exercise programmes. Others may be active at all times.

In those anorexics who engage in binge-eating and purging, patients may induce vomiting as well as using laxatives and **diuretics** to lose weight. Many patients who have anorexia nervosa are preoccupied with food and often are interested in preparing special meals for their family (Halmi, 2000).

Patients with anorexia nervosa have an intense fear of gaining weight and spend much time staring in the mirror to reassure themselves that they are not actually putting on weight. However, the significance of their body weight and shape is greatly distorted in their own perception. Some anorexics feel that they are globally overweight. Others realize that they are in fact too thin but nevertheless regard their abdomen and buttocks and thighs as being too fat. Overall, the anorexic cannot see his or her emaciation and values losing weight as being an achievement that boosts their self-esteem and gives them a sense of control at times that they feel is so lacking in other areas of their life. Sometimes food refusal is also to avoid gastrointestinal discomfort, (Rodin, personal communication). It has been suggested that the drive for thinness is a culture-bound phenomenon. Patients may also be obsessed with cleanliness and engage in compulsive studying whilst having difficulties in concentration, leading them to spend hours at their studies (Halmi, 2000). Anorexics often have little or no motivation to engage in treatment and have a delayed psychosocial sexual development with a decreased interest in sex (partly secondary to malnutrition).

Medical Complications of Anorexia Nervosa (Halmi, 2000)

1 Secondary to lowering of the **gonadotrophin-releasing hormone** (GnRH) there is suppression of the pituitary secretion of follicle stimulating hormone, and luteotrophic hormone leading to low levels of oestrogen and amenorrhoea in women.

2 As a result of the vomiting, diarrhoea and use of diuretics, patients have low levels of potassium and as a result of

purging may become hypokalaemic (diminished levels of potassium in the blood) with a metabolic alkalosis (accumulation of base in the body) and develop oedema (e.g., ankle swelling). Vomiting also leads to inflammation of the salivary glands (**parotid** hypertrophy).

3　Patients with over a year of amenorrhoea have a high risk of **osteopaenia** or **osteoporosis** (thinning of the bones).

4　As a result of starvation, patients may have delayed gastric emptying. This physiological change, in combination with reliance on laxatives, may lead to constipation. Underweight patients who also binge-eat may get dilatation of the stomach.

5　In the cardiovascular system, low levels of potassium may lead to heart arrhythmias and starvation may lead to a slowing of the heart. Starvation and fluid depletion may lead to a drop in blood pressure.

6　Starvation may lead to diminished levels of white cells and platelets (cells essential for blood clotting).

7　Dehydration and loss of subcutaneous fat will lead to a dry, cracking skin and, for unknown reasons, there is usually a characteristic baby hair known as 'lanugo hair'. In those patients who use their hands to induce vomiting, the friction of the hand against the teeth will cause a characteristic callous to develop on the dorsal part of the hand (Russell's Sign).

8　Pulmonary complications include the problem of aspiration of vomit with consequent pneumonia.

9　Dehydration, hypokalaemia (low serum potassium) and nutritional deprivation can lead to irreversible renal failure.

10　Muscle wasting can lead to extreme weakness and respiratory and cardiac failure.

Onset of Anorexia Nervosa

Anorexia nervosa has two peaks of onset – one between the ages of 14 and 15, and one at the age of 18. Rarely, it occurs in latency or is post-menopausal.

Treatment of Anorexia Nervosa

The type of treatment is very much dependent on the severity of the illness.

1 At the most extreme severity (weight less than 80 per cent of healthy weight; Anderson and Yager, 2005), the patient may require inpatient treatment in a specialized eating disorder unit. Medically, in all patients there should be an attempt at weight restoration, nutritional rehabilitation, rehydration and correction of the serum **electrolytes**. In the hospital setting, there should be daily monitoring of weight, food and calorie intake and urine output. Patients may respond to the use of the major tranquillizer olanzapine or else an antidepressant such as fluoxetine (Halmi, 2000).

2 In less severe cases the patient may respond to outpatient psychotherapy or else to a day-hospital programme. In controlled studies, it has been shown that those patients who are under 18 do better with family therapy than individual psychotherapy combined with nutritional counselling and pharmacological intervention. It may be very difficult to get the patient's cooperation and it is important to emphasize the benefits of treatment and to reassure the patient that it will help relieve other parts of the anorexia, such as their insomnia, their depression and obsessive thoughts about food and body weight and lead to an increase in energy, well-being and improved relationships with peers. Such outpatient treatments are best suited to those who have only had anorexia for less than six months, are not bingeing or vomiting and who have parents who are willing to cooperate in such a family therapy. Outpatients receiving treatment should be weighed on a weekly basis and given regular physical examinations and, if they are purging and vomiting, checks on their electrolytes (Halmi, 2000).

Bruch (1979), Crisp (1980) and Palazzoli (1978) described particular difficulties within the anorexic's family. Bruch wrote of how these families functioned as if members could read one another's minds. Sours (1980) emphasized the need of the family to maintain harmony and to disavow stress. Minuchin and colleagues identified five predominant characteristics as excessively present and detrimental to the overall functioning of the anorexic's family:

(a) enmeshment: enmeshment refers to a tight web of family relationships in which family members are over-sensitive to each other.
(b) over-protectiveness;
(c) rigidity;
(d) lack of conflict resolution;
(e) involvement of the sick child in unresolved parental conflicts.

(Minuchin et al., 1975)

Although there has been a lot of family research, none of these findings have been shown to be specific for anorexia nervosa (Rodin, personal communication). Family therapy is aimed at changing the behaviour of all family members. Such therapy enables the family to take responsibility for the resolution of the anorexic's symptoms (Sargent, Liebman and Silver, 1985). Dare argued for a more flexible, less confrontational, less blaming approach to these families (Dare et al., 1995). Here is a clinical example:

Case Study

Hannah had a two-year history of anorexia nervosa. The eating disorder became apparent when she was away from home in her second year at university in the north of England. She was brought home to London with a BMI of 12 (her pre-morbid BMI was 20), spent three months as an inpatient on a re-feeding regime, then became a day patient when her BMI had reached 14. As a result of the anorexia, she had developed osteoporosis in her spine and osteopoenia in her hip. She remained on the day programme for about 20 months and left when her BMI was 17.5.

In her family history (see Figure 6.1), her father Bob's father had died when Bob was only three years old and he was

NB: a cross on a square (male) or a circle (female) means that a significant illness occurred in this person.

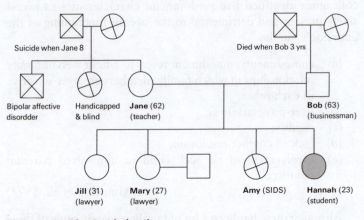

Figure 6.1 The Smith family

brought up by a mother who suffered considerable ill health, spending periods of time in hospital. Bob had been sent away to boarding school at the age of seven. He had coped with all this by escaping into his education and he was later to set a very high premium on education for his daughters. Jane, Hannah's mother, also had lost her father, who had committed suicide when she was eight, and both her brother and sister had died prematurely. She had coped with these traumas by having an intense and nurturing relationship with her own mother, which she sought to repeat with her daughters. After the couple's first two daughters, Jill and Mary, their third baby, Amy, died of Sudden Infant Death Syndrome (cot death), and then soon after this Hannah was born. Jane in particular did not appear to have properly mourned Amy's death.

In family therapy this couple presented as two intelligent, rather different people: Jane was a gentle, sensitive and nurturing teacher, while Bob was a practical, determined, achievement-oriented, and successful businessman. This dichotomy only appeared to become critical during the sensitive period when the children were leaving home. Both parents had high hopes for their daughters who had all gone to competitive girls' schools. However their hopes were very different, as Bob wanted them to attain academic success via Oxbridge, whereas Jane put more emphasis on the children's psychological stability and happiness. As a result, as they grew up, each of the daughters became involved in triangular relationships with the divided parents. This polarization of the couple's different outlooks on life and their difficulty in discussing this or being able to negotiate compromises imposed a conflict of loyalty on each daughter which each negotiated in a different way. As the family found it so difficult to address the issues verbally, the daughters resorted to dramatic actions in order to be heard. Jill as a teenager had **acted out** and ended up leaving home unhappily, and Mary had developed a serious **anxiety** disorder. Thus both managed to avoid Oxbridge, but did well enough in less prestigious universities, without ever having to overtly challenge the family situation. When her turn came, Hannah as the baby of the family found herself in a more difficult situation. Who would take her place if she were able to extricate herself? Both parents were well intentioned, caring and responsible people but they had become entangled in a situation that seemed too dangerous to address: focusing on their daughters had allowed them to deal with it. Hannah's anorexia, which put everything 'on hold', allowed the family to avoid addressing this situation and kept them linked together in an artificial closeness, creating an illusion of safety.

This family were seen monthly for 18 months by a male and female therapist working conjointly, as it was felt that, as there was such a dearth of men in the family, such a composition of therapists would mirror some of the issues that the parents needed to struggle with. The therapy focused on helping the family to find a way of expressing themselves verbally which might be heard and which would allow for discussion and negotiation. Bob seemed expert at offering solutions and planning strategies but did get not get listened to as it was felt that he was bullying. Jane was not listened to by Bob as, when she disagreed with him, she tended to route her disagreement through her daughters and he did not heed it as he experienced it as a criticism. Consequently there was no dialogue between the parents, and Hannah, who was caught in a conflict of loyalties with her parents pulling in opposite directions, needed to be helped to find her own voice and to challenge the status quo. As it was, she tended to keep a slim and silent profile, taking the easy option by adopting an 'I'm OK. Everything is fine' attitude.

Gradually the family were able to use the sessions to risk making changes. The parents began to talk together, rather than at each other: this allowed Hannah more space to work at her individual therapy, which she was also receiving, and to find a more effective voice which could now be heard. Mary had a baby girl which revived Jane's anxiety about Amy's death. However, it seemed that her ability to love this granddaughter and the granddaughter's survival allowed her finish her mourning. More importantly the arrival of this baby meant that Hannah was no longer the baby of the family, and she could now explore and review her long-held view that she had not been a wanted baby.

Towards the end of this family therapy a therapeutic injunction was put to the parents. This was that they should not get involved in any way in Hannah's plans and decisions for her future. It seemed almost with relief that this was followed and during subsequent sessions she revealed and discussed her plans. Bob, however, continued to try to advise Hannah, but with her growing robustness, she was better able to make her own decisions and only took the advice that suited her. She started a part-time job, while still attending the day programme part-time, and eventually left with a BMI of 17.5 and started back at her university, continuing to receive individual therapy weekly by telephone. (Arkell and Colahan, personal communication).

There have been no large-scale studies of cognitive behaviour therapy or psychoanalytic psychotherapy in anorexia nervosa, although Dare et al. (2001) conducted a randomized controlled trial of out-patient psychological treatments of adult anorexics. This is in contrast to research on treatments offered in bulimia nervosa, where there have been controlled studies of cognitive behaviour therapy and interpersonal therapy (Halmi, 2000).

Psychoanalytic Views

Crisp (1980) argues that, as puberty approaches, a girl may develop an intense fear of the impending changes to her body because these changes represent for her the threat of developing into a sexually mature adult, something she feels unable to cope with. Laufer and Laufer (1984) wrote of the adolescent's 'fear of the sexual body'. In order to prevent these changes, the anorexic girl tries to lose weight to maintain her pre-pubertal state and body shape. As Ritvo argues, the body is not only the first object of the drives and used early on as a metaphor but remains such an object: in his paper he illustrates how the body, its image and its functions are readily available for the representation and actualization of various aspects of psychic conflict during adolescence. Therefore, during this developmental phase there is 'an inescapable need to integrate the representation of the sexually mature body into the the eventual adult sexual organisation' (Ritvo, 1984).

Orbach, writing from a feminist perspective (1985), argues that body insecurity is bred into women by family psychodynamics and by contemporary western society, in which women's bodies are used as hidden persuaders in our consumer culture. Studies have shown that girls are often weaned earlier than boys and have less feeding time with their mothers, so receiving less holding than boys (Brunet and Lezine, 1966). Such a feeding relationship might therefore become a site for struggles between mother and child. Orbach argues that there could be continuity between these early feeding patterns in girls and accepted feeding patterns in adult women. If this first relationship had been experienced by the girl as one in which emotional nurturance was denied, it might have led to a mismatch between the daughter's desires and responses to them.

Classical psychoanalytic views
Originally psychoanalysts understood the symptoms of anorexia as a complex defence against positive and then negative Oedipal wishes. Ritvo argues that **genital conflicts** were transformed into oral conflicts to gain mastery over the genital conflict by a change of venue, shifting this Oedipal struggle to a safer, more familiar

and controllable ground (Ritvo, 1984). Waller, Kaufman and Deutsch (1940) postulated that refusal of food was a defence against ambivalently held **oral sadistic** and **cannibalistic phantasies**. Tuft (1958) thought it was to do with the fear of oral impregnation. Many other clinicians (Palazzoli, 1978; Sprince, 1984; Mushatt, 1992; and Wilson, 1992) look at pre-Oedipal mother–child conflicts in which the mode of relating was based on control and survival. Ego psychologists in the USA focused on the *early* **separation-individuation** struggles of these patients.

Self-psychological views
Bruch (1962) argued that the cardinal features of the anorexic are helplessness, passivity and ineffectiveness. Self-psychologists have seen the anorexic as deficient in a self-regulatory structure and too dependent on self-objects for well-being. The anorexic finds a compensation for the feelings of boredom, aimlessness and emptiness in being someone special (i.e., anorexic). By filling her life with rituals, she hopes to feel a sense of predictability and control, reducing her world to something more manageable. By devoting herself to the care, feeding and well-being of others, she can negate her own needs. Through self-starvation, she feels strengthened and temporarily superior to others. Goodsitt argues that psychotherapists tend to overestimate the capacities of anorexic patients to work in a psychotherapeutic setting (Goodsitt, 1982). He feels that anorexics frequently need the therapist to be a tension regulator, as these patients suffer with intense and recurrent tension states (Goodsitt, 1977, 1983) because they have no internalized psychic mechanism to soothe and regulate tension. They use starvation, bingeing, vomiting and physical exertion to diminish tension through such intense self-stimulatory activity.

Self-psychological treatment is aimed at enhancing self-organization by focusing attention on inner experiences and developing an awareness of the anorexic's own emotions. Anorexics often 'short-circuit', getting in touch with their feelings by taking self-stimulatory actions by means of starving, bingeing or hyperactivity. Such patients are terrified of intimacy and closeness so their motivation to be on their own with a therapist may be very poor. They need particularly sensitive feedback and cannot initially tolerate the usual silences of therapy. The anorexic is terrified of growing up and giving up the symbiotic or self-objects that are vital for their existence, cohesion and well-being. In this self-psychological view, guilt experienced by an anorexic is related to the problems of becoming a person separate from the parents, rather than to do with an achievement of any sort of Oedipal victory.

Kleinian views

Farrell argues that such active ways of psychotherapeutic relating are better replaced by work in countertransference so as to understand feelings aroused by early separation difficulties. She considers the possibility that the mother has used her child as an intermediate object to restore a missing element in her body image. Kleinians see the problems of the anorexic as being primarily narcissistic and have focused on the role of envy in these patients (Farrell, 1995). Crisp is wary of such views which seek to understand anorexia only and entirely in terms of the early mother–infant relationship, while seemingly ignoring the biological effects of puberty, including 'its own discrete and existential challenge' for character formation in adolescence (Crisp, 1980).

Case Study

Leah was a 22-year-old woman who had suffered from anorexia nervosa since the age of 14. She was significantly underweight as a result, restricting her food intake to the minimum: she drank large quantities of water and coffee. Although she was very weak, sleepless, had no menstrual periods and at times had a dangerously irregular heartbeat, she was able to dissociate herself from these alarming bodily experiences and continued to starve herself and to over-exercise.

She said of her body: 'I want it to be symmetrical, without any signs of femininity, such as my breasts or my bottom. I want it to disappear. I want my body to be pure. The thought of food staying inside my body makes me feel dirty and I want it to stay clean.'

During one of her psychotherapy sessions, when her therapist suggested that they might explore this fear of eating, she replied, 'If I eat, bad things will happen.' When the therapist asked her what kind of bad things might happen and whether bad things had happened in the past, she nodded. In subsequent sessions she told him how between the ages of seven and 14 she was repeatedly sexually abused by her father. The abuse only ceased when he died suddenly and unexpectedly. Leah could remember how she used to detach herself from her bodily feelings during the abuse so as to feel herself to be 'somewhere else, by thinking about other things'. At that time she felt she had no control over her body.

The anorexia, which developed after her father's death, was her way of controlling her body. By restricting her food intake she could prevent her body from becoming feminine and attractive to men. Tragically, the past sexual abuse was replaced by a different form of physical abuse which had life-threatening consequences. (Inspector, personal communication).

Much less is known about the psychopathology of anorexia nervosa in boys who only make up 10 per cent of patients with this condition. Certainly they also have a fear of becoming too fat, especially if one of the parents is overweight. There are feelings of inadequacy about sexual relations with girls, leading to the wish to remain pre-pubertal and not yet engage in sexual relations; fear of being too greedy; and rebellion against the parents, especially in enmeshed families where independence is difficult to achieve. Sometimes problems with sexual identity and identification with girls play a part (Wolff and Shoenberg, 1990).

Prognosis and Factors Influencing Outcome (Crisp, 1980)

Poorer prognosis is associated with

1 underlying personality potential: **borderline personality** (e.g., impulsivity, splitting and self-destructiveness);
2 male gender;
3 low social class;

4 major pre-morbid obesity, which may be associated with frequent vomiting and purging to maintain low body weight;
5 regular and frequent over-eating, vomiting and purging;
6 chronicity;
7 later age of onset;
8 pervasive despair and hopelessness;
9 lack of motivation for change;
10 poor social adjustment in childhood;
11 parental neurotic or affective disorder;
12 rigidity in parents, especially the father;
13 parental marital discord.

Its prognosis in the USA as studied by ten-year outcomes shows that 25 per cent make a full recovery, 50 per cent are markedly improved and functioning well, but 25 per cent do poorly and that includes 7 per cent who die at 10 years. Those doing poorly remain chronically underweight. In the UK and Sweden in a study over 20–30 years, there was mortality much higher at 18 per cent (Halmi, 2000). When these patients are followed over a longer period of time, the mortality rate increases when corrected for the expected mortality rate. Anorexia nervosa has the highest standardized mortality rate of any psychiatric disorder (Harris and Barraclough, 1998).

Bulimia Nervosa

This condition usually begins in a period of a few weeks to a year after the onset of dieting and may or may not allow the patient to lose weight. The weight loss is never sufficient to qualify for the diagnosis of anorexia nervosa. Restrained dieting eventually gives way to binge-eating episodes which are usually terminated by the development of abdominal pain, discomfort or self-induced vomiting. This is followed by feelings of guilt, depression and self-disparagement. In addition, some patients use laxatives and have a pattern of alternating bingeing and fasting. A minority also use diuretics to control weight. Such patients fear being unable to stop their eating voluntarily and so develop severe dieting interrupted by patterns of binge-eating. The food consumed has a dense caloric content and a specific texture to facilitate binge-eating. The result is that frequent weight fluctuations may occur. Bulimia nervosa is a common disorder found in 2–3 per cent of girls in the age of risk (Jones et al., 2001). The typical age of onset is 18–19 years.

A bingeing episode lasts for about one hour. Some patients have the characteristic abrasions and scars on the backs of their hands, described above, from sticking their fingers down their throat to induce vomiting. Most do not eat regular meals, have difficulty reaching satiety at the end of a meal and tend to eat alone at home. Binge-eating and vomiting relieve tension and anxiety and become, therefore, rewarding activities. Rodin argues that binge-eating and purging are often motivated by an attempt to regulate intolerable affect states. Often the lives of such patients are chaotic with troublesome interpersonal relationships and additional impulsive behaviours which are self-destructive. They may be anxious and suffer with low self-esteem. There is a high prevalence of mood disorder and substance abuse and compulsive stealing may also occur (Halmi, 2000).

The underlying psychopathology is often like that of anorexia nervosa. Fear of fatness is in conflict with an uncontrollable desire to eat excessively. Conflicts about sexuality and femininity, a disturbed body image and underlying depression, guilt and anxiety are common findings. The secret and solitary bingeing episodes bring about temporary relief but leave the patient feeling more guilty and depressed afterwards. As bingeing ceases during therapy, patients may experience a period of depression (Wolff and Shoenberg, 1990).

Medical Complications (Halmi, 2000)

1 The exposure to the gastric juices by vomiting causes severe erosion of the teeth;
2 Parotid gland enlargement;
3 Acute dilatation of the stomach and oesophageal tears;
4 Intoxication with laxative ipecac may cause cardiomyopathy (disease of the heart muscles), leading to cardiac failure;
5 Hypokalaemic alkalosis, as seen in the bulaemic form of anorexia nervosa.

Treatment of Bulmia Nervosa

Cognitive behaviour therapy (CBT) has been studied in 35 controlled psychosocial studies: it has been found that up to 40–50 per cent of patients have abstained from binge-eating and purging by the end of a 16–20 week treatment period with improvement through reduced binge-eating and purging in 75–95 per cent of patients. CBT also helps with the depression. Thirty per cent of patients without an initial improvement showed a full recovery at one year. CBT interrupts the self-maintained cycle of bingeing and dieting and is aimed at altering the dysfunctional cognitions and beliefs about food, weight, body image and overall self-concept (Halmi, 2000).

Such treatment is conducted on an outpatient basis, lasting approximately five months. It is semi-structured problem-oriented and mainly concerned with a patient's present and future rather than their past. The responsibility for change is with the patient. The therapist provides information, advice, support and encouragement.

In the first stage of therapy, emphasis is on establishing some control over eating, using mainly behavioural techniques. In the second stage, treatment is more cognitive, so that there is an attempt to identify and modify dysfunctional thoughts, beliefs and values. In the final stage, the focus is on maintaining change (Fairburn, 1985).

The alternative, **interpersonal therapy**, is not as effective as cognitive behaviour therapy. However Fairburn, Cooper and Shafran (2003) argue more recently for combining interpersonal therapy with cognitive behaviour therapy, so as to allow for potential resolution of interpersonal difficulties. In one controlled study, it was found that fluoxetine at 60 mg per day taken for up to six months was helpful in reducing episodes of bingeing and purging. In three studies, a combination of CBT and antidepressants was found to be superior to medication alone (Halmi, 2000).

Such short-term approaches to stop episodes of bingeing may need to be followed up by group analytic psychotherapy. If emotional and family problems persist in the long term, individual psychoanalytic psychotherapy or family therapy may be indicated (Wolff and Shoenberg, 1990).

Course and Prognosis of Bulmia Nervosa

After 5–10 years, 50 per cent of patients have fully recovered, 20 per cent still have bulimia nervosa, and 33 per cent will relapse at four years. Patients with personality disorders have the worst prognosis (Halmi, 2000). The mortality at 0–3 per cent is far lower than for anorexia nervosa.

Eating Disorder in Diabetes Mellitus

Type 1 diabetes mellitus is a common metabolic disorder where a deficiency in insulin secretion by the pancreas causes impaired glucose utilization. The treatment for this is multiple daily insulin injections with regular monitoring of blood sugar and restriction in the type and timing of food intake so as to bring the blood sugar to normal levels. Its aim is to diminish short-term complications of the condition, which include **ketoacidosis** and more long-term **microvascular complications** where there is damage to the kidney, the retina, the heart and the peripheral blood vessels.

Eating disorders typically occur in young women with type 1 diabetes and may do so on a coincidental basis. In eating disorders where there is binge-eating and insulin omission, there is consequent elevation of the blood sugar and so more frequent episodes of ketoacidosis. The effect of this behaviour is to lead to a threefold increase in **diabetic retinopathy**, which is a major complication of this type of diabetes.

Clinicians need to have a high index of suspicion of young women with diabetes with poor metabolic control and repeated episodes of ketoacidosis and weight fluctuations. A simple enquiry about body dysfunction and dieting, binge-eating and purging by deliberate omission of insulin, may lead to an identification of an underlying eating disorder (Rydall et al., 1997).

Maharaj et al. have demonstrated that eating disorders in young women with type 1 diabetes are associated with disturbances in empathic responsiveness in mother–daughter interactions (Maharaj et al., 2001).

Preliminary studies by Rodin have suggested that a six-session clinic-based psychoeducational intervention for girls with type 1 diabetes and their parents can lead to a reduction in disturbed eating attitudes and behaviour for up to six months (Olmsted et al., 2002). Diabetic patients with more severe eating disorders may benefit from a range of interventions for eating disorders, including CBT, interpersonal therapy and dynamic psychotherapy, and may, in more severe cases, require day hospital or inpatient treatment. The importance of this research is that it offers an opportunity to reduce the incidence of dangerous physical complications in a group of patients with unstable diabetes (i.e., diabetes that is difficult to control).

Further Reading

Bruch, H. (1979) *The Golden Cage* (New York: Vintage Books).

Goodsitt, A. (1986) 'Self-psychology and the treatment of anorexia nervosa', in *Handbook of Psychotherapy for Anorexia Nervosa and Bulimia*, ed. D. M. Garner and P. E. Garfinkel (New York: Guilford Press), pp. 55–83.

Halmi, K. A. (2000) 'Eating disorders', in *Comprehensive Textbook of Psychiatry*, 7th edn, ed. B. J. Sadock and B. A. Sadock (Philadelphia, PA: Lippincott, Williams and Wilkins), pp. 1663–76.

7 Obesity

Let me have men about me that are fat;
Sleek-headed men and such as sleep o' nights;
Yond Cassius has a lean and hungry look;
He thinks too much: such men are dangerous.

Shakespeare, *Julius Caesar*, I.ii.191

The western world is currently facing an epidemic of obesity, which represents a massive public health problem. It is now the leading cause of preventable death in the USA (Brownell, Wadden and Phelan, 2005). The prevalence of obesity has tripled since the early 1990s and has been highest in minority populations. Brownell and Wadden (2000) defined obesity as an excess of body fat in which there is greater than 25 per cent of the body weight taken up by fat in women and greater than 18 per cent of the body weight taken up by fat in men. The prevalence of obesity in Britain doubled from 8 per cent to 15 per cent between 1980 and 1995 (Wilding, 1997).

One useful measurement for obesity is the body mass index which is produced by dividing the weight of the individual in kilograms by the height of the individual (in metres) squared. The ideal body mass index should be between 20 and 25 kg/m^2. In the USA, 35 per cent of women and 31 per cent of men have a body mass index greater than 27. Over 60 per cent of African Americans have a body mass index greater than 27. Patients who are between 25 and 27 body mass index are at a slightly increased risk of the problems of obesity. If their body mass index is between 27 and 30 they are at a definitely increased risk and if above 30 they are at a greatly increased risk of the problems of obesity. Advances in treatment have improved weight loss but failed to stop the increase in prevalence (Brownell, Wadden and Phelan, 2005).

Overweight people often feel criticized and even blamed by not only the general public but also health professionals and this may deter them from seeking medical help. In normal individuals, weight gain is most pronounced between the ages of 25 and 44; after the age of 50 men's weight gain usually stabilizes but women's weight gain continues to increase until the age of 60.

Physical and Psychological Consequences of Obesity

When the body mass index is greater than 27, there is a clear correlation between obesity and the development of serious disease and mortality. Aside from factors associated with smoking, this level of obesity leads to an elevated cholesterol which increases the risk of major cardiovascular disease, in particular coronary artery disease, myocardial infarction and essential hypertension. Patients with this level of obesity are at risk from the development of **type 2 diabetes** (non-insulin dependent). The increased load bearing leads to degenerative joint disease. Obesity is also associated with **obstructive sleep apnoea**, some cancers, gall stones, gynaecological problems, problems with irregular periods and depressive illness. On the whole, body fat distribution is a better predictor of cardiovascular mortality than overall weight. The distribution of fat that puts the patient at risk is increased subcutaneous body fat in the upper body. This is also a high risk factor for type 2 diabetes.

Individuals who have grown up overweight may well have been ridiculed and tormented in their childhood by other children and indeed adults, as well as suffering from discrimination at school and when seeking jobs. The effects of obesity on the quality of life are as important as the risks of morbidity and mortality. Patients with obesity have poorer physical functioning, poor general health, a lower vitality, are subject to pain in their body, poorer social functioning and poorer mental health (Brownell and Wadden, 2000).

Psychological Factors

Apart from binge-eating, there is little evidence that overeating is a response to anxiety or depression. However, in women it has been found that adult obesity is associated with childhood depression – 50 per cent of obese binge-eaters present with clinically significant depression as compared with 5 per cent of obese non-bingers (Brownell, Wadden and Phelan, 2005). Food for obese individuals may be a means to escape and comfort. As one patient said to me: 'Eating is a buffer against disappointment.' There are two recognized psychogenic abnormal eating patterns:

- Binge-eating: about 30 per cent of obese individuals seeking help for obesity report binge-eating, which is not followed by vomiting or laxative abuse as a compensatory behaviour. Binge episodes are distressing and include rapid eating until uncomfortably full, either when not hungry or eaten alone. Often binge-eaters report being numb during such an episode and that they use the food to block out the world. This pattern of eating is caused by interpersonal distress.
- Night eating: a small percentage (1.5 per cent of the general population and 9 per cent of obese patients) consume 50 per cent of calories after the evening meal and a carbohydrate-high snack at least once during the night.

Causes of Obesity

The main causes of obesity are:

- High fat, high calorie, easily palatable diets, such as those provided by fast food and convenience food, combined with a decline in physical activity.
- Genetic: in the experimental mouse, called *ob/ob*, the mouse becomes obese because of a deficiency in the protein leptin, synthesized in the adipose tissue. This acts on central nerve networks to control normal food intake and energy expenditure. Leptin inhibits food intake and increases energy expenditure. Normally, as the adipose mass increases, leptin secretion also increases, reducing food intake. In the *ob/ob* mouse, because of a mutation in a gene called the *ob* gene, no leptin is produced. As a

result, the animal has an excessive appetite and is extremely inactive. If the animal is given recombinant leptin it returns to a rapid normalization of eating and activity. However, to date only a few human beings have been found to have the same anomaly as the *ob/ob* mouse. The overwhelming majority of obese subjects have high levels of leptin.

- Low basal metabolic rate: no specific gene for low energy or high energy expenditure has been found except in a very rare genetic syndrome called the Prader-Willi syndrome.
- Certain physical conditions which predispose a patient to become overweight. These include:

   (a) **Cushing's disease**, where too many steroids are produced; and *hypothyroidism*, where too little thyroid hormone is produced and the basal metabolic rate is lowered;
   (b) **hypogonadism**;
   (c) obesity, produced by administration of steroids for medical purposes;
   (d) the use of other medications which contribute to overeating including major tranquillizers such as the phenothiazines and antidepressants such as **tricyclics**.

Treatments for Obesity

These vary from helping patients who are grossly overweight to deal with the psychological stigma through supportive psychotherapy to helping patients to lose weight through a range of psychological and physical means. Common supportive psychological measures may be:

- Encouraging the patient to join a self-help group for obese patients (such as 'Weight Watchers');
- Setting realistic goals for weight loss rather than advising the patient to go on a drastic diet;

- Encouraging the patient to take more physical activity; and the prescription of medication to reduce food intake or to reduce the absorption of dietary fat.

Patients with a body mass index of more than 40, who are grossly overweight and in danger of severe damage to their health, may choose to have some form of bypass surgery that reduces the amount of food that can be eaten or that enables food to bypass the stomach, passing instead through a pouch linked to a loop of the small bowel. Such drastic measures may produce quite significant weight loss, in the region of 25–35 per cent, but such patients need be carefully selected from a psychological as well as a physical point of view. Gastric bypass surgery may lead to diarrhoea and metabolic disturbances. Where the stomach is stapled, in an operation known as vertical banded gastroplasty, there may initially be vomiting as a reaction.

Where the patient has a form of obesity in which bingeing is part of the cause, the use of cognitive behavioural therapy, as with bulimia nervosa, may be extremely helpful in reducing this pattern of eating. Interpersonal therapy has been found to be equally effective (Wilfrey et al., 2002). Here is an example of a patient whose obesity was linked to binge-eating and who was referred for psychoanalytic psychotherapy.

Case Study

Jane was a 50-year-old doctor referred for individual psychotherapy with problems of overweight and bingeing over the past twenty years. Her weight at the time of assessment was around 14½ stone and her height 5′5″. Her body mass index was 33. She was troubled by this weight because she felt it was interferring seriously with the possibility of finding a boyfriend. For the past ten years she had been living on her own and finding that, although she was able to maintain a normal diet during the day, when she was alone at home, the evening felt so long and empty that she would start to eat high carbohydrate foods which initially involved bingeing followed by vomiting. However, since stopping the vomiting pattern, her weight had increased over the previous three years from its more usual 12 stone to 14½ stone. She was now worried that not only was the obesity getting in the way of finding a partner but that it also might contribute to diabetes which was in her family history.

In her background, she had had a successful, long-term relationship with a man that had ended because he was not prepared to commit himself to marriage. She came from a strict Calvinistic family in Switzerland where her father was a successful lawyer. She felt worried that she had never been able to meet his expectations in her professional and personal life, in spite of having done so well. There was a history of sexual abuse by a middle-aged female friend of the family between the ages of five and seven which had left her with profound feelings of guilt and remorse. Now she wanted to explore these emotions, the depression and the reasons for her binge-eating pattern. She was motivated and insightful and it seemed possible that a psychodynamic psychotherapy would be extremely helpful for this intelligent, insightful person.

Helping Patients with Body Image Disturbance and Obesity

Obese people are more prone to distort body size. They are more easily dissatisfied and preoccupied with physical appearance and more avoidant in social situations. Most commonly, a patient complains about the size of their waist, abdomen, thighs, buttocks or, possibly, their whole body. More than one third are concerned with their facial features, especially the appearance of facial and head hair, along with skin blemishes and breast size or shape. The two groups most prone to negative body image are those with binge-eating disorders and those needing gastric bypass surgery. The GP can have a central role in the management of obesity, and Zalidis gives a very moving account of his work with one massively obese patient who received surgery and counselling (Zalidis, 2001).

Obese adolescents are likely to be more self-conscious than normal because of the stigmatizing experience of being stared at and subject to inappropriate comments from professionals and their peer group, amongst whom thinness is at a premium.

Numerous studies have attested to the effectiveness of body image cognitive behaviour therapy, carried out either as individual or group therapy or as a self-administered treatment. The overall aim in all treatments for obesity is to reduce caloric intake and to increase physical activity. The use of very low caloric diets (between 900 and 1000 calories per day) may also be recommended in some circumstances but is a drastic form of treatment.

Two drugs have been used in conjunction with diet in the long-term treatment of obesity. One is sibutramide, which inhibits reuptake of serotonin and noradrenaline (and also dopamine; all neurotransmitters), which has the side effects of increased heart rate and diastolic blood pressure. The other is orlistat, which reduces the absorption of dietary fat (selectively inhibiting gastric and pancreatic lipase) but its side effects include oily stools, flatulence and **faecal urgency**. Weight loss with these drugs slows after four to six months and leads to about 10 per cent loss of initial body weight.

Further Reading

Brownell, K. D., Wadden, T. A. and Phelan, S. (2005) 'Obesity', in *Comprehensive Textbook of Psychiatry*, 8th edn, ed. B. J. Sadock and A. Sadock (Philadelphia, PA: Lippincott Williams and Williams), pp. 2124–36.

Zalidis, S. (2001), *A General Practitioner, his Patients and their Feelings* (London: Free Association Books), pp. 164–75.

8 Gastrointestinal Disorders

Ventre affamé n'a point d'oreilles [A hungry stomach has no ears]

Jean de la Fontaine, 'Le Milan et le Rossignol'

Emotions and emotional conflicts can affect gastrointestinal functioning in many ways. These range from nausea and vomiting to abdominal cramps, diarrhoea, constipation, rectal bleeding, faecal incontinence, irritation of the anus and passing of excessive flatus (wind). As the psychoanalyst Engel pointed out (1975), some of these complaints are purely psychological in origin, others are psychophysiological phenomena or symptoms of organic bowel disorders, some of which may have psychological factors in their aetiology. Engel described how, in acute anxiety there may be nausea and vomiting with periodic **intestinal peristalsis** causing abdominal cramps and diarrhoea (Engel, 1975). Less commonly, in severe depression or with acute feeling of sadness and discouragement there may be severe constipation. The digestive system is so connected with our emotions that it has entered the language in metaphor. We say we cannot 'stomach' a situation, or that we have not the 'guts' to go through with a planned action or that we have a 'gut reaction' to something. When we are devastated we may say we feel 'gutted'.

Functional Disturbances

1 Globus Hystericus

In adults, conversion reactions may occur in the upper part of the gastrointestinal tract. Here, repressed rage may lead to the conversion symptom of *globus hystericus*, also called 'hysterical dysphagia', in which the patient complains of an acute difficulty in swallowing (see conversion disorder and also the case history

121

of *globus hystericus* in the section on psychosomatic incidents in psychotherapy in Chapter 3).

2 Pruritis Ani

Adults may develop *pruritis ani*, where there is itching and soreness around the anal margin, or there may be pain in the rectum. Engel argued that this itching and soreness might represent repressed fantasies and correspond to conversion manifestations linked with anal intercourse and repressed homosexual wishes.

3 Addiction to Laxatives

In adults, there may be an addiction to laxatives, to enemas and to having high colonic irrigation. Sometimes patients use excessive laxatives or enemas, not as part of a bulimic syndrome (see Chapter 6) but because they consider the contents of their bowel as bad or destructive.

4 Aerophagia

Some adults periodically swallow large amounts of air, developing symptoms such as belching.

5 Psychosis

In a psychosis, there may be bowel manifestations. Extreme constipation may develop during severe psychotic depression. Incontinence of the bowel may develop in acute or chronic schizophrenia with bizarre anal or rectal sensations which have a delusional or persecutory character. These may also be a presenting complaint of paranoid schizophrenia. Sometimes patients present with a monosymptomatic delusion, the fear of emitting a bad smell.

6 Irritable Bowel Syndrome

Irritable bowel syndrome is a common gastrointestinal disorder in which combinations of abdominal pain, altered bowel habit and bloating occur for more than three months. It is the commonest complaint seen in gastroenterology clinics, and accounts for 10–20 per cent of patients presenting in general practice. It is commoner in women than in men and its prevalence may be inversely related to household income (Drossman et al., 1993). The prevalence of anxiety and mood disorders, especially panic disorder, in patients attending gastroenterology clinics is twice that of inflammatory bowel disease (Drossman et al., 2000, 2002). The onset of anxiety or mood disorder precedes or coincides with the onset of irritable bowel in two-thirds of irritable bowel patients (Craig, 1989; Ford et al., 1987). The presence of untreated psychiatric disorder predicts a poor outcome. There is an association between reduction of psychiatric symptoms and reduction of bowel symptoms (Creed, 1999).

Clinical Features

The abdominal pain is commonly dull and aching or else sharp and cramping. It may be relieved by defecation, or associated with a change in frequency or consistency of the stool. It is usually associated with two or more of the following symptoms:

1 the passage of mucus with the faeces;
2 the sensation of bloating combined with abdominal distension;
3 altered stool form;
4 altered stool passage;
5 altered stool frequency, which may become diarrhoea or constipation or alternation between the two.

The pain may be associated with other non-gastrointestinal complaints such as fatigue, fibromyalgia (see Chapter 12), headaches or urological symptoms. Although milder forms of irritable bowel syndrome that last less than three months can occur, those forms that last more than three months are of significant cost to the country in terms of health care and sickness benefit.

These patients are excessively sensitive to visceral pain, which can be reproduced on balloon dilatation of the large bowel. High amplitude ileal contractions (i.e., in the small intestine) have been shown to be responsible for some of the abdominal pain in irritable bowel syndrome. Recent research by Gershon (1998) has emphasized the neural control of gut movements and secretions by a 'gut brain'[2] (the enteric component of the autonomic nervous system), resulting in secretion of serotonin into the gut lumen, which affects intestinal movement and is inhibited by the enzyme SERT; in patients with irritable bowel there is a deficiency of SERT, resulting in excessive serotonin in the gut which may also partly cause the symptoms of irritable bowel (i.e., at one level of secretion, diarrhoea results, and at a higher level constipation results).

Psychological Factors

Creed and colleagues (Creed, Craig and Farmer, 1988) showed that patients with irritable bowel have commonly had a severe life-event during the previous thirty-eight weeks, as have patients suffering with a depression or who had taken an overdose. If patients present with irritable bowel they should be carefully investigated for infections, inflammation or malignancy of the gut.

Treatment

1. *General*: treatment of the abdominal pain may be helped by the use of **anti-cholinergic** drugs and also, sometimes, the use of tricyclic antidepressants which have direct action on the bowel. If the main symptom is diarrhoea, this may be helped by anti-diarrhoeal agents, such as loperamide and constipation by dietary measures such as increasing dietary fibre. A new drug, Tegaserod, a 5-HT receptor partial agonist and a prokinetic in the gut, is effective in women with constipation-predominant irritable bowel syndrome although a Cochrane review showed no effect on pain and discomfort (Farthing, 2005; Evans et al., 2004).

2. *Psychotherapeutic*: in 1983, Svedlund made a controlled study of the use of psychodynamic psychotherapy in irritable

bowel syndrome and showed that it could be effective (Svedlund, 1983). Guthrie reported on a method of brief psychodynamic psychotherapy in 1991. She studied 102 patients with chronic irritable bowel syndrome whose symptoms had not responded to medical treatment and which had lasted for more than a year. They had abdominal pain, abdominal distension and altered bowel habits. She conducted a randomized controlled study of brief psychodynamic psychotherapy, comparing the use of seven sessions of psychodynamic interventions with a control group of patients, who had received five sessions of supportive 'listening therapy'. The bowel symptoms were independently and blindly assessed by gastroenterologists at the end of the trial. Any controls who reported continuing physical distress were then offered the psychodynamically-oriented psychotherapy of the model above. The treatment group showed a significant improvement over the control group in terms of gastrointestinal symptoms and in psychological outcome. The psychodynamic approach used was based on Hobson's conversational model (Hobson, 1985; Guthrie, 1991). In the first session, time was allowed for a strong therapeutic alliance to develop. The session might last for up to three hours and was intense. The subsequent six sessions lasted for 45 minutes each. The conversational model emphasized ways of generating a feeling language, using the bowel symptoms as a means of describing emotional states, e.g., 'you are bunged up'.

Randomized controlled trials of cognitive behavioural therapy in primary care irritable bowel patients demonstrated short- to medium-term improvements in treatment-resistant irritable bowel patients but these were not sustained beyond one year (Kennedy et al., 2005); in hospital-based patients, results are more equivocal (Drossman et al., 2003; Boyce et al., 2003). Until now, there has not been a comparison of cognitive behaviour therapy with psychodynamic psychotherapy in this condition.

Case Study

Maria suffered with irritable bowel syndrome and was referred to me by a surgeon. She felt that her physical condition had little to do with the grief over the loss of an aunt who had died some months earlier. Her crying had led her surgeon to be concerned. She was sure that her abdominal pain and intermittent constipation required further physical investigation. She was ambivalent about any commitment to psychotherapy but prepared to try some initial sessions.

Maria was an isolated person who worked as an accountant. She had had a close but conflictual relationship with a father, a craftsman, with whom she quarrelled in adolescence, and a lukewarm relationship with her mother. Both parents were now dead. She had grown up relatively securely until the age of 11, when she and her brother were separated from their parents on a number of occasions. These separations were painful.

Her bowel symptoms began shortly before she left home to marry and, since that time, they had occurred intermittently. Initially she was unsure about her capacity to use psychotherapy; she could be querulous and demanding and was curiously jealous, fantasising that my other patients were better able to use such therapy.

Some months into the therapy she cancelled a session because they were introducing computers at her office. She was worried that she would not be able to learn to use these new machines as quickly as the other, younger, accountants. At the last minute, before the cancelled session, she telephoned me and said she had changed her mind and now wanted the session. She said that a lot of thoughts had surfaced. When she came, she explained that she could now see a link between her irritable bowel and emotional stress. She told me that, over the last few weeks of psychotherapy, the irritable bowel had completely disappeared.

Over the weekend, however, her bowel symptoms had recurred as she had begun to worry about the impending computer course. This reminded her of how the irritable bowel had recurred after the death of her aunt, who had been like a mother to her. She had had to organize the funeral on her own and when afterwards she had commented on her sadness to her husband, he had told her to 'cheer up and enjoy the nice sunny day'. To better control these sad feelings, she thought of learning to drive a car. Her abdominal pains began after her first driving lesson.

In telling me this story, in which for the first time she made a link between her emotions and her bowel symptoms, she said, 'I know what you're going to say'. I asked what it was that she thought I was going to say and she replied, 'You're going to tell me how sad I look'. I said, 'Well, you do look sad.' She replied, 'That's right but I don't like it that you should be right.' We had reached the end of the session and I felt uncomfortable about the way it had ended. However, I remembered how she had described to me the argumentative relationship she had with her father in childhood and considered that this was being repeated with me in transference.

At the next session, I was surprised that she told me how helpful the last session had been. She reported her first dream, in which she was coming for therapy but I was not in my consulting room. Instead, I was standing in a small tree house. After arriving, she found herself sitting down with me at a small table to eat some cake. In her associations to the dream she could recall worrying that she would spill crumbs on the floor. In the dream I resembled her father. She then explained how, as a child, she loved waiting up for her father's return from work so as to share a small meal with him. She reported quarrels about tidiness they had had when she was a small child.

This dream, with its vivid and meaningful content, following her linking of her psychological distress with her somatic symptoms, demonstrated a capacity to work in a deeper way than I had originally anticipated might be possible. It slowly led to an understanding of the origins of her need to control her feelings through her bowels. She told me about experiences she had with her mother when she was much younger. The mother had worried about her children's bowel functions because she herself suffered with an anal fistula (a passage between the anal canal and the outside skin), and so she made them take massive quantities of the laxative cascara every day, which they hated.

Her irritable bowel syndrome eventually resolved. The therapy, with its use of transference and dream material, allowed us to appreciate the significance of the importance of her early relationship to a depressed mother, which had made her so insecurely attached and vulnerable to the later separations and losses in childhood and adult life. Her father's concern with tidiness and her mother's preoccupation with bowel control helped us both to link her need to control her bowels in order to control emotions which she regarded as messy and dangerous. (This patient is also discussed in the sections on assessment and the uses of symbolic interpretations in Chapter 3).

Peptic Ulcer Disease

Usually peptic ulceration is a chronic illness.[1] Emotional factors are thought to play a more significant role in duodenal ulcer than gastric ulcer. Peptic ulcer has been considered to be a disease of western civilization, as it is rarely seen in the developing world, such as in northern India or among the African population of South Africa. It is more prevalent in urban than rural areas, and amongst men in administrative and professional fields. Six to 15 per cent of the western world's population suffers with duodenal ulcer, although its incidence has been decreasing over the past 40 years. This trend is thought to be due to declining rates of infection with *Helicobacter pylori* (Parsonnet, 1995), presumably because of the introduction of successful antibiotic therapy. Gastric ulcer has a similar incidence, although its peak incidence is in the sixth decade which is ten years later than for duodenal ulcer. Duodenal ulcer is commoner in men than women and tends to occur in a younger age group, whereas gastric ulcer occurs with equal frequency in both sexes. Also, gastric carcinoma is associated with gastric ulcer, unlike duodenal ulcer.

Clinical Features

The main symptom of peptic ulcer is pain in the epigastrium (the upper part of the abdomen) occurring one to four hours after a meal and usually lasting for half an hour to one hour, relieved by eating food or taking alkalis. When the patient is examined they can usually point to the site of the pain with their finger. It is most intense in the afternoon and at night, usually between midnight and 2 a.m. The syndrome is periodic and chronic with remissions and exacerbations and can extend over a period of 10–25 years. The diagnosis is made from the patient's history, X-ray studies and direct inspection of the lining of the stomach or the duodenum by gastroscopy or duodenoscopy respectively. Various factors increase the risk of developing peptic ulcer, including infection with *Helicobacter pylori*, the use of non-steroidal anti-inflammatory drugs (e.g., ibruprofen for pain relief) and stress ,as well as the regular consumption of alcohol and cigarette smoking, which themselves may be linked to stress.

Psychological Factors

There is convincing evidence that the onset, perpetuation and recurrence of peptic ulcers are associated with stressful life-events (Creed and Olden, 2005). This has been shown after earthquakes, where the presence of *Helicobacter pylori* has been known to interact with stress (Matsushima et al., 1999).

In 1833, Beaumont carried out a study of Alexis St Martin, who had an opening from his stomach onto his abdominal wall (joined by a narrow passage called a gastric fistula), and noticed how psychological factors influenced the secretion of his gastric juices. Engel, Reichsman and Segal (1956) studied a baby, named Monica, with a similar fistula and found that, when relating to others, especially her nurse, she had high amounts of gastric secretions. When separated from her nurse, attention seeking, angry, anxious, or experiencing guilt or shame, she secreted low amounts of gastric juice (see Chapter 4 and also the photographs of Monica in Figure 4.2). Subsequently Wolf and Wolff (1947) demonstrated a relationship between human gastric functions and various emotional states in Tom, another patient with a gastric fistula.

There are important differences and similarities between duodenal and gastric ulcers:

1   In duodenal ulcers the levels of hydrochloric acid and the enzyme pepsin are increased, whereas in gastric ulcers the secretion of hydrochloric acid and pepsin is variable

and may often be normal or in half the cases of gastric ulcer even decrease). These patients have blood group type O. In duodenal ulcer there is a high level of serum pepsinogen which has a high somatic risk factor and is inherited as an autosomal dominant trait (Mirsky, 1958).

2   With gastric ulcer, hypersecreters of acid and pepsin are also like duodenal ulcer in that they have the blood group type O.

3   Other patients who are not hypersecreters and have gastric ulcers have blood group type A.

Weiner et al. (1957) successfully predicted which men in a large cohort of US army draftees would have duodenal ulcers by combining psychological criteria with the biological criterion of high baseline pepsinogen secretion. Given such differences in the genetics and pathophysiology of duodenal and gastric ulcers, we need to be careful about applying the same psychological theory to all types of ulcer.

Personality Factors

Dunbar, in 1947, argued that the patient with peptic ulcer was activity oriented, ambitious and striving. Alexander (1950) argued that the unconscious conflict in these patients had to do with an inner need to be loved, nourished and cared for, versus a sense of shame against which the patient defended. This led to a continuous tension produced by the oral drive to be loved and nourished and kept the patients in a state of physiological activation. Often these patients proved to be competitive and hard-driven people.

However, a study by the psychoanalysts de M'Uzan and Bonfils (1961) of 193 patients with peptic ulcer showed that only 25 per cent were like Alexander's patients. The remainder were not strongly competitive or hard-driving. Engel (1955, 1975) has argued that such hypersecretion of acid and pepsin in the infant might alter the mother–infant relationship, causing such babies to have a high oral drive, resulting in special demands on the mother for feeding which may be frustrated.

In adult life, the tendency to experience a loss with a sense of verbal rage and frustration could then lead to excessive production of acid, resulting in an ulcer.

Studies do show a consistent link between stress and the prevalence of peptic ulcer. Cobb and Rose (1973) studied the prevalence rate of peptic ulcer in air traffic controllers and found that it was twice that of second-class airmen. Castelnuovo-Tedesco (1962) retrospectively constructed a profile of the two or three weeks before the onset of 17 duodenal ulcers and three gastric ulcers in patients who had subsequently perforated (i.e., developed a perforation in the stomach or duodenal wall) and found that the patients had experienced a sense of omnipotent rage in a setting of impending personal defeat, prior to becoming aware of the defeat.

More recently Creed and Olden (2005) have argued that there is still no convincing relation between a particular personality type and duodenal ulcer, based on work by Lewin and Lewis (1995). However, they refer to studies by Craig and Brown (1984) and Ellard et al. (1990) that suggest that, where chronic stressors involve goal frustration, peptic ulcer disease is more persistent (Creed and Olden, 2005).

Treatment: the discovery of high serum levels of the bacterium *Helicobacter pylori*, and the possibility of treating this infection with antibiotics greatly improved the prognosis of peptic ulcer, which has led many doctors to underestimate the role of psychological factors in the aetiology of this condition. Although these patients respond to antibiotics, most uncomplicated cases of peptic ulceration will also improve within 4–8 weeks with **H$_2$ receptor antagonists** that reduce the basal acid secretion (cimetidine) or with **proton pump inhibitors**, e.g., omeprazole which inhibits gastric ATPase.

There is some evidence that psychoanalysis can affect the long-term course of peptic ulcer. Orgel (1958) studied 15 chronic peptic ulcer patients in psychoanalytic treatment. Although five discontinued their treatment, the ten who continued their treatment for 3–4 years had *no* recurrences of their peptic ulcers whereas of the five who discontinued their treatment there was a recurrence in four of these of their peptic ulcer symptoms.

Inflammatory Bowel Diseases: Ulcerative Colitis and Crohn's Disease

These are chronic relapsing diseases of the small and large bowel in which the bowel wall is damaged by an inflammatory process. Both illnesses cause diarrhoea that may be blood-stained, accompanied by abdominal cramps and weight loss. They run a chronic but intermittent course, with exacerbations and remissions. The two conditions differ in the nature of the inflammation, its location and its local and systemic complications. These are rare conditions: ulcerative colitis has an incidence of 6–8 cases per 100,000 population and Crohn's disease has an incidence of two cases per 100,000 population. Ulcerative colitis has a prevalence of 70–150 cases per 100,000 population.

Ulcerative Colitis

In ulcerative colitis, the mucosal surface (the lining of the bowel), as well as the submucosa of the wall of the large bowel (the colon and the rectum), is ulcerated and **oedematous**. The inflammation may be restricted to the rectum or it may involve the whole or parts of the colon. This disease can occur at any age but peak incidences are between 20 and 30 years and between 60 and 70 years. Its onset is usually gradual and the initial symptoms are of episodes of diarrhoea accompanied by blood and mucous in the stool, with abdominal pains and rectal cramps, anorexia and weight loss. It rarely has a severe acute onset. The disease is more common in women than in men and in Caucasians (it is commonest in Jews). There is a familial incidence in 2–5% and an important association with an arthritic condition called **ankylosing spondylitis**.

Immunological and psychological factors play an important role in its precipitation and causation (Kirsner and Shorter, 1982). An anticolon antibody (mainly IgM and IgG) is detectable in the majority of patients. This may play a part in causing the inflammation and be associated with the development of extra colonic (systemic) complications, but it is also found in healthy persons. It is possible that a rise in the titre of IgM is secondary to mucosal damage caused by the colitis. Also, there are circulating lymphocytes which may cause damage to the colonic epithelium (the colonic mucosal tissue) as a result of early sensitization in infancy (Strang, 1989). (See also the discussion of Maunder's research in the section on psychological factors in this chapter.)

Local complications include the development of:

- cancer of the colon or rectum in 0.6–14 per cent of patients;
- the development of strictures of the bowel;
- perforation of the bowel, toxic megacolon (gross swelling up of the colon to the point of disintegration);
- severe haemorrhage from the bowel wall.

Systemic (bodily) complications are:

- ankylosing spondylitis;
- **sacroilitis**;
- a peripheral arthritis affecting the small joints of the fingers;
- skin complications;
- eye complications (**uveitis, conjunctivitis** and **iritis**);
- liver complications;
- tension headaches and migraine;
- the development of **aphthous ulcers** in the mouth.

Crohn's Disease

This usually presents with similar symptoms to ulcerative colitis but the disease is characterized by damage to the whole of the bowel wall and may affect any part of the intestine. Typically, it affects the small bowel (in the ileum) and the colon. There is a characteristic distribution of the lesions, which are described as 'skip lesions'. Local complications, although similar to those of ulcerative colitis, are often more troublesome and can include the development of **fissures** in the bowel wall and the development of passages called *fistulae* between one part of the bowel and another, or another organ or the skin. Systemic (bodily) complications are similar to those of ulcerative colitis. Severe Crohn's disease is more difficult to manage than ulcerative colitis. The physical factors causing Crohn's disease are different from those causing ulcerative colitis and are not yet established.

In both conditions the extensive damage to the bowel wall may necessitate surgical removal, resulting in the need for a **stoma** (an ileostomy), or else an ileo-anal anastomosis which can each affect the patient's self-esteem, especially when young.

Psychological Factors in Inflammatory Bowel Disease

As early as 1930 Murray, a medical student at Columbia University, noted the emotional immaturity of 12 patients suffering with ulcerative colitis. He found that they were often over-fearful and had had too close a tie with their mother, described as being 'cramped' (Murray, 1930a and b). In 1955, Engel reviewed 44 published reports of 700 cases, including 29 of his own patients, of ulcerative colitis. These patients demonstrated inhibited anger, rigid attitudes to moral issues and often obsessive-compulsive traits (Engel, 1955), as also noted by Wittkower (1938). Occasionally, severe depression is associated with a relapse of inflammatory bowel disease, and there is a five-times the expected incidence of schizophrenia in 5–10 per cent of ulcerative colitics in some series. Most studies suggest that patients with ulcerative colitis are without major psychiatric morbidity.

Two studies by Feldman and colleagues on Crohn's and ulcerative colitis (Feldman et al., 1967a and b) failed to find any overt conscious stress or significant psychological precipitant in Crohn's disease and ulcerative colitis. Much was made of this study by gastroenterologists resistant to the idea of a psychological aetiology in these conditions. However a more recent study (Fava and Pavan, 1976–7) compared ulcerative colitis with irritable bowel and appendicitis. This suggested that the personalities of these different patients showed more pronounced alexithymic features (the inability to find words for feelings; see Chapter 3) in ulcerative colitis. Fava and Pavan also studied stressful life-events preceding ulcerative colitis as compared with irritable bowel and appendicitis. They found that with ulcerative colitis and irritable bowel disease, conditions were more frequently preceded by events involving losses or exits from the social field, as compared with appendicitis.

This second factor confirmed Lindemann's observation of 87 patients suffering with colitis that the onset of the disease had been preceded by a common life situation which involved the loss of a key person on whom the patient had been very dependent (Lindemann, 1950). More recently, North et al. (1991) reviewed 96 studies of patients with ulcerative colitis. Of these, 81 were uncontrolled and 15 were controlled. In both the controlled and uncontrolled studies, a relationship was found between stress and colitis in only half of them. Since 1990 there have been four more controlled studies. A gastroenterologist, Levenstein and colleagues (2000), studied 62 patients in remission prospectively and found relapses in 80 per cent under high stress, in 40 per cent under mild stress and in 40 per cent under medium level stress.

Maunder argues that this conflicting evidence for the role of psychological factors may be because only some patients with ulcerative colitis are sensitive to stress. Reviewing an intriguing study based on animal work with the siamang gibbon and the cottontop tamarin, he argues that patients who are negative for the antibody P-ANCA are more sensitive to stress than those who are positive. The cottontop tamarins were all also found to be ANCA-negative. ANCA is an antibody against neutrophils found in the cytoplasm of the cell. It was found in these animal studies that the cottontop tamarin, *Oedipus oedipus*, when held in captivity, developed colitis. Maunder and his colleagues are currently studying the relationship between ANCA-negative status in colitis and the development of colitis in avoidant personalities. In one study he has found that 60 per cent of colitics with **avoidant attachment styles** had ANCA-negative status. This has led him to propose that there may be a biological marker for colitics who are sensitive to stress, namely ANCA-negative status. These colitics who are sensitive to stress are more likely to have avoidant attachment styles (Maunder, 2000). This fascinating research helps us to understand why only some patients with ulcerative colitis are sensitive to stress, and so in future we may better select those patients suitable for psycho-analytic psychotherapy.

Psychodynamic Theories

Engel (1955) studying 30 relapses of colitis in 10 patients found that 24 of the relapses had occurred in a setting of threatened or symbolic separation or else on the anniversary of a loss, in which the patient had felt unable to meet the pressure or to assume the greater responsibility incurred. Engel argued that these patients were over-sensitive and extremely dependent on a key figure, either the mother or her substitute. He also found they were over-dependent in marriage and seemed to lack sexual desire. Often they had felt dominated by a rigid, fearful, over-protective and hostile mother, responding to this by over-conformity. The father was found to be absent or passive (Engel, 1952).

Alexander (1968) argued that colitis was precipitated when there were conflicts of compliance versus rebellion associated with a response of helplessness and resentment which, of itself, was guilt-provoking. Such conflicts were caused by having to face a life situation requiring outstanding accomplishments for which the patient felt inadequate. Hogan (1995) argues that the mothers of colitics have an unconscious hostility towards the child that might be the equivalent of their own unconscious, destructive, self-punitive fantasies about themselves. These mothers seem to choose one child to play the role of the helpless invalid in their own intrapsychic life. This child, who is often the oldest, might become a colitic. He or she has an ego which was poorly differentiated within itself and riddled by fragmented judgements (see the case history of the patient with Crohn's disease and alexithymia in Chapter 3).

Treatment

Medical and surgical treatments remain the mainstay of therapy for these two chronic disabling and life-threatening conditions. Althouth medication with anti-inflammatory drugs, for example, **mesalazine**; and sometimes also oral or topical steroids may be required throughout life, there is much to suggest that psycho-analytic psychotherapy can be very helpful in reducing the morbidity and mortality of ulcerative colitis and Crohn's.

Karush, Daniels, Flood and O'Connor (1977) studied the effects over three months of twice-weekly psychoanalytic psychotherapy for patients with ulcerative colitis, given by psychiatrists (who were also in psychoanalysis themselves). These studies although uncontrolled, suggested that such psychotherapeutic interventions were more effective in improving the physical prognosis in those patients who had a milder form of colitis and a more **individuated personality**. In patients with a more severe and extensive colitis and a more immature **symbiotic personality**, psychoanalytic therapy needed considerable modification so as to be more supportive in order to be helpful. A survey of the follow-up of 28 cases of psychoanalytic treatment of ulcerative colitis by a number of experienced American psychoanalysts (Weinstock, 1962) showed that after 2–3 years of psychoanalysis of patients at 3–18 years of age, ten had a good outcome of their psychoanalysis and 12 were totally symptom-free. It is not clear what the range of severity of colitis was in this interesting series.

All psychotherapy of such physically ill patients requires close cooperation with a hospital-based physician who can admit and treat them if necessary. Psychotherapy may help the patient to become less vulnerable psychologically as well as physically, but the underlying mucosal lesions may remain a problem.

Case Study

Caroline had developed a mild form of localized ulcerative colitis at the age of 16, while preparing for her GCE 'O' level examinations. At the time she had felt under considerable stress and was worried she would not do as well as the other pupils in her class. She worked in the media, was still living with her parents and was without a partner. She came for psychotherapy at the age of 33, having heard that it could be helpful for patients with ulcerative colitis.

There were conflicts in her parents' marriage, and she and her brother often found themselves having to act as go-betweens for the parents. Father was a difficult man who could humiliate her rather mild-mannered mother. Caroline was aware that her colitis might be triggered by emotional stress. She was under the care of a gastroenterologist and took anti-inflammatory medication to control her attacks of diarrhoea. When there were threats of an actual separation or loss, she reacted by developing rectal bleeding and diarrhoea that was resolved by treatment with steroid enemas. After a year of her therapy, she decided to move from her family home to a flat of her own. This move, together with her anxiety that her mother might not approve of the flat, triggered an attack of rectal bleeding which required topical steroid treatment by her physician.

In the once-weekly therapy she found it difficult to free associate and directly examine her feelings, which often centred on her fears of not being approved of by others. She was curiously passive, speaking of her therapy as if it were like taking a pill.

Psychotherapy helped Caroline to become a more independent person who could better express feelings such as anger that she had previously kept to herself. Her attacks of diarrhoea became less frequent. However, when the therapy ended, her colitis had not completely disappeared (she had an attack of rectal bleeding with diarrhoea whilst facing her anxieties about the ending) and she remained on her anti-inflammatory medication and under the care of her physician. (Also discussed in Chapter 3).

Other cases with ulcerative colitis referred by physicians may not be so promising.

Case Study

Janet, who had ulcerative colitis affecting the whole of her colon, was referred to me because of a severe depression with episodes of depersonalization. She had been told that she might have to have the whole of her colon removed, leaving her with an ileostomy (an opening onto the abdominal wall to allow the liquid bowel contents to empty). She saw a psychotherapist once weekly, but was dismissive of the therapist's attempts to relate to her and broke off her therapy after six months. One year later her colitis had completely cleared up (on endoscopic examination).

A few years later she had a recurrence of her colitis. Her surgeon told her that he planned a total colectomy but now wanted to join her small bowel to her anal canal to provide a conduit for her faecal contents that would be less unsightly (an ileoanal anastomosis). Before the operation she was depressed and distressed and had nightmares of old women with unsightly ileostomies coming towards her. After the operation the ileal pouch (the intra-abdominal reservoir attached to the ileoanal anastomosis) became inflamed (*pouchitis*) and she became more depressed. I tried to persuade her to come as an inpatient for treatment. She initially agreed, but then left the medical ward to recuperate with her father in France. When she returned her *pouchitis* still troubled her. She began a further psychotherapy on a once-weekly basis. By the end of one year her *pouchitis* had settled and she was less depressed but remained an intensely vulnerable and immature person (see Shoenberg, 1990).

These two case histories show the range of psychopathology and physical pathology in this worrying condition. At one extreme there are relatively individuated patients with mild colitis who will respond to an interpretative approach and, at the other end, there are more symbiotic and disturbed patients with more severe colitis, who are less **psychologically minded** and need more supportive and hospital-based psychotherapy.

Further Reading

Engel, G. L., Reichsman, F. and Segal, H. L. (1956) 'A study of an infant with a gastric fistula – I: Behaviour and the rate of hydrochloric acid secretion', *Psychosomatic Medicine*, 18: 374–98.

Engel, G. L. (1958) 'Studies of ulcerative colitis – V: Psychological aspects and their implications for treatment', *American Journal of Digestive Diseases*, 33: 315–37.

Guthrie, E. (1991) 'Brief psychotherapy with patients with refractory irritable bowel syndrome', *British Journal of Psychotherapy*, 8: 175–88.

Orgel, S. (1958) 'Effects of psychoanalysis on the course of peptic ulcer', *Psychosomatic Medicine*, 20: 117–25.

9   Skin Disorders

Il est bien dans son peau

French saying

Our skin communicates many feelings: we blush with embarrassment, blanch with extreme fear, sweat with anxiety and flush or grow pale when angry. Skin is referred to in a variety of metaphors and sayings. We speak of someone being thick- or thin-skinned or speak of something getting 'under the skin'.

In infancy, the skin is a medium for communication between a mother and infant (Pines, 1980) when a mother provides a 'holding' environment from which her infant can develop a primary identification of the self. There is an immediate soothing effect of skin-to-skin contact between a neonate and its mother, after the newborn has emerged from its mother's warm body into a cold and non-containing world (Leboyer, 1974; Pines, 1980). Skin contact re-establishes a mother's intimate feelings for her baby, allowing mother and baby once again to feel merged as they were in the womb, when the mother's skin had indeed contained both of them (Pines, 1980). The skin is also a medium for transmission of smell, touch, taste and warmth, giving pleasure and intimacy to both mother and infant. It is a primitive channel for pre-verbal communication through which non-verbalized affects can be somatically experienced and observed (Pines, 1980).

During a mother's handling of her child, her skin conveys the full range of her emotions from tenderness, warmth and love to disgust and hate (Pines, 1980). An infant may react through its skin to its mother's positive feelings with a sense of well-being, and to a mother's negative feelings with skin disorders which can take various forms. Winnicott wrote that it is the mother's successful holding and handling of the baby in these earliest stages of life that allows psychosomatic integration to be established (Shoenberg, 2001; Winnicott, 1970). Anzieu (1989) describes a 'skin-ego', a psychic envelope that contains, defines and protects the psyche.

Disorders of Skin Function

Itching: Pruritus

Itching occurs in many skin disorders, including some of the psychosomatic ones and it may be first manifestation of certain general medical disorders as well, such as the malignant disorder Hodgkin's disease. It has been shown that under emotional stress there is a prolongation of itching produced by an enlargement of the standardised **histamine response** in the skin (Cormia, 1952). Behind the symptoms of itching, there may be many different repressed emotions, including guilt, anger, boredom, irritation and sexual arousal (Musaph, 1964).

Itching and scratching may also be initiated by an organic factor, such as an infestation or else an irritating discharge; if itching fails to disappear after the presumed original organic cause has been cleared up, it may be serving as an outlet for an underlying emotional conflict (Engels, 1985). Engels gives the example of the patient whose need for affection had not been met and the feelings aroused had been repressed leading to frustration causing itching (Engels, 1985). Musaph proposed that itching occurred chiefly when aggressive impulses threatened to enter the conscious mind (Musaph, 1964).

Excessive Sweating (Hyperhidrosis)

Perspiration is regulated by the sympathetic nervous system via cholinergic nerve fibres. We perspire between 300–12,000 millilitres. of fluid a day. Excessive eccrine sweating on the palms, soles and axillae is made worse by emotional stress. In many cases intense preoccupation with one's appearance and odour accompanies the excessive sweating. Such ideas about personal offensiveness caused by hyperhidrosis may occasionally become delusional.

Treatment of excessive sweating includes the use of tranquillizers to alleviate anxiety. Sweating may also be alleviated by rest and topical application of aluminium chloride preparations. In severe cases, surgical **sympathectomy** may be considered but this can lead to other problems. In young people psychotherapy may help them to centre and to try and resolve underlying conflicts which are often associated with sexual issues (Engels, 1985).

Self-Induced Skin Disorders

Psychosis
In a psychosis, the skin may be the target for self-punishment or else the site for fear of self-destructive contamination or infestation, as in delusional parasitosis. Treatment is with anti-psychotic medication.

Compulsive Hair Pulling
Compulsive hair pulling, also called *trichotillomania*, may produce a superficial resemblance to other forms of hair loss. It occurs mainly in women and is common in children, where it tends to be a minor psychological disturbance. In adults, large areas of the scalp may become bald. This can lead to feelings of shame and social isolation. Often there is an underlying depression and when this condition occurs in adults they are found to be quite profoundly disturbed individuals, some of whom may respond to psychoanalytic psychotherapy.

Dermatitis Artefacta
Dermatitis artefacta is a skin condition in which the patient initially denies the fact that they are themselves inflicting the lesions. As well as scratching, a range of chemical and physical agents may be employed to induce bizarre imitations of other disease-like states. Here is an account of the early stages of psychotherapy of a young woman with a skin problem caused by scratching infected pimples on the face:

Case Study

Annette first saw her therapist when she was 40. When she was 20, her mother had committed suicide. Two years later an older brother, with whom she had been close, also committed suicide. Annette's parents had separated when she was only ten. She had been brought up by her mother who was chronically depressed and who had already attempted suicide on numerous occasions during Annette's adolescence. She was now living with her father, a successful television producer. She had made various attempts at having psychotherapy in the past but none had really worked.

She now presented with a rash around her mouth that at times became red, sore and blistered. It had not responded to conventional physical approaches and was generally regarded by her doctors as being of psychosomatic origin. She saw this rash as the 'outward sign of the burns inside' her. When she got the rash, she would say 'It feels as if the hurt and anger from before is exploding.' She felt that her first therapist had been too detached and too rigorously analytic, and that her second therapist had been too familiar. She was still suffering from recurrent nightmares about her mother's and brother's deaths. In one such nightmare, her brother was digging his nails into her arms. Psychotherapy had been her decision. She felt that at the root of her skin problem were her difficulties with anger that interfered with her relationship with her partner, an equally vulnerable person who had grown up with a disturbed mother.

After the first meeting with the therapist, Annette developed a large rash on the right side of her face. She and her therapist took this to be a warning of the difficulties that lay ahead in the therapy. She told the therapist off for having asked her so many questions in the first session. She said, 'If you take a history, you needn't have it all at once. You should just get it piecemeal as it comes in the sessions.' There were difficulties about finding the right time for the session and, in the end, the patient had to wait some time before therapy could start properly. She came for the next session some weeks later with two red spots on the right side of her mouth. She laughed, but then told the therapist what a terrible time she had been having in the interval between the sessions. It had culminated in a disastrous holiday with her partner when things had come to a head because he had decided at the end of the holiday to go on a further holiday with an ex-girlfriend. Referring to her face which had been very bad, Annette asked the therapist, 'What do you think of it?' The therapist said that she did not think her face looked so bad.

In the next session these two spots had been replaced by a red spot on her chin. Annette began the session by pointing to her chin and asking the therapist, 'How do you think my face looks now? It doesn't help to have another spot and it makes me feel depressed. It's just a vicious circle. The Spanish assistant in my office is making me leave my job. You'll think that I can't work with anybody.' The therapist said, 'Just another vicious circle.' Annette said, 'Well, I earn so little an hour it's just beneath me. The heat in the office is too much. I trained as a secretary, but I can't take the bullying that goes on. My best job was working with Professor "X". But then my brother committed suicide. I can't tolerate the feeling of being blamed.' She then spoke of wanting to do something more worthwhile with her life. She said she had not been able to get on with the previous therapist. So the therapist said, 'So I have been warned'. Annette, however, said she was determined to make this therapy work. Then she added, 'My face doesn't help. I feel ashamed. Can you see this scar along the left side of my face?' (It was a large, long blister). 'The spots I get always remind me of the very traumatic time when I had to become a recluse for a year. This was after I had an abortion, after I had become pregnant by my partner.' (Loden, personal communication)

Structural Disorders

Atopic Eczema (Infantile Eczema)

The term atopy means an inherited predisposition to the disorders of asthma, hay fever and eczema. The respiratory symptoms of hay fever and asthma may develop later in life or else at the same time as the eczema. Ten per cent of children have some form of atopic eczema (which translates from the Greek 'to boil over'). In 70 per cent of sufferers there is a family history of asthma, eczema or hay fever (see Figure 9.1). Atopy is caused by an inherited non-specific reactivity accompanied by an

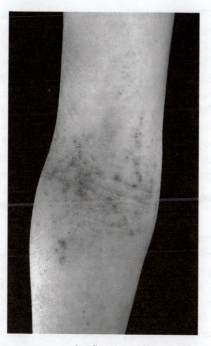

Figure 9.1 Acute eczema on the flexure of the elbow

increase in the immunoglobulins IgE-IgG and a lowered resistance to viral infections. The skin capillaries in atopy react to stimulation by light and firm pressure, with a prolonged contraction leading to the phenomenon of white dermographism. This literally means that one can write by means of pressure on the skin.

Eczema starts in infants in their third or fourth month with redness and scaling on the scalp. It soon spreads to the cheeks and leads to itchy red **papules** which erupt and weep. Often the infant is too young to scratch but will rub its head and face on the pillow. In severe cases the eruption spreads to the limbs and napkin area. Because of the discomfort, the child cannot sleep and its crying keeps its parents awake. In more severe cases the whole body surface is involved and the child tears at its skin in a frenzy, drawing blood with its fingernails. This is obviously also distressing for the parents. Cold weather will aggravate eczema and intense heat will lead to sweating which brings problems because of the interference with the inflamed skin (Sneddon and Church, 1971).

Many mild cases of eczema clear spontaneously by the age of two. In children whose eczema has not cleared, while the facial eruption goes, the eczema persists in the flexures and on the fingers. Its hallmark is a leathery, dry, erythema (redness) in the flexures and around the neck (Sneddon and Church, 1971). Only a small group of sufferers begin to have eczema *after* puberty. In one series of 500 patients with infantile eczema, only 10 per cent had significant disability ten years later. These were the ones who had a poor family history of atopic disorders as well as adverse psychological factors.

Psychological Factors

Pines argued that the mother of the child with eczema is faced with an impossible task of soothing a restless and fretful baby. The child's demands might have exceeded the patient care of her 'good-enough mothering', so her baby not only has physical discomfort but also may have had to experience its mother's potential **narcissistic disappointment** at her infant's appearance, and this could be reflected in her response to its demands. This could leave the baby very vulnerable to feeling overwhelmed by uncontained aggression and also deprive it of additional maternal '**mirroring**' by admiration and love. Such failure of mirroring might also have longer-term effects on the child's narcissistic structure (Pines, 1980). Pines referred to Spitz who had quoted a study by Katherine Wolf of 22 children suffering with eczema, where it was found that mothers had been afraid to touch their children.

Patients with eczema may have an intense craving for physical closeness (Engels, 1985). In Wittkower's and Russell's study of 90 patients with eczema compared to matched controls (Wittkower and Russell, 1953), the onset and relapse of attacks of eczema were often precipitated by threats to life and existence, or the threat of losing an outside source of emotional support. Alternatively there were disturbances to inner established patterns caused by blows to self-esteem or else conflicts over sex or aggressivity. Their retrospective studies showed that children with eczema had either felt unwanted or had been spoilt: this had resulted in an insecure, clinging nature that sought reassurance. Often such eczema sufferers disguised their sense of feeling unwanted by seeking the limelight or else by expressing resentment.

The physical treatments essential to the successful management of eczema are described elsewhere (Sneddon and Church, 1971; Graham-Brown and Burns, 1996). Engels recommended that psychotherapy might usefully focus on repressed feelings of aggression (Engels, 1985). Pines beautifully describes the analysis of a patient with eczema who feared re-experiencing her primary narcissistic hurt and shame at being a blemished infant. In the transference, there was a wish to '**merge with the analyst**', but also a fear of such regression with its threat of loss of self. In other patients, Pines found a more secure sense of self and a greater degree of independence. Nevertheless, she noted there were also intense anxieties in these patients about attachment and ambivalence towards the mother that could be reactivated in the transference. In the analytic situation, with its absence of physical contact, this could become a particular frustration for such patients. The verbalization of long-repressed intense rage and anger could be facilitated by giving up such a regressed position (Pines, 1980).

Urticaria

> '*It's not the milk that gives me skin bumps – it's mater!*'
> Joyce McDougall (1989)

Urticaria, also called nettle-rash, is characterized by an eruption of transient weals. It is often allergic in origin. The weals are formed by an extreme dilatation (swelling) of skin capillaries which allows serum to escape into the surrounding dermis. The capillary dilatation is produced by histamine released by mast cells within the dermis. Many substances in plants and animals can cause this release of histamine; aspirin, a salicylate, may potentiate any cause of urticaria.

In acute urticaria, weals erupt across the body surface and last between eight and twenty-four hours, accompanied by joint swelling, fever and sometimes an enlarged spleen and lymph glands. Urticaria may take different forms, including dermographism (in which weals occur under scratch marks), giant urticaria and angioneurotic oedema (which involve the subcutaneous tissues with resultant swelling of the eyelids, lips, tongue and larynx), emotional urticaria, heat urticaria and solar and cold urticaria (where there is acquired hypersensitivity to actinic light or to cold). In heat and cold urticaria there is a generalized eruption of small erythematous (red) weals precipitated by physical exercise, rises in temperature or emotional tension. Each factor causes a release of **acetylcholine** which in turn results in histamine release by the sweat glands.

Chronic urticaria presents often after an initial interval of severe pruritis with large or small weals that are scattered over an otherwise normal skin. The distribution is usually on the trunk and extremities. It is seen between the second and fourth decades and occurs more commonly in women than men. The treatment of urticaria is with antihistamines which, although helpful, may also have a sedative effect. Psychotherapy focused on repressed aggressive feelings may help (Engels, 1985). Musaph's study found that the majority of cases had experienced a hidden annoyance before the eruption of the urticaria (Musaph, 1964).

Rosacea

This is a common condition occurring more often in women than men, with a peak incidence in the fourth and fifth decade. It is caused by an increase in the vascularity of the skin with papule and **pustule** formation on the blush area of the face and the upper chest. The skin of the sufferer is tense, shiny and red, with small visible collections of capillaries called *telangiectasiae*. Patients with rosacea may go on to develop ophthalmic inflammations and unpleasant swellings on the nose, called rhinophymia. The skin has a primary oedema (swelling) from dilated blood vessels in its upper dermis. The papules have dense, leukocytic (white cell) infiltration and may proceed to granuloma formation (a granuloma is a tumour made up of granulation tissue).

Engels describes psychological studies linking rosacea with a disordered blushing reaction (Engels, 1985). He refers to personality studies indicating that rosacea occurs in rather perfectionistic individuals with a strong need to please and a predisposition to guilt and shame. He argues that treatment approaches require the physical use of intermittent oral antibiotics to reduce papule and pustule formation but points out that this would not change the reddening. Psychotherapy can help to modify the intense demands of the superego that have resulted in the perfectionistic character trait.

Alopecia Areata

This is a condition of unknown causation in which there is sudden patchy hair loss. It occurs at any age but is often seen in childhood. The diagnosis is made by the special appearance of what are called 'exclamation mark hairs' which are short and stumpy. Mehlman and Griesemer have described a series of young patients with alopecia areata (Mehlman and Griesemer, 1968). In these patients they found an earlier loss of an important symbiotic relationship which had only been partially adjusted to. In their series it emerged that a traumatic event had occurred which echoed this earlier loss and that this traumatic event precipitated the development of the sudden hair loss after a two-week interval. Clinically, with alopecia areata, hair does regrow and brief psychotherapy may also be helpful (Engels, 1985).

Psoriasis

Psoriasis is a fairly common chronic inflammatory disease of unknown aetiology that may affect people at any age with varying severity. It occurs in 1–2 per cent of the world's population. It can be aggravated by systemic infections, excessive or insufficient sunlight, damp or cold, as well as emotional stress. It presents with large red plaques (flat areas) that are covered with thick white scales, especially on the knees and elbows, and, commonly, there is an additional nail deformity. Underlying this condition histologically there is an increase in **basal cell proliferation** with rapid epidermal development. There may be an associated rheumatoid-like arthritis of the small joints of the hand. The condition often runs in families and immune factors are important in its pathogenesis. Life-events may trigger an episode of psoriasis.

The conventional physical treatments include the use of ultraviolet radiation with or without additional medication as well as topical steroids, tar and salicylate ointments. More severe cases may require treatment with a **cytotoxic** drug such as methotrexate. Engels says that there has been poor documentation of the psychological interventions which can help patients to avoid the social isolation that can be consequent on psoriasis (Engels, 1985).

Further Reading

Pines, D. (1980) 'Skin Communication', *International Journal of Psychoanalysis*, **61**: 312–22.

10 Cardiovascular Disorders

To feel with the heart

Zulu saying

Over three hundred years ago, Harvey (1578–1657), the discoverer of the circulation of the blood, wrote: 'Every affection of the mind that is attended with either pain or pleasure, hope or fear, is the cause of an agitation whose influence extends to the heart.' The heart responds to many emotions: it beats faster with excitement or anxiety and palpitations may be experienced. The word 'heart' occurs in many expressions referring to emotion: something is 'heartfelt', someone is 'hearty', someone's 'heart sinks'; a loved one is called a heart-throb; an unfeeling person is spoken of as 'heartless'; a committed person gives his 'wholehearted' support to a cause. One may be 'light-' or 'heavy-hearted'. In medieval times the heart was considered as the seat of the soul. Pascal (1623–62) wrote: 'The heart has its reasons, which reason knows nothing of' (Pascal, 1962).

Anxiety Disorders

In anxiety, the heart may develop a chronic condition which has been called irritable heart, DaCosta's syndrome, effort syndrome or cardiac neurosis. This condition is associated with chest pain, difficulty in breathing, fatigue and fainting. Palpitations, weakness and dizziness may occur and are associated with anxiety. The patient often worries that they have heart disease and fears dying. The underlying anxiety may sometimes lead to hyperventilation which lowers the pH of the blood and produces an alkalosis (accumulation of base in the blood), lowering the PCO_2 which in turn may cause the additional physical symptoms of hyperventilation (see Chapter 11) causing further anxiety. Nowadays this condition is regarded as a form of **anxiety**

neurosis in which there is no structural cardiac abnormality (Wolff and Shoenberg, 1990). Although symptomatic approaches may be helpful, in many cases psychoanalytic psychotherapy should be considered.

Essential Hypertension

Our blood pressure varies with posture, salt intake, exercise, heat, cold, noise, pain, as well as with emotional and sexual excitement, mental concentration, and the experience of novel situations. It tends to go up with ageing and is usually lowered during sleep (Weiner, 1977).

In secondary hypertension there is a chronic elevation of blood pressure secondary to a primary disease: this may be because of a variety of conditions, including raised intracranial pressure, a variety of kidney diseases, **coarctation of the aorta**, renal artery stenosis (narrowing), **aldosteronomas, reninomas, phaeochromocytomas**, the use of the contraceptive pill in women, **polycythaemia** and the two endocrine conditions – Cushing's disease and **Graves' disease**.

Essential hypertension (that is hypertension which is not secondary) is a vascular disorder in which the blood pressure is chronically elevated, with a raised systolic pressure of greater than 140 mm of mercury and a raised diastolic pressure greater than 90 mm of mercury.[1] It afflicts up to 18 per cent of the population. Clinically, it can occur in a benign or a malignant form. In **malignant hypertension,** vascular disease (resulting from the hypertension) develops rapidly and is severe with dangerous effects on the body. The exact causes of essential hypertension are not yet known.

Clinical Features

Patients may complain of non-specific problems like headache (typically occipital), weakness, nervousness, flatulence, palpitations or dizziness. However, often there are no symptoms or signs in this condition. In more advanced hypertension, there may be symptoms and signs of cerebral arterial disease, coronary artery disease, **congestive heart failure** or renal failure. Patients with hypertension are at twice the risk of having cardiovascular disease.

Epistaxis (nose bleeding) and intermittent haematuria (blood in the urine) with some proteinuria (protein in the urine) are also common findings. These urinary signs may signify damage to the kidney.

On examination, changes to the blood vessels of the retina may be seen (arteriovenous nipping and haemorrhages and white exudates) and later blurring of the margins of the optic disc (the part of the optic nerve seen at the back of the eye). In severe hypertension, there may be a marked rise in blood pressure and this occurs most commonly with kidney disease and can lead to brain changes known as hypertensive encephalopathy.

Pathological Effects of Essential Hypertension

Once established, sustained high levels of blood pressure lead to damage to the arterioles with fibrinoid necrosis (a form of tissue death). This process occurs most often in the brain and the kidney and leads, over a long period of time, to hyperplasia (an overgrowth) of the intima (the inner layer) of the **arterioles**. This results in:

1 reduced blood flow to vital organs;
2 a contribution to the development of arteriosclerosis;
3 hypertension, which may also cause microaneurisms in the small vessels and also cardiac hypertrophy and dilatation (enlargement of the heart), leading to left ventricular failure of the heart;
4 persistent high levels of blood pressure, which may cause necrosis in part of the ascending portion of the aorta, leading to **aneurisms** (Barr Taylor and Fortmann, 1985).

When hypertension exists with other major risk factors for heart disease, these risks are additive (Barr Taylor and Fortmann, 1985). In the Hypertension Detection and Follow-up Programme (Simpson, 1979), 10,000 men were followed up and randomized into those receiving intensive drug care and those receiving standard care. It was found that very aggressive treatment of high blood pressure (in the range 90–104 mm of mercury diastolic) was associated with a decrease in morbidity and mortality from stroke and acute myocardial infarction over five years.

Aetiology
Family and twin studies suggest that essential hypertension is:

1   partly an inherited condition (Hamilton et al., 1954; Pickering, 1955);
2   partly related to increased weight and salt intake;
3   partly related to stress.

Role of stress
People living in towns have higher blood pressure and higher mortality rates than those living in the countryside. In the USA, it has also been found that African-American city dwellers have higher blood pressure levels than their Caucasian counterparts, especially when they live in parts of the city marked by low socio-economic status, high crime, police brutality and high rates of marital separation and divorce (these studies were carried out in Detroit). Blood pressure tends to fluctuate more in people who have stressful occupations, such as air traffic controllers. Animal studies (such as crowding mice into small boxes) show that territorial conflict and defensive vigilance over prolonged periods of time result in sustained increases in blood pressure.

The role of the nervous system
The autonomic nervous sympathetic activity affects blood pressure and volume through its direct effect on the kidneys, causing increased sodium reabsorption and increased plasma **renin** activity. When animals are given drugs that cause a generalized sympathectomy, profound drops in blood pressure are recorded. In some hypertensive patients, sympathetic activity has been shown to be altered. Elevated **catecholamines** have been found more consistently in patients who have labile hypertension (Eide et al., 1978).

*The role of the renin **angiotensin** system*
Whilst the central nervous system is partly responsible for blood pressure elevation, there is also evidence that changes in the renin

angiotensin system and changes in the blood volume control of the kidneys contribute to sustained essential hypertension.

Personality Factors

In 1968, Alexander argued that hypertensive patients struggled with depressive feelings and had difficulty in asserting themselves. He argued that they tried to control the expression of their hostility because of their fear of losing the affection of others. He also argued that in childhood they had been prone to outbursts of rage and aggression but as they grew up they learnt to control these attacks and became overtly compliant and unassertive. In executive positions, however, they found they could not assert themselves and tended to take on too much responsibility and become over-conscientious, making them resentful. The onset of their hypertension was triggered by events that mobilized hostility in them and prompted an urge for self-assertion, which was now inhibited (Alexander et al., 1968).

Although Alexander's formulation has not been confirmed, hypertensive patients do seem to have more difficulty in coping with expressing feelings, especially anger, in interpersonal situations (Sapira, et al., 1971; Harburg et al., 1979; Pilowsky, et al., 1973). But such personality difficulties are not unique to hypertensive patients. In an important study undertaken by Thomas and colleagues, a battery of psychological tests were administered to graduates of Johns Hopkins Medical School between 1948 and 1964. Thomas followed these subjects well into the 1970s, showing that initial significant systolic and diastolic pressure, heart rate and relative body weight were associated with the subsequent development of hypertension. However, he found no difference between these individuals and the controls on measures of anger, anxiety or depression (Thomas and Greenstreet, 1973).

In a more recent cross-sectional correlation of psychological variables with mild hypertension, measured in clinic visits or by ambulatory monitoring in 283 middle-aged men, there were no significant differences between normotensive and hypertensive men in any of the psychological variables assessed, including type A behaviour, state and trait anger, anger expression, anxiety, psychological distress, locus of control, or attributional style (Friedman et al., 2001).

Treatment

The mainstays of treatment are:

1   attention to weight reduction;
2   lowering of blood cholesterol if elevated;
3   salt restriction;
4   medication: often there are problems about patient compliance with their medication and a good physician/patient relationship has an enormous impact on this;
5   stress control. There have been more than 50 studies on relaxation and related techniques to reduce blood pressure. Twelve of them were carefully controlled (for review see Taylor, 1980). Depending on the initial blood pressure, these techniques will produce pre-treatment to post-treatment changes of as much as 0–26 per cent systolic and/or 1–18 per cent diastolic blood pressure, significantly better than in the control subjects. The use of psychotherapy with hypertensive patients has been reported in uncontrolled single case studies but its efficacy is uncertain.

Coronary Heart Disease: Psychological Factors

> *Out-worn heart, in a time out-worn*
> W. B. Yeats, 'Into the Twilight'

In the USA, 11 million people suffer with coronary artery disease and 1.5 million people have a myocardial infarct (a heart attack) each year. Thirty per cent of these myocardial infarcts result in death, of whom half die before they have reached a hospital.

Personality

In a lecture on angina pectoris in 1910, the physician William Osler (1849–1919) suggested that certain personalities might be more prone to develop coronary artery disease than others. He described them as 'keen and ambitious men, the indicator of whose engine is always at full speed ahead' (Osler, 1910). In 1974, Friedman and Rosenman proposed that patients who had this specific type of personality, 'type A personality', were prone to the development of coronary artery disease. Such a personality was characterized by an excessive competitive drive and an enhanced sense of time urgency (i.e., the drive to be ahead of oneself). Time urgency was derived from the associated intense desires to achieve success, gain recognition and take on new tasks. These personalities were possessed, in addition, of a free-floating hostility.

Friedman and Rosenman followed up a large group of healthy men, aged between 30 and 59, in California over 8½ years. Approximately half the group were found to have type A personalities. The other type of personality was referred to as type B. The type B personality was described as more relaxed and easy-going, and often as successful as type A. At 8½ years of follow-up, over twice as many of the type A personalities had developed coronary heart disease as those with type B personalities, and twice as many in the type A group also had a fatal myocardial infarction. However, there has been a failure to replicate these findings in a more well-developed prospective study (Shekelle et al., 1985). Other studies have also raised serious concerns about the hypothesis.

While many studies have shown that stress is one of the eight most important contributors to coronary heart disease, other risk factors are also important.[2] These range from maternal health development and diet before and during pregnancy to a parental history of coronary heart disease, low birth weight, socio-economic deprivation from childhood onwards, poor growth in childhood, short leg length in childhood, obesity in childhood, certain infections acquired in childhood, diet from childhood onwards and high blood pressure in late adolescence, high serum cholesterol in late adolescence, smoking from late adolescence onwards, little physical activity from late adolescence, blood pressure in adulthood, serum cholesterol levels in adulthood, obesity in adulthood, job insecurity and unemployment in adulthood, short stature in adulthood, binge alcohol drinking in adulthood, diabetes in adulthood, elevated levels of

fibrinogen and other acute phase reactants in adulthood, and certain infections acquired in adulthood.

More recent psychological studies suggest that hostility may be a more reliable psychological risk factor for coronary heart disease than the type A personality. However, this variable also predicts for a wide range of other life-threatening and minor illnesses. Hostility can be measured on a rating scale of the Minnesota Multiphasic Personality Index (MMPI) called the Cook-Medley Hostility Scale. There is a prospective association between high hostility scores and the subsequent development of coronary heart disease (Williams, Haney, Lee, Blumenthal and Kong, 1980). However, these and other studies have failed to confirm that hostility is a unique factor in causing coronary heart disease. Three clusters of behaviour seem to predict such hostility – mistrust, anger and aggression.

Other studies have indicated that there is an association between depression and the causation and prognosis of coronary heart disease (Stansfeld and Fuhrer, 2002). Depression is regarded unequivocally as a risk factor for a poor prognosis in those patients recovering from a recent heart attack.

Psychosocial Factors

Other researchers have identified aspects of a social environment as causing an increased risk of coronary heart disease and a poorer prognosis for patients with existing coronary heart disease. These factors are social isolation, a lack of relationships to provide tangible emotional support, consistent stress at work and a lower socio-economic status.

Cardiovascular mortality has been declining in the developed economic world, particularly in countries such as North America, Australia and many countries in Western Europe. By contrast, in countries in central and eastern Europe and the newly independent states of the Soviet Union, it has been rising. There is now a six-year life expectancy gap between eastern and western Europe, half of which is the direct result of cardiovascular disease, especially coronary artery disease. This difference in life expectancy has increased since the late 1960s. More recently there has been a decline in coronary heart disease mortality in the USA and the UK, enjoyed by higher socio-economic groups, leading to a widening of the gap with lower socio-economic groups in the same countries (Marmot and Bartley, 2002).

In 1991, Marmot, Smith, Stansfield and colleagues conducted an important study on health inequalities amongst British civil servants, known as 'the Whitehall Study'.

This study showed that the probable or possible risk as measured on an electrocardiogram of cardiac ischaemia, of angina, of average or worse self-reported health combined with the likelihood of a regular phlegmy cough in winter, of obesity, of being a regular smoker and of longstanding illness all increased as the grade of employment decreased.

Karasek developed the concept that 'job strain', produced by a combination of high levels of demand associated with low levels of personal control over the pace and scheduling of work, produced increased cardiovascular risk factors, such as higher blood pressure, and eventually led to heart disease itself (Karasek et al., 1981). Siegrist has developed an alternative concept of what he called the 'effort/reward imbalance'. He argues that many jobs require a high degree of effort but provide too low a level of reward in terms of job security, remuneration and prospects for promotion. It is this imbalance that represents a high risk factor for several of the precursors of a heart attack (Siegrist, 1996).

Biobehavioural Pathways

Anger is a potent trigger of acute ischaemic episodes, as much as is strenuous exertion. Episodes of intense anger may be responsible for triggering as many as 36,000 instances of acute myocardial infarction each year in the USA (Verrier and Mittleman, 1996). Anger produces an increased activation of the sympathetic nervous system in individuals who already have free-floating hostility and this clearly affects the heart. Depression also increases the activity of the sympathetic nervous system. Clearly, early life experiences may have influenced many of the individual's psychological characteristics, especially in this context with regard to hostility, depression and future social isolation.

Management

It is vital that medical help is sought as quickly as possible after the onset of cardiac symptoms, including the symptoms of chest pain. Persistent pain and anxiety may themselves contribute to death within the first few hours of the onset of cardiac symptoms. It is worrying, therefore, that some patients take so long to decide whether or not to get help, which inevitably worsens their prognosis. Clearly the use of painkillers and sedatives and other medical resources is essential. Finding oneself in an acute coronary care unit may be a very frightening experience,[3] especially when surrounded by other coronary patients undergoing cardiac resuscitation.

As the patient recovers from their heart attack, the doctor should reassure them that they will eventually be able to return to a normal life although limitations may have to be accepted. Such early physical rehabilitation, combined with psychological encouragement and support, plays an important part in diminishing the patient's anxieties about their future. It is common for patients to feel depressed and anxious after a heart attack and it is important that these symptoms are treated with supportive psychotherapy but they may also require additional antidepressants or tranquilizers. Depression, if untreated, is likely to increase the chances of the patient having a poor prognosis. It is important to consider the patient's lifestyle but attempting to make the patient less active and ambitious may only cause increased anxiety and depression because the patient needs such defences against their self-doubts and feelings of inadequacy.

A number of behavioural interventions have been studied, in particular by the National Heart, Lung, and Blood Institute in the USA, which is supporting a trial, the ENRICHD Study (2000), aimed at enhancing recovery from coronary heart disease. This is the first large-scale multicentric randomized clinical trial of a behavioural intervention in coronary artery disease. It is trying to target depression and social isolation in order to reduce emotional distress in patients with heart disease and so improve their medical prognosis.

To date, it has been found that group therapy is more efficient than individual psychotherapy in helping patients with coronary heart disease to make an adjustment to their illness. Relaxation techniques, such as meditation and breathing exercises that help to reduce autonomic arousal, are also useful as they enable patients to become more aware of their negative emotions. Williams and Williams have developed a life-skills workshop which trains people to reduce their psychosocial risk factors. Gidron, Davidson and Bata (1999) have developed a specific hostility reduction intervention programme for patients with coronary heart disease. Occasionally, more long-term individual supportive psychotherapy may be helpful, especially if the emotional problems and difficulties in relationships persist.

Further Reading

Barr Taylor, C. and Fortmann, S. P. (1985) 'Essential hypertension', in *Psychosomatic Illness Review*, ed. W. Dorfman and L. Cristofar (New York: Macmillan), pp. 90–107.

Stansfield, S. and Fuhrer, R. (2002) 'Depression and coronary heart disease', in *Stress and the Heart*, ed. S. A. Stansfield and M. G. Marmot (London: BMJ Books), pp. 101–24.

11 Respiratory Disorders

A being breathing thoughtful breath
                    William Wordsworth, 'Perfect Woman' (1804)

Changes in the rate, depth and regularity of breathing may be caused voluntarily or else occur in relation to a variety of emotional states, changes in temperature, stages of sleep or physical diseases (for example, raised intracranial pressure slows the respiratory rate; obesity, which may lead to sleep apnoea; chronic obstructive airways disease; and morphine, which suppresses respiration). A surprised or pain-stricken person gasps; a bored person yawns. Love and sorrow are often accompanied by sighing, and fear and anxiety may cause hyperventilation (Weiner, 1985).

Hyperventilation

This is a common condition occurring in as many as 6–10 per cent of all medical outpatients (Lum, 1976) and 4–6 per cent of a general practitioner's consultations (Zalidis, 2001). In this condition, irregular sighing and upper thoracic breathing lead to carbon dioxide deficiency. Zalidis argues that this upper thoracic breathing is part of the somatic component of emotional arousal, produced by intense emotion (panic, rage, sorrow), of which a patient may be unaware, which has not been expressed in automatic action, i.e., fight or flight (see Chapter 4). The symptoms of hyperventilation make the sufferer frightened. Darwin suffered from hyperventilation (Bowlby, 1990). Patients with hyperventilation feel that they cannot get enough air and so tend to increase their breathing rate, which, in turn, makes their physical symptoms worse. The clinical features of this condition are as follows:

1 *Respiratory system*: shortness of breath at rest or after but not during exertion; inability to take a deep enough breath; tightness in the chest; a dry and irritable cough; sighing, yawning and sniffing; sometimes waking up early in the morning, fighting for breath.

2 *Central nervous system*: light-headedness; blurred vision; headache; sudden loss of consciousness.

3 *Cardiovascular system*: palpitations and areas of thoracic tenderness.

4 *General symptoms*: tiredness; muscular stiffness; dry mouth and belching.

5 *The excessive blowing off of the carbon dioxide by hyperventilation*: this results in carbon dioxide deficiency and this leads to a respiratory alkalosis (loss of acid in the body). This, in turn, reduces the cerebral blood flow, leading to anoxia (diminished oxygen in the brain with loss of carbonate in the urine and fatigue in the muscles).

6 *A shift in the intracellular calcium*: this resulting in increased neuronal activity causing the syndrome of tetany, in which there is carpopedal spasm (spasm of the muscles of the hand and the foot).

Management

Zalidis describes a simple and effective management for cases of hyperventilation in general practice. He tries, with the patient, to recognize the hidden emotions that might be behind the state of hyperventilation. This management involves taking a good history to elicit the symptoms and any fears the patient might have, followed by careful physical examination and explanation of the diagnosis. The patient is then shown how over-breathing results in carbon dioxide deficiency and they are made aware that they are using the upper chest to breathe at the expense of the diaphragm. The aim is to help them to learn diaphragmatic breathing from the lower part of the body, and to ventilate the underlying feelings (Zalidis, 2001).

Bronchial Asthma

Asthma is characterized by episodes of breathing difficulty due to a widespread narrowing of the airways of the lungs. It may be due to mucus in the airways, a swelling of the lining of the airways, or else a spasm of the muscle walls or a combination of these factors. The patient suffers with episodic wheezy breathlessness and has more difficulty in breathing out (expiration) than in breathing in (inspiration). Attacks are accompanied by a sense of tightness, congestion and wheezing that occur in paroxysms lasting for minutes or up to an hour. Asthma is a very common condition occurring in 4–5 per cent of the population of the USA. Half of the cases develop before the age of ten and another one third develop before the age of forty.

Often, before an attack and as the symptoms approach, the patient experiences a heaviness of the chest, a sluggishness when doing accustomed work and mood change which is often alternating apprehension and depression. Also there may be coughing and skin irritation. At the height of an attack, the sufferer is pale and anxious with cold clammy skin and rapid pulse and sweating. He may sit forward, his elbows on his knees, on the edge of the chair, looking frightened and distressed. Whitish phlegm along with whitish pellets that are casts of mucus may be produced. After an attack, the patient's tension relaxes and his mood improves but there is a need for rest (Lane and Storr, 1981).

Asthmatics are often sensitive to their physical environment, including cold weather, petrol fumes, gas fires, smoke, exercise and pollen, which may also cause hay fever (seasonal asthma). Often symptoms are worse at night and in the mornings (Lane and Storr, 1981). Characteristically asthmatics, when tested with a measuring device called a peak flow meter, have a reduced peak expiratory flow.

Causes of Asthma

In 1958, Williams and his colleagues made a study of 487 asthmatic outpatients. They found that in 29 per cent of these, extrinsic factors had played a predominant role in the causation of their asthma (that is, exposure to extrinsic allergens); 40 per cent had respiratory insufficiency that played a predominant role in causation (of these, 22 per cent also had an allergic precipitant); in only 30 per cent psychological factors play a predominant role in causation. Of these, 50 per cent also had an allergic factor. Their study showed that more than one causative factor was present in 60–77 per cent of asthmatic cases.

Other factors causing asthma include genetic factors, the use of beta blocking drugs, aspirin, premenstrual syndrome, smoking and the fungal infection aspergillosis. Great care must be taken in separately evaluating the role of psychological factors in initiating a first attack, and the role they play in causing recurrences of asthma and in sustaining this condition or altering the course of any single attack.

Psychological Studies

In 1886, Sir James Mackenzie described 'rose asthma' in women who developed asthma at the mere sight of a paper rose. Godfrey and Silverman (1973) found that, in as many as 20 of their 44 cases, exercise-induced asthma could be inhibited by a placebo, as well as by anti-asthmatic medication. In their classic paper, Luparello and his colleagues showed that when asthmatics were given the non-irritant physiological saline (salt solution) to inhale but told in addition that it contained an allergen or irritant, 19 out of 40 responded with a significant amount of increased airways resistance (as occurs in an asthmatic attack). Twelve of these cases experienced a full-blown asthmatic attack which could be reversed by the same solution of saline now given as a placebo. This was in contrast to 40 control non-asthmatic patients suffering with restrictive lung disease who had no response to the treatment with saline, either in provoking an attack or in relieving an attack (Luparello et al., 1968). These studies support the idea that psychological factors are important in asthma. They predominate more often as factors in childhood and late-onset asthma than they do in adult-onset asthma.

Neural Pathways

Any increase in nervous tension or anxiety may lead to hyperventilation, which itself can precipitate or aggravate asthma. It has been shown that the autonomic nervous system acts to modulate the release of the substances that mediate the allergic response causing asthma. In asthmatics, stimulation of the parasympathetic vagus nerve (of the autonomic nervous system) produces a transient and reversible asthma-like response in the bronchial tree. In addition, the adrenal medulla (part of the adrenal gland that secretes adrenaline into the blood) affects asthma and is itself regulated by the central nervous system, especially by the posterior hypothalamus in the brain (see Chapter 4). These neural mechanisms may be active under the psychological influence of a stressful situation and produce asthmatic attacks in vulnerable subjects (Knapp, 1989).

Psychodynamic Factors

In 1922, the psychoanalyst Eduardo Weiss wrote that asthma represented, in distorted form, the expression of intense feeling and described it as 'a suppressed cry for the mother'. Two psychodynamic hypotheses were subsequently put forward:

1   Alexander, French and Pollock (1968) hypothesized that the asthmatic attack united the crying child with the caring mother who, whilst capable of holding her child closely, was also alienated by her child's desire for intense closeness. This led to conflict in the child.

2   In contrast, Deutsch (1953), Fenichel (1945; 1953, p. 221) and Sperling (1963) proposed that asthma represented an unconsciously learned pattern of expression in which there was a conversion of unconscious conflict into a learned, symbolically relevant somatic expressive pattern. This conversion resulted from a persistent attachment to the mother with whom the child had a dependent but seductively tinged relationship, experiencing intense angry, often sadistic, urges against which they struggled.

The writer Proust never stopped grieving for his adored mother after she died and hoped that he would be reunited with her after his own death. Once, after a quarrel with her, he had had an intense asthma attack. He later wrote: 'I would rather have asthma and please you' (Hayman, 1990). After her death he moved her furniture into the Paris brothel where he lived and regularly engaged in sadomasochistic activity!

Weiner argues that there is no one personality type with asthma (Weiner, 1985). Up to half of all patients have a strong unconscious wish for protection and a need to be encompassed by another person. However, whereas in some cases these wishes merely sensitize the patient to the effects of maternal separation, in others they cause such intense conflict that separation results in a remission of the asthma. The mothers of asthmatic children, in turn, may be overprotective and overambitious or else perfectionistic or domineering. Knapp described the intense passivity and dependency in asthmatic patients who have a need to maintain gratification from and the support of key figures. He argued that asthmatic symptoms are intensified by arousal of guilty feelings of unacknowledged hostility to the key figures (Knapp et al., 1970).

Family studies by Minuchin and colleagues (1975) suggest that enmeshment, overprotectiveness, rigidity and lack of conflict resolution in families are a cluster of transactional behaviours that encourage somatization (see the section on family therapy in anorexia nervosa in Chapter 6). These unconscious dynamics may reinforce illness in asthmatic children (Liebman et al., 1974). Kleiger and Jones (1980) found that the role of alexithymia (i.e., difficulty in finding words for feelings) seems applicable to only a few asthmatic patients.

Winnicott described the development of an asthmatic attack in a baby he was observing during the course of his 'spatula game'. In this game Winnicott observed a child's capacity for play, using a wooden spatula he had given the child, in particular focusing on the child's excitement:

> The baby sat on her mother's lap with the table between them and me. The mother held the child round the chest with her two hands, supporting her body. It was therefore very

easy to see when at a certain point the child developed bronchial spasm. The mother's hands indicated the exaggerated movement of the chest, both the deep inspiration and the prolonged obstructed expiration were shown up, and the noisy expiration could be heard. The mother could see as well as I did when the baby had asthma. *The asthma occurred on both occasions over the period in which the child hesitated about taking the spatula.* She put her hand to the spatula and then, as she controlled her body, her hand and her environment, she developed asthma, which involves an involuntary control of expiration. At the moment when she came to feel confident about the spatula which was at her mouth when saliva flowed, when stillness changed to the enjoyment of activity and when watching changed into self-confidence, at this moment the asthma ceased. (Winnicott, 1941, p. 58)

Psychological Treatments

Some asthmatic children may benefit from separation from their parents (Abrahamson and Peshkin, 1961). In a study by Purcell et al. (1969), parents went away to a hotel and a nurse came in to care for a child, recording the medicines used, respiratory symptoms and peak flow. About half the children in this study showed a significant improvement, suggesting differences in reactivity to separation amongst asthmatic children.

All patients with asthma will need help medically as well as psychologically, specifically anti-asthmatic medication in the form of bronchodilators and, possibly, steroid medication. Psychological intervention may be necessary when symptoms are refractory to medication; when there has been too great a dependence on steroids (particularly oral steroids); when the parents of the child are finding difficulty in recognizing their unconscious need for their child to be ill, or are over-anxious or indifferent. Simple educational or relaxation techniques may be helpful but more specific help may be required in a paediatric psychosomatic unit or in individual psychotherapy.

Case Study

Laura was a 47-year-old housewife who was referred to me for psychotherapy because of severe recurrent attacks of bronchial asthma which had started a year previously. By the time she saw me, she had been admitted to hospital five times in the space of five months; she was very dependent on her steroid medication and her bronchodilators. She said: 'The doctors think I prefer to be in hospital ... I've been saying all along it's related to stress ... I don't want to have asthma but to me it's like saying to everyone, "Go away and leave me alone".' She acknowledged that two of her admissions had followed conversations with a friend about her mother.

She described herself as being caught up in complex rivalries between her sisters, subject to the whims of a jealous mother who, when Laura became engaged, bought herself an engagement ring. Her mother had never been able to show her affection and had often threatened suicide in front of her children when Laura was growing up. She had, in spite of this, achieved a happy but childless marriage to a chemist.

I arranged to see her in a general medical hospital setting where she could get urgent medical help, should an asthmatic attack occur during therapy. She came for therapy on the advice of her doctor and also because a friend had found therapy helpful. She saw her asthma as a sort of 'breakdown' after 'years of not being in control'. It had begun shortly after her husband was diagnosed with cancer, which was a big threat to her security and after a friend had told her she was childish which greatly upset her. She felt still at the beck and call of her mother and described herself as too compliant.

In her first session, she spoke of a dream in which her mother fell down the stairs and reported her fear that her mother would break her hip. Shortly after this, she was readmitted to an intensive care unit with a severe attack of asthma. She was then unable to come to therapy for three months, after which I received a letter from her husband saying that although she was now out of hospital she needed to go to the chest clinic once a week and was now on a higher dose of steroids. He said it would be too difficult for him to bring her for further psychotherapy, so they had decided to discontinue it.

Nevertheless, when seen for review ten years later, she reported that she had come off all systemic steroids a year after seeing me. She attributed her improvement to the realization that by taking steroids she was trying to draw her family's attention to herself. Within a year of stopping this medication, she had recovered to the extent that she only had infrequent attacks of asthma.

This case illustrates how difficult it can be to engage psychotherapeutically with such patients, as well as the medical and psychological hazards involved in setting up psychotherapy. Although it may be possible to help patients to become more confident, it is usually very difficult to help them wean themselves off steroids.

Further Reading

Knapp, P. H. (1989) 'Psychosomatic aspects of bronchial asthma', in *Psychosomatic Medicine*, vol. 2, ed. S. Cheren (Madison: International Universities Press), pp. 503–65.

Lane, J. D. and Storr, A. (1981) *Asthma: The Facts* (Oxford: Oxford University Press).

Zalidis, S. (2001) 'Breathing and feeling', in *A General Practitioner, his Patients and their Feelings* (London: Free Association Books), pp. 66–88.

12 Musculoskeletal Disorders

*I would never have
imagined the slow passion
to that deliberate progress.*

Thom Gunn, 'Considering the Snail' (1969)

Chronic Recurrent Low Backache

Chronic recurrent backache, especially lower back pain, is very common. It causes more time off work than any other condition in the United Kingdom or the United States of America. Although certain numbers of patients who consult their doctors clearly have significant organic or spinal disease, such as arthritis or prolapsed intervertebral discs, osteoporosis or even a secondary carcinoma, in many the pain is due to muscular tension caused by additional emotional stress and may be associated as well with a faulty posture and muscular strain caused by poorly coordinated movements. The persistence of pain causes further anxiety and depression. So although the main treatments for lower back pain need to be physical, especially the use of physiotherapy and exercise, psychological considerations should also be taken into account. Approaches such as the Alexander Technique (Barlow, 1973) and Pilates help a patient to pay attention to both psychological and physical aspects of their condition and to develop better posture and control of the lower back (Wolff and Shoenberg,1990, p. 42).

Fibromyalgia Syndrome

This syndrome is characterized by complaints of generalized musculoskeletal pain, with tenderness in characteristic regions. These are the neck, the low back, the buttocks, the thighs and the

171

knees. It is a fairly common condition which is costly in terms of medical care. Originally Gowers (1904) called this condition 'fibrositis'.

The pains and tenderness in the musculoskeletal system are accompanied by non-restorative sleep in which there is frequent disturbance so that there is fatigue and muscle stiffness on wakening. In a general population survey in Wichita, Kansas, fibromyalgia syndrome was found in 3.4 per cent of women and 0.5 per cent of men (Wolfe et al., 1995). It occurs more commonly with age. Its highest prevalence is in the 70–79 year age group. Patients often complain of poor memory, subjective muscle weakness and poor stamina, but there are no central or peripheral components to the muscle fatigue. Moldofsky and his colleagues (Moldofsky et al., 1975) argue that non-restorative sleep might cause this syndrome but the sleep anomaly, alpha non-REM sleep, does not appear to correlate with the pain severity in this condition.

Psychological Factors

Originally Halliday (1941) described patients with fibromyalgia as being 'unhappy, distraught individuals' and Wolfe et al. (1984) found that as many as one third of sufferers with fibromyalgia were psychologically disturbed. However, there seems to have been little progress in understanding possible psychosomatic aetiology in this disorder nor evidence to suggest a strong role for psychoanalytic psychotherapy in its treatment. On the whole, education, support and reassurance are the mainstays of psychological management with additional instruction in pain management. Some researchers have reported a role for cognitive behavioural therapy in the treatment of this condition.

Chronic Fatigue Syndrome

The term 'chronic fatigue syndrome' describes a group of non-specific symptoms which include sore throat, tender lymph nodes, muscle pains, joint pains, headache, unrefreshing sleep and post-exertional malaise, combined sometimes with problems with concentration and memory associated with persistent or relapsing fatigue. In 1869, the New York neurologist Beard introduced the term 'neurasthenia' to describe a condition characterized by chronic fatigue, observing that women were more commonly affected than men. Freud used this neurasthenic construct to define anxiety neurosis (Freud, 1894) and ten years later some of the obsessive and phobic features of this disorder were considered to indicate another, newly named specific mental disorder, 'psychasthenia' (Janet, 1903). Although neurasthenia is not included in the North American DSM (Diagnostic Standards Manual of Psychiatric Diagnosis), it is included in the ICD (the International Classification of Diseases) and other parts of the world as a separate category.

A modern definition of chronic fatigue syndrome has been provided by Holmes and his colleagues (Holmes et al., 1988). In 1994 the Centre for Disease Control and Prevention defined chronic fatigue as 'the presence of a persistent or relapsing chronic fatigue of new or definite onset which was unexplained after clinical evaluation and not the result of ongoing exertion and not substantially alleviated by rest, which produces a significant reduction in previous levels of occupational and social activity'. Associated with this condition was an occurrence of at least four of the following symptoms:

- substantial impairment in short-term memory and concentration;
- sore throat;
- tender cervical or axillary lymph nodes;
- muscle pain;
- multi-joint pains without other signs of arthritis;
- headaches of a new type, pattern and severity;
- unrefreshing sleep;
- post-exertional malaise lasting for more than 24 hours.

Four or more concurrent symptoms from the above list need to have persisted or occurred during six or more consecutive months of the fatiguing illness and not pre-date the onset of fatigue.

In a single urban community in the USA, a screening survey mailed to 4,000 randomly selected members of a managed care system revealed that 19 per cent reported having fatigue that had significantly interfered with their activities in the preceding six months, but only three individuals were given a final diagnosis of chronic fatigue syndrome (Buchwald et al., 1995). A prevalence study in a Boston primary care setting found its prevalence to be 0.3% (Bates et al., 1993). By contrast, in hospital medical outpatients, prevalence was found to be 5 per cent. This condition is commoner in women than men and is often accompanied by symptoms of depression and sometimes associated with the features of somatization disorder (described in Chapter 5). It is perhaps of interest that with such a low prevalence, it has been estimated that the cost of chronic fatigue syndrome in the USA might be at least $200 million per year, taking into account the high costs of specialist care, comprehensive immunological testing and the use of MRI scans (Manu and Mathews, 1998).

There are no useful laboratory or imaging tests that can positively identify this condition. Attempts have been made to identify infectious processes: only some patients have been found to have Epstein-Barr virus, herpes viruses and human herpes virus type 6 and two retroviruses and human T-lymphocyte lymphotrophic virus types 1 and 2 as well as enteroviruses. Studies of immunological dysfunction have shown some abnormalities of humoral and cellular immunity in some patients, but there seems to be no definitive or consistent evidence. Comparison of randomized, controlled trials of treatment show no significant evidence to suggest any satisfactory response to immunological treatments aimed at tackling an underlying cause.

Clinicians, when assessing a patient with chronic fatigue syndrome, need to exclude certain physiological states producing fatigue, such as pregnancy, sleep deprivation and excessive muscular activity performed by persons in poor physical condition, as well as physical disorders such as **obstructive sleep apnoea syndrome** and **narcolepsy**, neuromuscular disorders (e.g., multiple sclerosis and myasthenia gravis), low output heart failure, hypothyroidism and hyperthyroidism. **Collagen** and vascular diseases should also be considered, as well as the side effects of medications including tranquillizers such as benzodiazepines and antihypertensives that may produce fatigue.

Psychological Approaches

Although there are a few interesting single-case reports[1] in the literature about successful psychoanalytic treatment of patients with chronic fatigue, the overwhelming medical and psychiatric view has been to treat this condition with cognitive behavioural therapy (Whiting et al., 2001), or with graded exercise therapy (Fulcher and White, 1998). White and Naish (2001) report on a consecutive series of 59 patients with chronic fatigue syndrome treated by a physiotherapist using graded exercise therapy and compared with a series done in 1998 (Fulcher and White): they concluded that this treatment is useful in about half the patients referred to a physiotherapist. Ridsdale and her colleagues found that counselling had as powerful an effect as cognitive behavioural therapy when used in primary care settings (Ridsdale et al., 2001). Here is an example of a psychodynamic approach to chronic fatigue:

Case Study

Joanna suffered with quite severe chronic fatigue syndrome. She often went to bed at 8 pm, unable to stay awake any longer. Her sleep was fitful and rarely refreshing. Occasionally she woke up in the night drenched in sweat. On some days any physical effort (e.g., climbing the underground exit stairs) exhausted her. She had grown up in a relatively cold family environment in which emotions were not expressed. She felt that she had been brought up more severely than her younger brother. She had married a physically abusive man from whom she was now separated. She spent her days looking after her adult children who were unreasonably demanding. She seemed over-identified with her family's problems and many of the early sessions were focused on these family members' problems rather than her own. Gradually she began to see herself as a person in her own right who was entitled to have her own feelings.

With therapy, her symptoms of fatigue initially got worse: she felt physically drained and started to complain of nausea and vomiting, but remained very active in the household, where her family were even less supportive when she felt weak. During the therapy she began to make links between her fatigue and the contact she had with her family. The family was large, demanding and lively, yet no one found time to listen to her needs.

She was afraid of upsetting them and always tried too hard to please. As she began to express her feelings and wishes and became more independent, her depression and fatigue lessened. (Gubert, personal communication).

Rheumatoid Arthritis

This painful, deforming and often crippling disease was first described by Garrod in 1858. It is relatively uncommon, occurring in 0.8 per cent of the population. It is commoner in women than men with a peak incidence between 20 and 40 years. Its clinical features include the presence of morning stiffness and pain on movement or tenderness of at least one joint with swelling in one or more joints as well as pain on motion or tenderness in at least one joint. In addition, there is symmetrical swelling of joints for at least six weeks. It is common for the small joints of the hand to be involved. In addition there may be subcutaneous nodules with characteristic radiological changes to the joints.

Sometimes rheumatoid arthritis can begin with a sudden high fever and extensive inflammation of many joints followed by rapid development of joint deformities. More often, the onset of this condition is slow with less discomfort and only a gradual development of deformity. Rheumatoid arthritis begins with general bodily complaints, such as fatigue and weight loss caused by anorexia. Later there are fleeting or more long-lasting pains in the muscles and certain joints, such as the knees, the joints of the hands and feet, which are symmetrically distributed.

Deformities will develop secondarily to the shortening of muscle tendons associated with a myositis (an inflammation of the muscles). In severe forms of the disease, there are subcutaneous lesions just below the elbow as well as other bodily disturbances involving the eye, the lymph glands, the spleen and peripheral nerves. After twenty years, as many as 15 per cent of patients become totally incapacitated.

Investigation shows characteristic changes in the blood where there are high levels of white cells, rheumatoid factor and anti-nuclear antibodies. The synovial fluid of the joints is abnormal and X-ray reveals characteristic changes in the affected joints demonstrating the damaging effects of this disease.

Although many studies have shown an increased prevalence of rheumatoid arthritis amongst the relatives of rheumatoid patients, there is no clear-cut evidence for a hereditary influence. There is strong evidence to suggest that the immune system is involved and that an as yet unidentified antigen stimulates the production of antibody which eventually leads to tissue damage and inflammation through the deposition of IgG-IgMRF complexes in the capillaries of the joints. In addition, the hormone prostaglandin E causes inflammation, oedema and joint damage.

Psychological Factors

Psychological factors have been reported since the 12th century when a Persian text of AD 1155 attributed rheumatoid arthritis to the inability to express aggression. Rimón in 1969 argued that there might be different populations with rheumatoid arthritis and that some patients clearly had a greater biological predisposition to develop this disease. In such people, psychological factors were less significant than in the remaining group of patients. The sudden onset of rheumatoid arthritis may follow bereavement or disappointment or else infection, pregnancy, surgery or physical trauma. I have seen one person who developed rheumatoid arthritis shortly after jumping from the first floor of her house which was on fire. Often, however, the onset is gradual. Certain personality features, such as the constant struggle to contain unconscious hostile feelings, may accompany rheumatoid arthritis (Rimón, 1989). Crown, Crown and Fleming (1975) found psychological factors to be more relevant in the less severe forms of the condition. In a 15-year follow-up study of 74 female patients with rheumatoid arthritis, 41 per cent exhibited overt psychopathology of whom the majority had depressive reactions (Rimón and Laakso, 1984).

Treatment

Treatment of this condition is initially conservative, with non-steroidal anti-inflammatory pain relief. If this fails to alleviate the symptoms, then more radical treatments will include the use of gold, penicillamine, anti-malarial and, ultimately, cytotoxic drugs to induce a remission. Patients also often require steroids to remain well. Steroids and cytotoxic drugs have many undesirable side effects, not least the major changes in bodily appearance generated by steroid use. Joint surgery may also be required. Exercise, diet and appropriate rest also can play an important role in management

Patients require a good psychological attitude and care from a doctor who needs to have a deep understanding of the problems of chronicity and likely feelings of helplessness. Where the disease is rapidly progressive, a resultant depression may interfere with the outcome of any operation. Supportive psychotherapy may help save a patient from the terrible despair and sense of awful hopelessness in the face of such advancing disability (Rimón, 1969). If the depression in rheumatoid arthritis patients becomes persistent, the rheumatological state tends to deteriorate or become therapy-resistant (Rimón, 1974). Severely depressed patients are less likely to respond to their medical regime. If adequate rehabilitative measures, including psychiatric therapy modalities, are instituted then there may be realistic expectations for improved health.

Systemic Lupus Erythematosus (SLE)

This is an autoimmune disorder of unknown causation characterized by immune dysregulation with tissue damage caused by pathogenic **autoantibodies, immune complexes** and T-lymphocytes. Ninety per cent of cases are in women of child-bearing age. It is rare, with an incidence of 2.4 per 100,000 population. Its clinical manifestations include a variety of cutaneous lesions, constitutional symptoms (fatigue, weight loss and fevers), **arthralgias** and arthritis, **pericarditis** and **pleurisy**, renal disease, neuropsychiatric disorders and haematological disorders including anaemia and leukopenia (lowering of the white blood cell count). The neuropsychiatric disorders range from stroke, seizures, headaches, neuropathy and movement disorders to depression, **mania,** anxiety, delirium and cognitive deficits (Dickens, Levenson and Cohen, 2005).

Coping with this condition is clearly extremely challenging, given its chronic, debilitating multisystem nature and unpredictable course. Lupus flares clearly cause stress, but several studies also indicate that stress may cause a lupus flare. These latter studies show that stress may induce immune dysregulation in SLE. Compared with healthy controls, in SLE patients the normal increase in B- and T-suppressor or cytotoxic lymphocytes, and decrease in T-helper lymphocytes, is blunted in response to acoustic, psychological and exercise-induced stress. (Ferstl et al., 1992; Hinrichsen et al., 1989). Dickens, Levenson and Cohen discuss the ways in which such immune dysregulation may cause a lupus flare-up (2005).

Further Reading

Rimón, R. H. (1989) 'Connective tissue diseases', in *Psychosomatic Medicine,* vol. 2, ed. S. Cheren (Madison: International Universities Press), pp. 565–611.

Sharpe, M. C. and O'Malley, P. G. (2005) 'Chronic fatigue and fibromyalgia syndrome', in *The American Psychiatric Publishing Textbook of Psychosomatic Medicine*, ed. J. L. Levenson (Washington, DC: American Psychiatric Publishing), pp. 555–77.

13 Headache

When you're lying awake with a dismal headache and repose is tabooed by anxiety.

Sir W. S. Gilbert, *Iolanthe*

Headaches are a common complaint and, usually, these are mild and self-limiting or responsive to treatment with mild analgesics such as aspirin. Head pain is one of the 10 commonest symptoms in general practice (Leviton, 1978). Chronic daily headache affects about 5 per cent of the population of the United States (Lake and Saper, 2002). In most cases the pain is either produced by muscle contraction (tension headache) or vascular spasm (migraine). Severe headache is a very common cause of incapacity.

It is important to realize that headache may also occur as a result of trauma, **meningitis**, cerebral abscess, a brain tumour, subarachnoid haemorrhage, a **subdural haematoma**, sinusitis, **glaucoma, temporal arteritis**, malignant hypertension, and the use of certain drugs such as calcium channel antagonists. It also occurs with carbon monoxide poisoning and anoxia.

Muscle Contraction (Tension) Headache

In these headaches there is a sensation of tightness, pressure or constriction, as well as an ache. Usually and typically they are bilateral headaches. Their intensity, frequency and duration are variable. Also their site varies, although the sub-occipital region (at the base of the skull at the back of the head) is common. The headache is associated with the sustained contraction of skeletal muscles, but there is no permanent structural change. The symptoms are most often part of a person's reaction to an emotionally stressful situation. On examination, the occipital and sub-occipital areas of the head are tender. There is a significant association between tension headaches and depression (Davis et al., 1976; Martin, 1985).

Treatment

With repetitive tension headaches, EMG and biofeedback will relieve the tension headache in a high proportion of cases, but not all studies have confirmed this (Jessup et al., 1979). The use of tricyclic antidepressants may also be helpful (Diamond and Baltes, 1971). Here is an example of the usefulness of psychoanalytic psychotherapy for one patient with a continuous, severe and incapacitating tension headache occurring during the daytime:

Case Study

A young woman in her early twenties presented with a continuous dull headache which persisted throughout the day, only going away when she fell asleep at night. It had begun shortly after she discovered that the teacher with whom she was in love was homosexual. Her parents split up when she was just beginning puberty. Shortly after her disappointment in love, her younger sister had a major psychotic illness. It was very difficult to engage this woman in psychotherapy. She was convinced that the cause of her headaches was organic although investigations by many physicians proved this was not the case.

Behind her headache lay a depression and, although she had been put on antidepressants, she had failed to respond to these. Subsequently, in psychotherapy, she was able to cry for the first time about the significant events that had led to the development of her headache (also discussed in the section on psychotherapy assessment in Chapter 3).

Migraine

A migraine is a physical event which may also be from the start or later become, an emotional or symbolic event. A migraine

> *expresses both physiological and emotional needs: it is the prototype of a psychophysiological reaction.*
>
> Sacks (1981)

Migraine has been defined as pain on one side of the head, associated with nausea or vomiting as prodromal symptoms (i.e., symptoms that occur before the pain develops in the head). Over the lifespan, 18 per cent of women and 6 per cent of men will suffer from migraine (Lipton et al., 1997). Although its causation is different from that of tension headache, there are many similarities with regard to sex ratio (i.e., women more than men), age of onset, natural history, psychological data and response to medication (Raskin, 1985).

We still do not know the exact mechanism that underlies the production of this type of headache. It may arise from the displacement of pain sensitive intracranial structures that are vascular or it may be a genetic disorder of the brainstem pain-modulation system in which there is a defect in the turnover of the neurotransmitters, especially serotonin (Sicuteri et al., 1974). Vascular headaches may also be secondary to lumbar puncture, systemic lupus erythematosus or cerebral infarction.

Common triggers are psychological factors such as anxiety, stress or worry. The migraine (in contrast to tension headache) may begin when the stress is over. Physical factors include head trauma, lack of sleep, certain foods and alcohol, physical exertion, menstruation, hunger, temperature changes and the use of oral contraceptives. Often there are warning (prodromal) symptoms with visual disturbances that may include flashes of colour, wavy lines, spots or stars (spectral fortification may follow an initial alteration of visual acuity). In half of migraines there is an associated tingling (paraesthesia) or numbness of the hand or forearm or elsewhere. The headache may be described as throbbing in quality and associated with nausea, sometimes ending when the individual vomits. The headache may be relieved by lying in a darkened room.

Simple management of migraine may only require the use of a mild analgesic such as aspirin or else moderate use of a non-steroidal anti-inflammatory drug. Nowadays selective serotonin agonists are used, which will avert a full attack of migraine if taken during the prodromal phase of the migraine (i.e., during the aura) but these may be followed by rebound headaches. In more severe attacks of migraine, ergotamine is helpful. However, with this drug there is a danger of causing peripheral circulatory disorders. The drug methysergide has been used as a prophylactic to prevent further recurrence. However, connective tissue damage may follow with this medication with subsequent damage to the kidney, heart and lung function. Beta-blocking drugs (i.e., drugs which block the beta-adrenergic effects of the sympathetic nervous system), such as propranolol, have also been used successfully to treat migraine.

Psychological Approaches

Wolff observed that migrainous headaches were often responses to repressed hostility and frustration (Wolff, 1937). Paulley and Haskell (1975) stressed the perfectionistic and self-driving characteristics of migraine patients and their inability to relax. Psychotherapy has often been used for migraine but no adequately controlled studies have been carried out (Raskin, 1985). Relaxation therapy may also be helpful.

14 Psychosomatic Aspects of Gynaecology

A good gynaecologist needs particular sensitivity in listening to and handling the range of psychosomatic problems that may occur in his or her patients.[1] These problems include a number of menstrual disorders, complaints of vaginal discharges, certain aspects of infertility, pelvic pain, problems associated with pregnancy and labour (as well as miscarriage and termination of pregnancy), problems to do with the menopause and problems surrounding the after-effects of gynaecological surgery, for example, hysterectomy. Discussions about the functioning of and complaints around the genital tract, even menstruation, may be embarrassing or distasteful for a patient. A psycho-analytical psychotherapist is liable to encounter these problems together with problems surrounding adolescent promiscuity, non-adherence to contraceptives, motherhood, the menopause and problems of old age, all of which reflect on a woman's use of her body for unconscious purposes (Pines, 1993, pp. 151–66).

Menstrual Disorders

These are very common. Even minor emotional disturbances can affect the heaviness, regularity and occurrence of menstruation.

Case Study

Marguerite was a young woman from the Middle East with irregular periods for which no physical pathology had been found. These had begun during her second marriage when her husband had begun to travel abroad and she feared he would be unfaithful to her, as her first husband had been. During her childhood her father, to whom she had been very close, had frequently travelled abroad and had died when she was only ten.

1 Amenorrhoea (Absence of Menstruation)

(a) Primary Amenorrhoea

This is considered pathological when menarche is significantly delayed, especially in the absence of developing secondary sexual characteristics, where investigations show no physical cause. Then a psychological explanation needs to be considered.

(b) Secondary Ammenorrhoea

Any subsequent amenorrhoea is deemed to be secondary. Pregnancy, abnormal thyroid or adrenal function, diabetes and the menopause are the common physical causes. When these have been excluded, psychological factors should be considered, including anorexia nervosa and depression. Severe prolonged emotional stress may also lead to a loss of periods (such as the experience of a major trauma, for example torture and experience of prisoner-of-war camps). Also less severe stress-linked disturbances of the hypothalamic-pituitary-adrenal axis or hypothalamic-pituitary-gonadal axis may cause secondary amenorrhoea. Intrapsychic conflicts about sexuality and pregnancy may also cause secondary amenorrhoea. All of these psychological difficulties may require long-term psychotherapy.

2 Menorrhagia (Heavy Periods)

A patient's estimation of the excessiveness of her menstruation is highly subjective. If she regards her periods with disgust, then any period is likely to be seen as excessive. Physical conditions such as fibroids, thyroid dysfunction and bleeding disorders may also cause heavy periods. There is individual variability in menstrual flow. In some patients there are significant emotional factors and the menorrhagia resolves once the emotional disturbance has resolved. Some of these patients who complain of heavy periods but, in fact, have a normal menstrual flow may proceed to go through a number of different doctors, changing from an initial hormonal therapy to surgical procedures like dilatation and curettage and on to a potentially unnecessary hysterectomy, which may worsen their psychological situation.

3 Primary Dysmenorrhoea (Painful Menstruation)

Primary dysmenorrhoea begins at the menarche. Pain begins in this condition just before or with the menstrual flow and is worse for the first day and then slowly eases. Up to 50 per cent of teenage girls may have some pain with their periods but by their early twenties between only 5–10 per cent have severe pain for several hours with each period. Pain is caused by the excessive contraction of the uterus, leading to ischaemia (diminished blood supply) and may be accompanied by smooth muscle contraction elsewhere, leading to pallor or even fainting, with associated nausea, vomiting and looseness of stools. It is often relieved by pregnancy. The severe cramping pain may be caused by a narrow cervical canal, uterine malformation and immaturity, retroversion hormonal influences or constipation. It is, nowadays, thought to be a response to excessive prostaglandins. Life-events may increase the severity of dysmenorrhoea. Sometimes there is a family background in which the mother's negative attitudes to her own menstruation have been relevant in the development of her daughter's attitude to her menstruation and the development of dysmenorrhoea.

Management includes the exclusion of underlying pathology and the use of analgesics and, sometimes, the induction of anovular menstruation by using the contraceptive pill as well as the use of prostaglandin inhibitors to render the menstruation less painful.

4 Secondary Dysmenorrhoea

Secondary dysmenorrhoea starts after months or years of pain-free menstruation. The pain occurs for one or two days before menstruation commences and is a protracted severe deep pelvic ache. It may be made worse by passing water or faeces. Often, pelvic examination shows that there are small implants of endometriosis. It may be associated with heavy periods and pain on intercourse.

5 Premenstrual Syndrome

Originally called premenstrual tension by Robert Frank (1931), in this condition a combination of common psychological and physical symptoms occur premenstrually, including sadness, irritability, tension or anxiety, with bloating or breast tenderness. Other symptoms may include a change in appetite or sleep, with difficulty in concentrating and working. Five per cent of women experience severe premenstrual symptoms that impact on their functioning.

The DSM IV-TR describes the following criteria for Premenstrual Dysphoric Disorder (PMDD): in most menstrual cycles over the past year, five or more of the following symptoms which were present during the last week of the luteal phase,[2] began to remit within a few days after the onset of the follicular phase, and were absent in the week post-menses:

- markedly depressed mood, feelings of hopelessness or low self-worth;
- anxiety, tension;
- affective lability;
- persistent irritability;
- decreased interest in usual activities;
- difficulty in concentrating;
- lethargy and easy fatiguability;
- changed appetite/overeating;
- hypersomnia or insomnia;
- feeling out of control;
- breast tenderness or swelling/headaches, joint or muscle pain, sensation of bloating, weight gain.

The cause is unknown but a combination of physical (hormonal) and psychological factors are likely. Stressors to do with marital and sexual disharmony, family crises, losses and bereavements may increase the liability to premenstrual tension

(Gath et al., 1987) and more long-standing personality problems, including attitudes to sexuality and menstruation, may also play a part.

Menopausal Symptoms

During this phase of a woman's life, she must change her view of herself, her body, her body image and the self-esteem that has often been gained by other's admiration of her youthful appearance. Adolescent anxieties may be revived in the anxieties of a menopausal and post-menopausal woman, so that her body image and attractiveness to others again become important factors in a woman's view of herself (Pines, 1993).

The common recurrence of somatic symptoms in the perimenopausal years, including hot flushes, excessive sweating and vaginal atrophy, is directly due to low oestrogen levels but, when depression and anxiety develop, these may also be the result of changes in the woman's personal and social awareness. The somatic symptoms may contribute to the anxiety and depression but the depression itself is no different from depression at any other time in life.

Post-menopausal women often experience decreased sexual interest and frequency of orgasm. If there has been good previous sexual interest and if sexual activity has been important, this correlates with higher frequency of sexual activity in later life. For some, the menopause may coincide with a lessening of responsibility for children who have now grown up, with being more available for career or leisure activities and having more time to be with a partner. These factors together with the freedom from the need to be concerned with contraception may actually lead to an enhancement of the sexual relationship. Although hormone replacement therapy has been found to be helpful for hot flushes of the perimenopause, its use has been called into question because of the slightly increased risk of breast cancer. Depression and anxiety occurring in the menopause may require psychotherapy and antidepressants and are sometimes helped by oestradiol.

Chronic Pelvic Pain

This is a common condition in women, requiring very careful initial assessment. It has an estimated prevalence of 3.8 per cent in adult women which is similar to that of asthma and back pain (Zondervan et al., 1999). Two physical conditions are most often associated with chronic pelvic pain, namely endometriosis and **pelvic adhesions**. These may be very difficult to detect on physical examination and imaging. Pain that has lasted for more than six months and is accompanied by altered mood and altered physical activity, including sexual activity, is significant in determining whether there is chronic pelvic pain.

General pelvic pain may be present either on one side or over the entire lower pelvic area. It may occur cyclically or continuously. Cyclic discomforts are typically associated with endometriosis, but may also be associated with pelvic adhesions which may also be cyclical. A continuous pain is more often due to pelvic adhesions, that is, caused by a previous infection, or else by surgery.

It should be noted that dyspareunia (painful sexual intercourse) is either localized at the introitus, i.e., around the opening of the vagina, or else felt deeply during sexual intercourse. A deep dyspareunia is usually due to organic factors, whereas introital dyspareunia is more often psychologically-based, or due to vulvodynia or vulvovaginitis.

When no organic pathology has been found for pelvic pain on laparoscopy, there may still be a physical contribution from various conditions, including **trigonitis**, **urethritis**, functional pelvic musculoskeletal problems, postural changes or irritable bowel syndrome.

Psychological Factors

Many reports suggest the importance of psychological factors in women with pelvic pain and these may be associated with underlying physical disease. Various workers have found a higher incidence of sexual trauma, including sexual molestation, incest and rape (Beard et al., 1977) but others failed to confirm this (Rapkin et al., 1990). There is often an associated decrease in sexual desire with pelvic pain and also vaginismus with this condition. Women referred for psychological help will have had a negative laparoscopy and often women with some physical pathology may have been subjected to many futile medical and surgical measures to relieve the pain.

In this condition of pelvic pain, there is a real opportunity for collaboration between the gynaecologist and the psychiatrist or psychotherapist. Psychological approaches may involve spouses or families and include sexual counselling, as well as the use of relaxation techniques and antidepressants where indicated. Psychotherapy may be helpful as well.

Vulvodynia

This is a chronic burning sensation, stinging or pain in the vulva, without objective clinical or laboratory findings, which may or may not be caused by touch. In a survey by Edwards in the USA, 16 per cent of women reported lower genital tract discomfort persisting for three months or longer (Edwards, 2003). Depression and anxiety commonly accompany this syndrome (Stewart et al., 1994) which may respond to SSRI antidepressants (e.g., fluoxetine) and to gabapentin, used for neuropathic pain (Stotland et al., 2005).

Infertility

This is usually defined as a failure to conceive after twelve months of appropriately-timed sexual intercourse. About 40 per cent of infertility problems are attributable to the female and 60 per cent are either attributable to the male or are of unknown aetiology (Klock, 1998, pp. 349–88). Eight to twelve per cent of couples experience some type of fertility problem during their reproductive life (World Health Organization Programme of Maternal and Child Health and Family Planning Unit, 1991). Recent studies have emphasized the effect of stressful investigations and treatment as well as intercurrent psychiatric morbidity on fertility and outcomes of fertility treatment (Burns and

Greenfield, 1991). Eating disorders, including bulimia nervosa, are associated with infertility and lower pregnancy rates (Stotland et al., 2005, p. 734). Women report that the diagnosis and treatment of infertility are deeply painful experiences that affect the quality of their lives and may result in poorer sexual and marital adjustments (Weaver et al., 1997).

Further Reading

Pines, D. (1993) 'The menopause', in *A Woman's Unconscious Use of Her Body* (London: Virago), pp. 151–67.

Stotland, N. L., Stewart, D. E., Munce, S. E. and Rolfe, D. E. (2005) 'Obstetrics and gynaecology', in *The American Psychiatric Publishing Textbook of Psychosomatic Medicine*, ed. J. L. Levenson, (Washington, DC: American Psychiatric Publishing), pp. 733–59.

15 Psychosomatic Approaches to Cancer

It's the uncertainty of it all
> Patient with inoperable duodenal cancer,
> receiving palliative chemotherapy

Cancer is a common and a frightening disease (Sikora, 1994, pp. ix–x). One in three of us develops a cancer. Many patients notice the first signs of illness several months, or even years, before consulting their doctor. Up to 60 per cent of patients put off making an appointment (Henderson, 1966). This delay is prolonged where defence mechanisms, such as denial, predominate and also where there is social isolation, significant depression and anxiety (Magarey et al., 1977).

Diagnosis

The diagnosis of cancer is liable to turn the patient's whole life upside down (Guex, 1994). There is a danger that the patient may come to feel that they belong to a world apart, having contracted a disease with such a shocking reputation. Patients may fear being alienated or mutilated by surgical treatment; they may also fear the sudden confrontation with their own vulnerability and subsequent loss of control (Guex, 1994). The time of diagnosis is one of great vulnerability. At this time between 20 and 50 per cent of people may show signs of depression, most recognizable in their body language, somatization (including presentation with pain), unexpected side effects of cancer treatment and social and emotional withdrawal, than in more overt manifestations.

Psychological Adaptation

Adapting to cancer means facing up to the problems that the disease gives rise to: namely, the disruption to life, the pain and disability, and the management of the side effects of the treatments (hair loss, nausea and so on) as well as the restrictions it imposes on normal life. It is vital that a patient develop a good relationship with the medical team and to be able to come to terms with the necessary life changes. Such an adaptation may nevertheless involve the use of defences such as denial, avoidance, projection and rationalization. There is some evidence that denial may, in fact, enhance survival in breast cancer. Ultimately, each person has to come to terms with living with a degree of uncertainty.

Poor Adaptation

An over-compliance with the treatment, without any significant emotional reaction to the diagnosis, suggests poor adaptation. On the other hand, there may be over-reaction, for instance poor compliance with the treatment, or a relinquishing of work and social interaction with a consequent loss of self-esteem.

When cancer occurs in a young adult, they are less likely to be familiar with being ill and may have difficulty in learning to take care of themselves. For them it is a major setback which may also entail the parents regaining power, forcing the younger person back into a position of dependence. Single young people may be worried that they may not be able to have a normal love life because of their potential physical handicap. When cancer occurs in middle or old age, it may be a worrying reminder of mortality and this may lead to depression.

Depression

Assessing depression in the medically ill is generally harder than in medically well patients (Rodin er al., 2005, pp. 193–217). This particularly applies where symptoms that can occur in depression, such as fatigue or anorexia, are in fact being produced by the cancer itself or by treatment for the cancer. Certain hormone-secreting tumours and central nervous system tumours may also cause major mood change. Urea from kidney failure or electrolyte imbalance may also cause depression. Similarly, treatment with steroids or anti-cancer drugs such as procarbazine, rim-blastin, tamoxifen, interferon or l-asparginase may cause mood change. In addition, addictive narcotics, when used as analgesics, may cause mood change.

Anxiety

Anxiety is also liable to occur in cancer and may be linked to the fear of death and dying, the unknown nature of the suffering, loss of control and feelings of abandonment. It may be at its height after the therapeutic regime has finished and the patient feels abandoned by the medical team (Guex, 1994). This may be a good moment to offer psychotherapy if it is indicated.

Quality of Life

The quality of life will be damaged by a variety of symptoms that can disturb social and physical activity:

1 Nausea and vomiting may be caused by the cancer itself (as with cerebral metastases) or else by its treatment with radiotherapy or chemotherapy.
2 Nutritional disturbances are liable to occur, with anorexia and loss of weight, which may be secondary to depression or else to the disease and its treatment.
3 Sexual problems may occur, especially after surgery to the genito-urinary system, such as pelvic surgery and hysterectomy. Some treatments may reduce the patient's libido, sexual desire and fertility, as well as affecting the patient's body image and sense of sexual attractiveness. In addition, a reaction of a partner may have important consequences: Jamison et al. (1978), investigating the husbands of mastectomy patients, found that 20 per cent had never seen their wives naked after their surgery which was attributed to distaste on the part of the husband rather than the shame or discomfort of the wife. Much can be done to improve the quality of life by careful medical and psychiatric attention to treatment as well as to the

possibilities for cosmetic approaches such as breast reconstruction following a mastectomy or the use of wigs
during the period of hair loss resulting from chemotherapy. Sensitive psychotherapeutic work, combined with
body therapeutic techniques, can also help a woman better
to accept her body image and this in turn may facilitate a
better acceptance by her husband. (Macdonald, personal
communication)

Pain Relief

Pain is a common complex and important symptom, involving
acute and chronic elements. Its adequate management at all
phases of the illness is essential for improving quality of life.
Depression may lower the threshold for pain and needs to be
taken into account when planning treatment. The management
of pain in terminal cancer is especially important. Here the main
concern will be to make a patient as comfortable as possible.
At this stage analgesics should not be restricted and will be part
of good hospice or terminal care (Saunders, 1982). Minor and
major analgesics, ranging from aspirin to morphine, may need to
be supplemented with anaesthetic and neurosurgical approaches.
Relaxation techniques such as feedback desensitization or self-
hypnosis may also be helpful.

Psychosomatic Theories about Cancer

Much has been made of possible psychosomatic factors in
cancer, since Galen who in the second century AD argued that
melancholic women were predisposed to cancer. Longitudinal
prospective studies are rare (Guex 1994). Retrospective studies
have often shown that the experience of separation in the course
of a patient's life, such as a painful bereavement or divorce, has
been a key life-event preceding the presentation of a cancer.
However, we now know that tumours may be a long time in their
cellular development and are therefore disguised before they
present symptomatically as a lump or pain. This means that their
true time of onset may have antedated these life-events found in
retrospective studies.

Some patients with cancer have been described as having a typical personality. Various associated attributes include over-conscientiousness, cordiality, submissiveness to authority and social norms, and an over-readiness to neglect one's own feelings and behave as others expect (Bammer, 1981). Morris (1980) described a type C personality as submissive, emotionally inhibited, aggressively inhibited and conformist (see also Temoshok, 1987; Temoshok and Dreher, 1992). These views have not found wide acceptance or been substantiated by other studies. Such ideas have sometimes contributed negatively to the self-esteem of cancer sufferers and led to unnecessary anxiety. Apart from some animal studies, there would appear to be no conclusive evidence supporting a link between stress and cancer (Rodin, personal communication).

Psychological Treatment Approaches

It is clear that adopting a psychosomatic approach to the patient with cancer has an enormous impact at all stages in its treatment on their capacity to cope with such a threatening experience. This includes the way in which the discussion of the diagnosis is handled and also covers the adequate management of psychiatric sequelae of the condition and the close attention to the medical, psychological and social issues arising from the treatment of the illness.

Liaison-consultation psychiatry has a vital role in this complex medical and psychological situation where the relationship between the doctor and patient is at such a premium. Feelings of hopelessness and helplessness can easily give rise to a sense of impotence or omnipotence in carers, who need support and understanding from psychiatric colleagues, as well as possible psychiatric interventions, so as to improve their patients' capacity to cope with their condition and its effects on their life. Such interventions may include effective psychopharmacological treatments for mood disorders in patients and the recognition and understanding of the role of the cancer in the patient's life. Patients may need short-term or long-term psychodynamic intervention. Guex writes very movingly about the way in which his team in Switzerland work with cancer surgeons and oncologists to provide such integrated psycho-oncological care for cancer patients (Guex, 1994). Goldie has also written a very helpful account of his lifetime experience as psychoanalytic psychotherapist at the Royal Marsden Hospital, a national treatment centre for cancer, in the UK (Goldie and Desmarais, 2005).

Group Therapy

Spiegel has used group therapy for cancer patients in which patients are offered short- or long-term group analytic psychotherapy (Spiegel and Classen, 2000). In the groups, which are supportive and exploratory, the main emphasis is on the patient's relationship to his cancer. The groups are very much rooted in the here and now. In such groups boundaries are less rigorously kept so that group members have the opportunity to interact and support each other outside the group.

Initially the results of these groups were very striking, showing a marked improvement, not only in the quality of life but also in life expectancy over controls that had been randomly allocated (Spiegel et al., 1989). In subsequent prospective studies, while it has been clear that these groups enhanced the quality of life, there has been no evidence that they enhanced survival prospects.

Guex and MacDonald have developed a special form of group psychotherapy which included the use of relaxation and a special form of physiotherapy (Eutonie) to counter the patient's fears of bodily fragmentation by their cancer (Guex and MacDonald, 1984).

Family Therapy

This kind of illness often involves the whole family of the cancer patient. It may reinforce and enhance relationships or lead to withdrawal, with overprotective or denying ways of relating, which can make the patient feel even lonelier with his illness. In such situations a systemic family therapy may be very helpful.

Case Study

A young man in his second year of law studies, still living with his parents but with plans to move into a flat of his own, developed headaches. He was diagnosed as having a brain tumour, which was operated on. Six months later a second tumour was found. He commenced chemotherapy: soon he was complaining of anxiety and insomnia. He was then referred for relaxation therapy.

He was a rather timid and awkward man who liked this therapeutic approach. He told his therapist that it was the first experience he had had in which nothing was being demanded of him. He was treated with relaxation therapy for a year. Then sadly his brain tumour recurred but was inoperable.

At home he was finding it difficult to be with his mother who was over-protective. For the first time in his life he had fallen in love with a girl but was afraid to tell her about his cancer. Also as a result of his illness he was finding it increasingly it difficult to concentrate on his studies. So he had stopped his course at university and had taken up secretarial work; but he had to abandon this as his tumour was now causing a loss of sensation in his fingers.

A combination of psychotherapy and body work allowed him to experience his emotions for the first time: he began to speak to his therapist about his hopes and his inner world. Sadly his physical condition deteriorated. He now became angry with his therapist for helping him to discover his feelings, complaining that with the worsening of his condition he would no longer be able to use this newfound ability. His therapist was concerned about this outcome of her work with him. However on his next visit he reflected on the last session: He said he now realised that it would have been far worse if he were to die without having been alive in this way which had allowed him to experience his emotions so fully (Macdonald, personal communication).

Palliative Care

Modern medicine has been based too much on an acute disease/ curative model (Spiegel and Classen, 2000). Whilst there has been dramatic progress in curing some cancers such as Hodgkin's Lymphoma, testicular cancer and childhood leukaemias, and it may be reasonable to be optimistic with some tumours, people with a cancer have much cause to worry. Those who work with cancer should bear in mind the old adage, 'to cure rarely, to relieve suffering often, to comfort always'.

Palliative care for the dying and terminally ill has evolved in the last 50 years or so as a speciality in its own right, especially with the hospice movement started by Saunders, and also the potential for adequate terminal care to be provided at home. Specialist nurses (e.g., Macmillan nurses) can help the dying patient to arrive at the end of their life psychologically as well as physically. Such care helps them not to feel abandoned by their carers, friends or family and allows them to safely discuss the issues surrounding their death.

Rodin and his colleagues (Tan, Zimmermann and Rodin, 2005) argue that the progression of advanced cancer brings adaptational challenges related to the loss of capacity to be self-sufficient, with an increased need for support. That need for support may reactivate earlier difficulties in making and sustaining close relationships, resulting in the patient feeling more vulnerable and threatened by this new dependency on care givers. Care givers can find this very challenging and may be helped by the psychotherapist to consider the earlier insecure attachment styles of such individuals. This can help them to develop better ways of providing more effective long-term palliative care.

Further Reading

Guex, P. (1994) *An Introduction to Psycho-Oncology* (London: Routledge).

Rodin, G. M., Nolan, R. P. and Katz, M. R. (2005) 'Depression', in *The American Psychiatric Publishing Textbook of Psychosomatic Medicine*, ed. J. L. Levensen (Washington, DC: American Psychiatric Publishing), pp. 193–219.

Spiegel, D. and Classen, C. (2000) *Group Therapy for Cancer Patients* (New York: Basic Books).

16 Developing a Psychosomatic Imagination

Writing prescriptions is easy, but to communicate with people beyond that is difficult

Franz Kafka, *A Country Doctor* (1919)

The story of the medical student and the young man with atypical facial pain at the beginning of this book (Chapter 1, 'Introduction') shows how students can learn from clinical encounters with psychosomatic patients. A recent survey of 1593 doctors and 227 medical students in Geneva, which looked at the relative importance of psychiatric topics in undergraduate teaching, found that learning about the doctor–patient relationship was considered the most important topic (Georg et al., 1999). In British medical schools there has been new emphasis on helping medical students to develop a professional attitude towards their patients, alongside teaching communication skills so as to help them to become better doctors. However, much of this teaching is problem-oriented and tends to be prescriptive in its approach. Psychotherapy teaching can help medical students to learn about the doctor–patient relationship and to develop a *psychosomatic approach* towards their patients.

A British Approach to Psychotherapy Teaching

Our Department of Psychotherapy (at University College Hospital) is located within a large medical school and teaching hospital in central London. Clinical medical students receive one or two formal lectures about psychodynamic psychotherapy during their psychiatric attachment. During this attachment, they have an opportunity to join a short-term weekly discussion group run by a senior psychotherapist, to help them think about their emotional experiences of seeing mental illness for the first time, (Brafman, 2003). A very small number of students – three every five weeks are attached for a three-week period to our department and the Department of Psychological Medicine. During this placement, they are given an opportunity to interview patients prior to their psychotherapy assessment. Some of these are patients with psychosomatic disorders and so give the student the important opportunity to develop insights into psychosomatic conditions (see the Case Study in Chapter 1).

Medical Student Psychotherapy Schemes

Students get enormous inspiration from such rewarding and revealing encounters with psychosomatic and other patients referred for psychotherapy. Nearly fifty years ago, two psychotherapists, Ball and Wolff, and Tredgold, a psychiatrist working in our department, recognized this and began a scheme in which first-year clinical medical students were invited to see carefully selected patients for ongoing once-weekly individual psychodynamic psychotherapy (Ball and Wolff, 1963). This psychotherapy was supervised by a senior member of our team. The scheme has remained a very popular option for students who want to learn in greater depth about the doctor–patient relationship (Shoenberg, 1992). While similar projects have been initiated independently in medical schools in north America, our scheme has been followed and studied by other medical schools in Britain (in Bristol and Oxford), Canada (in Toronto) and Europe (in Heidelberg and Lausanne).

Often students do well with patients who are somatizers and with young people presenting with personality disorders. The gentleness and relative lack of intellectual sophistication of the medical students may make them better at emotional contact with their patient in such an introduction to psychotherapy than their counterparts amongst the psychiatric trainees who are often overloaded with psychiatric theory. Our students participate in the scheme on an entirely voluntary basis, whereas the psychiatric trainees have to do psychotherapy as a prerequisite for specialization in psychiatry.

Students who have participated in this scheme have reported in a recent ten-year retrospective study that it has been very helpful to them in learning to relate to patients (Yakeley, Shoenberg and Heady, 2004). We can see how they have begun to understand the patient's unconscious communications and appreciate the significance of childhood emotional development in the production of adult psychopathology. They are better able to handle discussion of embarrassing topics and feel more confident when managing patients who are aggressive or angry. They also feel less disturbed in their encounters with death and dying. Students often report that it has helped them with medical patients in more general ways and it is clear that they have begun to appreciate the links between *psyche* and *soma*.

Such an experience gives students the opportunity to learn to listen to a patient and to appreciate the value of continuity of care, as compared with the fragmentary nature of contact they have with patients during the rest of the medical curriculum. Students bring to this project enormous enthusiasm and a capacity to be gentle and unintrusive, which are vital qualities in any therapist.

Although some patients drop out of treatment early on, the majority respond well to this introductory period of what is in effect a relatively supportive and exploratory psychotherapy. After the therapy has ended, the patient is given the opportunity to consider having longer-term psychodynamic psychotherapy. In a study of a similar scheme in Heidelberg (Knauss and Senf, 1983), 30 of 38 patients completed the full course of psychotherapy with the student and in follow-up interviews, 52 per cent considered this opportunity to talk to an independent non-judgemental person to have been the most important experience during their therapy.

Psychodynamic psychotherapy gives the student a unique experience of handling the dependency needs of a patient through the student's understanding of, interpretation of and working through of transference situations. This provides profound insights into the doctor–patient relationship. At the end of the psychotherapy, which usually lasts for one year, students make an evaluation of their work in the form of a summary of their treatment. Recently a student wrote this interesting account of her work with a patient demonstrating unexplained medical symptoms:

Case Study

The problems that Jenny was experiencing with her bladder
and her bowels were a constant theme during the psychotherapy. In the first few sessions she spoke almost exclusively
about them. I thought that they were safe topics she could
discuss as I was a medical student, when other things were too
difficult. It was interesting as, because she knew I was a
medical student, I never commented on them as I explained it
was not my role, but it was difficult not to get drawn into
making some sort of diagnosis.

Her symptoms were of recurrent urinary tract infections
and bowel problems associated with pelvic floor and lower
back muscle tightening and pain. She also suffered with
headaches and lethargy. Jenny was initially reluctant to think
that her symptoms were linked to her feelings or emotions. . . .
However, by looking at examples of how the mind can affect
the body and vice versa, such as the migraine she always got
on returning from her parents' house and the strange mood
she felt during her periods, she was able to see that her mood
did affect her symptoms. For example, she had fewer urinary
tract infections whilst feeling happier compared with when
she was feeling lower.

We explored the significance of her symptoms for Jenny
and she remembered that as child she had been very anxious
about not making it to the toilet on time, and she feared that
she would have an accident in the classroom. As a result, she
often spent much of break-time sitting on the toilet, making
sure she went to the toilet just before the school bell rang, so as
to ensure there would be no susequent accidents in the
classroom. At home she had been taught that to use the toilet
was dirty and in some way wrong, and should *never* be
discussed. This was similar to the way in which emotions were
treated at home: we now explored the link between the use of
the toilet and her expression of her emotions and wondered if
sometimes the toilet was her way to express these feelings.
Although she claimed not to understand how this might be,
she gained insight into the way she expressed her emotions
and eventually could interpret new symptoms in this light. For
example, when trying to express her feelings about the ending

of the therapy, she developed a cough that interrupted her: she now interpreted this as meaning that she did not want to discuss her feelings about this forthcoming ending which would be so difficult for her.

As we discussed the end of the therapy, she compared it to an antibiotic, by which she meant that she thought it would continue to have an effect after it had ended. This was interesting for me, as it showed her ability to link the medical and emotional side of her complaints to the medical and emotional side of me, a medical student and her psychotherapist. It appeared that I had come to symbolize and indeed replace the antibiotics on which Jenny had been so dependent when we had first begun the psychotherapy. (Sallnow, personal communication)

Such long-term experiences for students who do psychotherapy are clearly deeply rewarding, as well as very helpful to their patients. They also teach the student a psychosomatic approach to illness.

Balint Groups for First-Year Clinical Medical Students

Our scheme, for reasons of clinical safety and because of the limited numbers of supervisors available, has had to be limited to a handful of students. So as to allow more students to learn about the doctor–patient relationship, we developed a new project based on the ideas of Balint in his groups for GPs and medical students (Balint, Ball and Hare, 1969). Such medical student Balint groups have also been initiated in the USA (Turner, 2005; Margo et al., 2004), various European countries (Luban-Plozza, 1989) and South Africa (Levenstein, 1980).

We offered 11 of the first-year clinical students whom we had not been able to place on the Student Psychotherapy Scheme the chance to join a weekly discussion group which would run for 12 weeks. In this group the students were encouraged to discuss clinical cases that they had found interesting from an emotional point of view during the previous week. Initially a Balint-trained GP (Dr Suckling) and I ran very small separate groups but within a month we decided to merge the two groups into one. The following is a brief account of our new experience:

Case Study

In the first group, which I ran on my own, the four students who came talked about how difficult it felt just to go up to patients who might be asleep, or not in a fit state to speak. One of them described how frightened she had felt about seeing a very ill patient, who was somehow repellent to her. She said how difficult it felt to get close to him. The one male student in the group told us how surprised he had been when a patient with chronic obstructive airways disease had waved to him on the ward, having seen him the day before in the casualty department. Seeing this patient again had made him realize suddenly how important continuity of care was. Another student talked about helping a patient she had taken to the X-ray department by telling him about the anatomy of his trachea, which was under examination and which he was very frightened about, and that she had noticed how patients were often not given explanations. My only comment in this group was that we seemed to be talking about trying to find something of the person in each of the patients who had been described.

By the fourth session, my group had begun to share a lot more feelings with each other. One of the students talked about seeing a poor wizened old man in his eighties with severe peripheral arterial disease. She said he was so emaciated she could see his ribs and his emaciated abdomen as he lay on the bed. She said he was hardly able to talk and looked like a bag of bones, with one leg amputated. She expressed how shocking it had been when his remaining leg had moved. It had all been so upsetting that she had burst into tears afterwards when she was speaking to her mother on the phone. It led to a discussion about the relationship between what you see and what you feel, and the fear that this man had aroused in her of growing old herself. We then talked about the fear of touching patients. Another student described a patient who had come to the casualty department who was so badly burned that one could not tell the colour of his skin. All that could be seen was the ash covering his body and his charred hair. The student had got ash on her skin from examining him. It had all been very threatening and frightening. She said she had wanted to cry and realised it would help her to cry. The group expressed the view that one needed to be objective if one were to become competent.

The student who had told us the previous story now told us about taking the history of a man in a cardiology ward. He kept on interrupting her to talk about the loss of his wife. He said, 'I'm sorry, I want to talk about Kate.' By his bedside was a picture of Kate. Apparently he had looked after his wife who suffered from Parkinson's disease and during this time he had lost four stone in weight. The group wondered what the student should do because the patient had refused to have counselling, yet he obviously wanted to talk. It was suggested that this student should return to this man later, but what would happen if he began to talk about something the students could not handle? Another student suggested that when somebody talked about something that was difficult, it was better just to say nothing and listen. I commented that this case showed how important emotions were, and how important it was for the student to be able to have real emotions themselves, in order to empathise better with the patient.

After a month the other group leader had an accident and so I merged the two groups. In retrospect, this larger group of 9 rather than 4 or 5 students with (eventually) 2 leaders functioned better than the separate groups.

By now, this big group had begun to consider much deeper issues. One student described her first experience of seeing a patient dying in Casualty. He died of a third heart attack: she described her surprise at the very peaceful expression on his face, which contrasted with the heart-rending screams of the relatives in the corridor and the anxieties of the Casualty doctors that they might have missed his high serum potassium and so created a bigger medical problem for him. The group discussed how this first experience of seeing a death had affected the student. She denied that it had been upsetting, yet I noticed that her eyes were filled with tears.

In this larger group, our discussions explored the histories of patients who did not fit into the hospital system. One student described a very demanding and abusive young home-less drug addict who wanted her to make a phone call to a

Homeless Persons Unit and then demanded that she fetch some orange juice for her: the student had refused to do this, as she did not consider it to be her role. Another student presented an angry, rather litiginous patient, who was convinced that the ENT surgeons who had put grommets in her ears had caused her subsequently to develop tinnitus. She described how the two consultants had listened patiently to this aggressive patient, yet she remained unsatisfied, even when the doctors offered to take the grommets out again. The students discussed why people were angry and why they were hypochondriacal; I was pleased when one student suggested that it might be to do with their private unhappiness and even perhaps a broken marriage in the background.

Another student described a case of a woman who came to an incontinence clinic complaining that she became incontinent of urine only when she passed a certain building. We all agreed that this might be a psychosomatic case in which one might have to take into account the patient's personality as well as their illness.

On another occasion, a student described a man who had already had a coronary bypass but who was now presenting with unstable angina pectoris. The social history in the doctor's notes only recorded that the patient lived with his wife. However, the student had been able to take a long psycho-social history during which the patient had told her his wife was becoming increasingly frail. The man had wanted to move from their house, which he felt was too big, but the wife was unwilling. On the day of his admission to hospital, the weather had been very cold, he had been busy all day and then he had eaten a very heavy meal, after which he had to do the washing-up. It was then that his angina came on. He had ignored it for one and a half hours before feeling able to call for help. The student commented that the doctor seemed only interested in the medical problems when it was clear that this man's social and personal circumstances were very relevant. Another student remarked this was not the case with geriatricians, while another said nor was it with GPs.

The ensuing sessions included discussions of patients with dementia and facial disfigurement, and how doctors dealt with these frightening and painful situations. Another group talked about patients who were difficult historians and who were devious with the students. The students wondered if it was because they *were* only students, after all. In another session, a student described a young patient with ulcerative colitis who said he preferred to talk to her, rather than the doctors, because she was nearer his age. She had found the closeness in age a challenge. Two students said they preferred to be with younger people, but another student said he preferred older patients with whom he felt safer.

A theme that recurred throughout the group sessions was the problem the students had in finding sufficient time with the patient, both to listen to their story and to obtain a systematic medical history. The students said how much they had appreciated being given time to talk about their work with patients and to hear other people's views, and that this had given them a fresh outlook and helped them to see things in a new light. They said it had been a revelation to realize that they, as students, could be useful to patients, and that it had stopped patients feeling so alone with difficult problems.

We have now enlarged this scheme so that we can offer up to four Balint groups each year to our first-year clinical medical students, with the possibility of giving our medical school feedback on the emotional problems these students experience in their first encounters with patients.

Balint's original work was with General Practitioners where he pioneered longer-term groups for GPs to meet regularly to present and discuss the emotional aspects of their work in a safe environment with an experienced group leader. The chief aim of these groups was to help doctors to gain a deeper understanding of their relationship with their patients (Balint, 1964). Often the clinical problems discussed in these groups were psychosomatic ones. There are now Balint groups in many countries as well as an International Balint Federation.

Conclusion

Psychotherapists who work in general medical hospitals have a unique opportunity to enhance the work of their hospital, where increasingly medical services are becoming more specialized and often separate from psychiatric services. Nowadays there is too much emphasis on speed of treatment to reduce the cost of medical care. The links between *psyche* and *soma* are precarious, not only in the psychosomatic patients we see, but also between the Departments of Medicine and of Psychological Treatment. Psychotherapy teaching can offer the medical student who is trying to navigate this brave new world a chance to find his own and his patient's emotions in the diseases he or she encounters on this journey through the hospital. In this way a psychosomatic imagination can be developed in the doctors of the future.

Further Reading

Shoenberg, P. (1992) 'The student psychotherapy scheme at the University College and Middlesex School of Medicine: its role in helping medical students to learn about the doctor–patient relationship', *Journal of the Balint Society*, 20: 10–15.

17 Conclusion

A psychosomatic illness can happen to anyone, be they a patient or a therapist. Indeed, if a therapist has had such an experience it will make it easier to empathize with their psychosomatic patient, and also to appreciate the impact of a patient's transference on their body, as well as their mind.

To attempt to reduce psychosomatics to its symbolic psychological meaning is as futile as to confine each psychosomatic event to a neural register of emotions and their somatic display. Each system or category of thinking has a place within the far more complex array of systems at work in the psychology of medicine described in this book. At times one or other system will have more coherence and relevance to the individual's psychosomatic story. To help an individual with a psychosomatic disorder, we should always examine the natural history of their medical condition as well as their personal narrative.

Contemporary medicine, with its emphasis on the speed and efficiency of treatment, often leaves too little time for patients to recover fully. The psychosomatic approach to illness has the virtue that it includes the concern to allow time for true healing to occur.

There is a place for the non-medical as well as the medical psychotherapist in this endeavour; but each type of psychotherapist is at risk of behaving omnipotently towards their psychosomatic patients (Shoenberg, 1999). While the non-medical psychotherapist is in danger of making psychological interpretations of psychosomatic events, in ignorance of the possibility of a non-psychological cause, the medical psychotherapist may search too vigorously for a physical cause. A useful psychosomatic imagination should be tempered with an accurate appreciation of the body both in health and disease: this allows the care of the psychosomatic patient to be shared with a physician.

Notes

Notes to Chapter 1

1. Even though from a biophysicist's point of view 'we are no more than the behaviour of a vast assembly of nerve cells and their associated molecules' (Crick, 1994).
2. A view he later changed to one in which he considered that often the patient had had a phantasy of being sexually abused in childhood.
3. Inevitably the case studies in this and other chapters are short and often simplified, which means that they may miss some of the complexities of the actual clinical experience. This is mainly to preserve confidentiality. Wherever possible, I have obtained written consent from the patients whose stories are described here. Each vignette has been heavily disguised to protect the individual's anonymity.

Notes to Chapter 2

1. In writing this chapter, I am indebted to Ackerknecht for his article 'The history of psychosomatic medicine' (1982), to Ellenberger for his account of hypnosis in *The Discovery of the Unconscious* (1970) and to Taylor for his account of the early psychoanalysts' interest in psychosomatic disorders in *Psychosomatic Medicine and Contemporary Psychoanalysis* (1987).

Notes to Chapter 3

1. Much of this discussion about psychoanalytic psychotherapy concerns long-term once or twice-weekly psychotherapies (as opposed to more intensive psychoanalytic psychotherapies), very often conducted in hospital settings.
2. For a more recent discussion of this French school, see *The Psychosomatic Paradox* by Smadja (2005).

Notes to Chapter 4

1. In writing this section, I am indebted to Sapolsky for his article, 'Taming stress', in *Scientific American* (10 August 2003).
2. I am indebted to Taylor for his account of stressful life events and general susceptibility to disease in his book *Psychosomatic Medicine and Contemporary Psychoanalysis* (1987), pp. 39–73.
3. Marasmus: a condition in infants in which there is a progressive wasting and emaciation.

Notes to Chapter 5

1. 'Prevalence' refers to the number of cases in existence at a certain time in a designated area. 'Incidence' is an expression of the rate at which a certain event occurs as the number of new cases of a specific disease occurring during a certain period.
2. In writing this section I am indebted to Taylor for his chapter on somatoform disorders in *Disorders of Affect Regulation* (1997), pp. 114–38.

Notes to Chapter 8

1. Acute ulceration of the stomach and duodenum may occur as a result of stress or excessive steroids (Cushing's ulcer), or as a result of Cushing's disease. Some duodenal ulcers are caused by physical factors alone, such as in Zollinger-Ellison syndrome, carcinoid tumours of the stomach and rarer conditions such as mastocytosis.
2. The entire structure of the enteric nervous system (ENS) is arranged in two ganglionated plexuses (the myenteric and the submucosal plexuses) responsible for gut motility and mediating enzyme output of adjacent organs. The ENS is responsible for self-cleaning, regulating the gut's luminal environment, working with the immune system to defend the bowel and modifying the rate of proliferation and growth of mucosal cells. (It is perhaps interesting that the writer D. H. Lawrence believed that the solar plexus (the autonomic nervous system network of sympathetic nerves behind the stomach) was the first seat of primal consciousness in man (Lawrence, 1923, 1974).

Notes to Chapter 10

1. During systole the heart pumps blood into the pulmonary trunk (to take it to the lungs for oxygenation) and the aorta (to take oxygenated blood to the tissues) and during diastole the heart dilates and fills with blood.

2. Nine out of ten heart attacks can be predicted on the basis of eight worldwide risk factors, regardless of sex or ethnic type: (1) abnormal ratio of apolipoprotein A to apolipoprotein B; (2) smoking; (3) high blood pressure; (4) diabetes; (5) abdominal obesity; (6) low daily fruit and vegetable consumption; (7) lack of exercise; (8) Stress. (C. White, News, *BMJ*: **329**: p. 527, Sept. 2004).

3. Winnicott is reputed to have ripped off all his ECG monitor wires and to have demanded to see 'a human doctor' after his first heart attack in New York (R. Taylor, personal communication).

Notes to Chapter 12

1. Benett (2005) has recently reviewed Jungian approaches to psychotherapy and in her own experience has been able to help five patients with a psychodynamic approach in long-term psychotherapy. See also Taerk and Gnam (1994) for a consideration of psychoanalytic psychotherapy.

Notes to Chapter 14

1. In writing this chapter, I am indebted to Stewart and Stotland for their book *Psychological Aspects of Women's Health Care* (1993) and to Stotland, Stewart, Munce and Rolfe for their chapter on 'Obstetrics and gynecology' in *the American Psychiatric Publishing Textbook of Psychosomatic Medicine* (2005), pp. 733–59.

2. The *luteal* phase is between ovulation and menstruation. The *follicular* phase begins with menstruation.

Glossary

Acetylcholine A chemical substance secreted at the nerve endings, including synaptic junctions, neuromuscular junctions and in the autonomic nervous system.

Acting Out The replacement of thought by action, characteristic of the anti-social and borderline personality.

Adrenal cortex This is part of the adrenal gland that lies on the outside layer of the gland. It is situated on the top of each kidney. It is an endocrine gland which secrets cortisone/cortisol, the steroid hormone.

Adrenal medulla The central portion of the adrenal gland (situated above the kidney) that secrets adrenalin.

Affect A general term for feelings and emotions, used extensively in discussions about the psychopathology of psychosomatic disorders in relation to the regulation of affects and the effects of dysregulation on the production of psychosomatic symptoms, especially in somatization.

Agoraphobia A type of phobia in which a patient avoids open spaces and is anxious when he or she has to go into one.

Aldosteronoma A tumour secreting excessive amounts of the hormone aldosterone that regulates electrolyte metabolism and controls electrolyte balance in the body tissues and blood.

Alpha 2 adrenaline receptor A pharmacological site on the membrane of nerve cells, cardiac muscle and blood vessel walls that responds to adrenaline as a neurotransmitter from the sympathetic nerve terminals.

Aneurism A blood-filled sac formed by the dilatation of the walls of an artery or vein.

Angina pectoris A paroxysmal thoracic pain accompanying a feeling of suffocation and impending death due most often to shortage of oxygen to the heart muscle. It is precipitated by effort and excitement.

Angiotensin   Any of three polypeptide hormones, one of which is a vasoconstrictor, that function to control the blood pressure.

Ankylosing spondylitis   An inflammation of the vertebrae, with pathological changes similar to those that occur in the joints in rheumatoid arthritis. It eventually leads to a rigid vertebral column.

Anterior cingulate gyrus   The anterior part of the cingular gyrus (in the cortex of the brain) which arches over the corpus callosum (a commissure which connects the two cerebral hemispheres).

Anticholinergic drugs   Drugs which oppose the action of the chemical neurotransmitter acetylcholine and in this way reduce spasm in the gut in irritable bowel syndrome.

Anxiety neurosis   A neurosis in which anxiety is the predominant symptom, accompanied by somatic symptoms mostly arising from sympathetic nervous overactivity.

Aphthous ulcer   A small whitish, benign ulcer which occurs on the tongue or on the gums.

Arteriole   Any of the small subdivisions of an artery that eventually end in capillaries.

Arthralgia   Pain coming from a joint or joints.

Autoantibody   Antibodies capable of reacting with 'self' components, causing autoimmune diseases, e.g., primary myxoedema (underactivity of the thyroid gland) and thyrotoxicosis (over-activity of the thyroid gland).

Autonomic nervous system   The portion of the nervous system that is concerned with the regulation of activity of smooth muscle, cardiac muscle and also glands. It consists of the sympathetic nervous system and the parasympathetic nervous system.

Avoidant attachment style   A type of insecure attachment between the mother and the baby resulting from a deficient attunement of the mother to the behavioural emotional expressions of her infant, because the mother is often low in emotional expressiveness. Insecure-avoidant children develop problems with the recognition and expression of affect and learn to rely on cognition (Taylor, Bagby and Parker,1997).

B-Lymphocyte These are bursa-dependent and involved in the synthesis of circulating (humoral) antibody

Basal cell A type of cell in the skin's epithelium.

Bipolar disorder Manic-depressive psychosis, in which there are periodic episodes of major mood disorder, alternating between mania and depression. One of the two functional psychoses.

Blood–brain barrier This is a barrier between the blood and the brain which probably functions to maintain the constancy of the neuronal environment in the central nervous system. This is because the cortical neurons are extremely sensitive to ionic changes and so need protection.

Borderline personality A type of personality disorder, characterized by impulsivity and self-destructiveness, in which the affects of anger and depression dominate the clinical picture and in which interpersonal relationships are often superficial and transient. There is a tendency to develop psychotic symptoms which are stress-related and transient.

Brainstem reticular activating system A part of the brainstem concerned with regulation of the autonomic nervous system and of sleep and wakefulness.

Bronchospasm A spasm of the bronchial tubes in the lung.

Cannibalistic phantasies A psychoanalytic term for phantasies of the infant occurring during the oral phase of development, characterized by incorporation and appropriation of the **object** and its properties. This idea of cannibalism implies close connections existing between the oral object-relationship and the earliest modes of identification (Laplanche and Pontalis, 1973).

Catecholamine Amine derived from catechol acting as a neurotransmitter or hormone; includes adrenalin, noradrenalin and dopamine.

Cholera An infectious condition characterized by diarrhoea and vomiting.

Circle of Willis A circular artery at the base of the brain.

Circumventricular organs Organs situated by the ventricles of the brain which are small cavities containing cerebrospinal fluid.

Coarctation of the aorta A malformation of the aorta characterized by a deformity of its component tissues (the media). It causes a narrowing (usually severe) of the lumen of the vessel.

Collagen diseases These are a group of connective tissue diseases including rheumatic fever, rheumatoid arthritis, polyarteritis nodosa, scleroderma, systemic lupus erythematosis, dermatomyositis, Sjøgren's syndrome and serum sickness. It is believed that the lesions in each disease are caused by the development of autoantibodies against the connective and other tissues.

Congestive heart failure That stage in heart failure when the heart is overloaded with blood.

Conjunctivitis An inflammation of the conjunctiva (the delicate lining membrane of the eyelids).

Conversion A psychoanalytic term referring to the process whereby a psychological complex of ideas, wishes or feelings, or an unconscious conflict is replaced by a physical symptom; a defence mechanism.

Corticotrophin releasing hormone A peptide hormone which acts as a central neurotransmitter in the brain and it is also a hormone which causes the pituitary gland to release adrenocorticotrophic hormone (ACTH), which in turn stimulates the adrenal cortex to secrete cortisol.

Countertransference A psychoanalytic term that describes the psychoanalyst's transference to his or her patient, and so is a distorting and disturbing element of this treatment; it may include his or her emotional attitudes towards the patient including his responses to the patient's **transferences** to the analyst (Rycroft, 1968).

Cushing's disease An endocrine disease in which excessive steroids are produced as a result of hyperfunction of the outer layer of the adrenal gland called the adrenal cortex.

Cytokine Any of numerous hormone-like, low-molecular-weight-proteins secreted by various cell types, that regulate the intensity and length of the immune response and mediate cell–cell communication.

Cytotoxic lymphocytes Lymphocytes capable of destroying other cells.

Denying Using the defence mechanism of denial, whereby some painful experience is denied or else some impulse or aspect of the self is denied (Rycroft, 1968).

Depersonalization This describes the distressing experience of feeling oneself to be unreal and not one's normal self or else detached from and outside oneself, while retaining insight into what is happening.

Diabetic retinopathy A condition in which the retina (at the back of the eye) is damaged by diabetes.

Disavowal A term used by Freud to describe a defence in which the subject refuses to recognize the reality of a traumatic perception; similar to denial (Laplanche and Pontalis, 1973).

Diuretic A type of drug used in heart failure and in essential hypertension. It encourages the kidneys to produce urine and results in a reduction of swelling of the tissues produced by oedema (in heart failure).

Dream associations Those thoughts, images, phantasies or feelings arising in a patient in association with aspects of a dream reported during psychoanalysis that facilitate a deeper understanding of the meaning of the dream; it is part of the 'basic rule' of psychoanalysis that the patient should free associate.

DSM Diagnostic Standards Manual.

Dynamic A term frequently used to describe psychoanalytic psychology because its concepts of process, instinct and development imply movement, in contrast to psychologies which are static and enumerate attributes of the mind; synonymous with 'psychodynamic' (Rycroft, 1968).

Ego deficit/defect The absence of an ego function.

Electrolytes in the blood (serum electrolytes) These are the sodium, potassium and bicarbonate circulating in the blood.

Endometriosis A disease in which the uterine musculature is abnormal, resulting in mennorhagia (heavy periods), and in which there may also be deposits of endometrium anywhere outside the uterus; often leading to pelvic pain.

Enzyme Intracellular biological catalysts made up of proteins, each with a unique structure specific for a given biochemical reaction within or outside the cell e.g., the proteolytic digestive enzymes responsible for the breakdown of protein in ingested food.

Faecal urgency The symptom of the urgent need to pass stools (faeces).

Fibrinogen A protein in the plasma of the blood converted to fibrin by the action of thrombin, resulting in an increasing coagulability of the blood. It is part of the mechanism of blood clotting.

Fissure Any cleft or groove in an organ or tissue.

Fixation A psychoanalytic term referring to a pattern of relating appropriate to an earlier phase of development; it is evidence of a failure to progress satisfactorily through the stages of libidinal development postulated by Freud.

Free association An essential part of psychoanalytic technique, referring to all the ideas, thoughts, images, phantasies or feelings that the patient experiences during the course of an analytic session that the 'basic rule' of psychoanalysis invites him or her to speak about to the analyst.

Frontal cortex Part of the brain made up of the two frontal lobes responsible for cognitive and other higher functions of the brain (the prefontal cortex is a part of this).

Functional somatic symptoms Bodily symptoms that are attributable to disturbed physiology without necessarily incurring concomitant damage to the tissues.

Ganglionated This means provided with ganglia, i.e., groups of nerve cell bodies that are located outside the central nervous system.

General paralysis of the insane A form of the infection tertiary syphilis in which there is paralysis and dementia accompanied by grandiose delusions.

Genital conflict A psychoanalytic term referring to the internal psychological conflict between the instinctual impulses arising from the Oedipal phase of emotional development that precedes the latency period in childhood.

Glaucoma An eye disease in which there is raised intraocular pressure which can lead to damage to the optic nerve (atrophy).

Glycogen This is a polysaccharide which is the chief carbohydrate storage material in animals. It is stored mainly in the liver and can be depolymerized to glucose and liberated when needed.

Gonadotrophin-releasing hormone (GnRH) A hormone secreted by the hypothalamus which stimulates the pituitary gland to secret follicle stimulating hormone (FSH) and luteotrophic hormone (LTH). These, in turn, act on the ovary to stimulate the production of ova and regulate the phases of the menstrual cycle.

Good-enough mother A psychoanalytic concept introduced by Winnicott, referring to the capacity of a mother to meet the omnipotence of her infant and to some extent to make sense of it (Winnicott, 1960). She achieves this through her successful adaptation to the needs of her baby (by her emotional attunement, and by means of adequate holding and handling).

Graves' disease A disease of the thyroid gland (situated in the neck) in which there is enlargement of the thyroid (goitre) with swelling of the front of the neck and exophthalmos (bulging of the eyes).

H2 receptor antagonists Drugs given in peptic ulcer disease to reduce the basal nocturnal and stimulated acid secretion of the stomach. This results in a reduction in both volume and acidity of gastric juice. The action of these drugs is to accelerate peptic ulcer healing and to reduce peptic ulcer relapse rate, e.g., cimetidine.

Histamine response The response in which the chemical histamine is released, occurring in many allergic states. In urticaria histamine released in the epithelium of the skin has to diffuse to the blood vessels before it can produce its extrinsic effects.

Hodgkin's Disease A malignant disorder of the lymphatic system in which there is enlargement of the lymph nodes and the spleen.

Hypogonadism A condition in which the gonads (the testicles) in the male are too small.

Hypothalamic pituitary adrenal system or axis This is the system that provides an axis beginning with the hypothalamus producing corticotrophin releasing factor (CRF), a hormone and neurotransmitter that stimulates the pituitary gland to secrete adrenocorticotrophic hormone (ACTH), which in turn stimulates the adrenal cortex to produce cortisol.

Hypothalamus A collection of brain nuclei (at the base of the brain) which exert control over visceral activities, water balance, temperature and sleep, etc., via links with the pituitary gland (an endocrine gland situated just behind the eye, underneath the brain) and also via the autonomic nervous system.

ICD The International Classification of Diseases.

Idealizing transference A psychoanalytic term referring to the patient's defensive relating to the psychoanalyst in which ambivalent feelings are denied and the analyst is seen to be ideally good. Idealization is a defence against the consequences of recognizing such ambivalence and allows a patient to be free from guilt and depression at the cost of a loss of self-esteem (Rycroft, 1968).

Immune complexes Complexes of antigen and antibody and compliment.

Individuated personality A psychoanalytic term used in the research of Karush and colleagues to describe the more independent type of personality they encountered amongst their patients with chronic ulcerative colitis, as opposed to the **symbiotic personality** (Karush et al., 1977).

Infantile psychotic anxieties A psychoanalytic term used mainly by Kleinian psychoanalysts to refer to depressive and paranoid (persecutory) anxieties, associated with the earliest phases of emotional development in the first year of life and deriving from the threat of annihilation.

Insulin The peptide hormone secreted by the pancreas, an endocrine and exocrine gland which also secretes digestive enzymes. It lowers blood sugar. There is a deficiency of insulin in type 1 diabetes mellitus.

Interpersonal therapy A form of psychotherapy in which the focus is on the patient's relationship with peers and family members. Its goal is to help the individual to identify and modify interpersonal problems and to understand and manage relationship problems.

Intestinal peristalsis The worm-like involuntary movements of the gut (produced by longitudinal and circular smooth muscle action) that pump food and other contents along the lumen of the gut. It consists of a wave of contraction that passes along the intestinal tube.

Iritis An inflammation confined to the iris of the eye.

Ketoacidosis A pathological condition in which there are high levels of acid and ketones in the blood.

Libido A psychoanalytic term which refers to a hypothetical form of mental energy with which processes, structures and are **object**-representations are invested (Rycroft, 1968).

Lymphocyte A white blood cell involved in the immune response. **T-lymphocytes** are produced by the thymus and are responsible for cell-mediated immunity.

Malignant hypertension A rare disease in which there is the most severe form of hypertension characterized by a high diastolic blood pressure (usually over 140 mm/Hg) and marked by arterial changes in the retina with papilloedema (swelling of the optic disc) and by progressive renal failure. It can lead to hypertensive encephalopathy.

Mania A functional psychosis that may be part of a **bipolar disorder,** Characterized by elation, excitement with increased physical and mental activity, severe insomnia, flight of ideas and often an eventual state of exhaustion; sometimes accompanied by grandiose delusions and hallucinations.

Maternal separation A psychological term referring to significant childhood episodes of separation from the mother; these can interfere with healthy emotional development by causing insecurity, increased hostility and ambivalence, and initiating a grieving process when a child is too immature to complete it, resulting in despair or depression and later mental illness in adult life.

Meningitis This is an inflammation of the lining membranes (the meninges) of the brain and spinal cord, produced by infection.

Merging with the analyst A psychoanalytic term referring to a state of mind in the patient in which there are no boundaries between himself or herself and the analyst. It may occur as a transference phenomenon, especially with borderline personalities and psychotic patients.

Mesalazine An anti-inflammatory drug, based on the sulpha-containing drug sulfasalazine, consisting of an active salicylate molecule linked to a sulphapyridene carrier. It reduces the frequency of colitic attacks in ulcerative colitis.

Microvascular complications Damage to the smallest blood vessels, that complicates a systemic disease, e.g., diabetes mellitus.

Mirroring A psychoanalytic term, used by British psycho-analysts following Winnicott and by American self-psychologists, to refer to the earliest phase of infantile emotional development when the mother reflects back the baby's nascent self; may also be used to describe certain empathic attitudes of the psycho-analyst towards his or her patient, often used in **self-psychology** approaches.

Morbid anatomy The study of the effects of disease on the body.

Mucosal cell The cell that forms part of the mucosal lining of an organ, e.g., the lining to the inner lumen of the bronchi or the intestine.

Myocardial Infarction   A disease of the heart in which a shortage of blood supply leads to persistent damage to its structure and function. A technical term for a heart attack.

Narcissistic disappointment   A psychoanalytic term referring to a disappointment that wounds the patient's self-esteem; this is likely to occur in narcissistic and borderline personalities, but can occur with other psychopathologies and in normal life. Narcissistic injuries will result from more severe psychological trauma.

Narcissistic character   This is a psychiatric term referring to a group of patients who are excessively self-centred and grandiose and require praise and appreciation from others, and who form shallow and short-lived relationships; they crave affection but are unable to return it. Their inner world is full of fears of emptiness, insecurity and low self-esteem.

Narcolepsy   A sleep disorder characterized by attacks of sudden drowsiness several times during the day, each followed by an episode of irresistible sleep; often these patients develop cataplexy in which they suddenly lose muscle tone and fall to the ground. Hypnogogic hallucinations when falling asleep are common.

Negating   A psychoanalytic term referring to the process whereby a perception or thought comes to consciousness in a negative form (Rycroft, 1968).

Neural atrophy   The shrinkage of the nervous tissue caused by cell death.

Neuropeptide   These are peptides secreted in the brain. Peptides are building blocks of protein molecules, made up of chains of amino acids in unique sequences specific for a given function. These sequences are determined by the sequences of base pairs in DNA of the genome (the genetic material in the nucleus of the cell).

Object   A psychoanalytic term referring to that to which the subject relates himself or herself; also that which the subject requires to achieve instinctual satisfaction and towards which an action or a desire is directed. This is a confusing term for the non-psychoanalytic reader for whom an object is a thing rather than a person (Rycroft, 1968).

Object loss   The loss of an **object**, usually a good one, i.e., benevolent and satisfactory; this precedes mourning (Rycroft, 1968).

Obstructive sleep apnoea syndrome   This is a disorder characterized by intermittent closure/collapse of the pharyngeal airway resulting in apnoeic episodes during sleep, which are terminated by partial arousal.

Oedematous   Swollen by the presence of an abnormally large amount of fluid in an intercellular space of the body.

Oral conflicts   A psychoanalytic term referring to psychological conflicts occurring during the earliest oral phase of emotional development in the child when the mouth is the main source of pleasure.

Oral sadism   A psychoanalytic term referring to pleasure in hurting or biting, or phantasies of these activities (e.g., **cannibalistic phantasies**).

Orbitofrontal areas   The part of the frontal cortex close to the orbits.

Osteopaenia   A milder form of osteoporosis.

Osteoporosis   The abnormal rarifaction of bone caused by failure of the osteoblasts (primitive bone cells) to lay down bone matrix.

Papule   This is a small circumscribed solid elevation of the skin.

Parotid gland   The largest of the three paired salivary glands which produce saliva.

Pelvic adhesions   Areas within the pelvis where tissues have become stuck to each other, sometimes as a result of previous surgical interventions in this region of the body.

Pepsinogen   It is a protein found in and secreted by gastric cells, changed to pepsin by hydrochloric acid. Pepsin is one of the digestive enzymes needed for digestion of food.

Pericarditis An inflammation of the membranous sack (pericardium) that contains the heart.

Peripheral nervous system That part of the nervous system consisting of nerves and ganglia that is outside the brain and the spinal cord.

Phaeochromocytoma A small vascular tumour of the chromaffin tissue of the central portion of the adrenal gland (medulla) or the sympathetic paraganglia. It secretes adrenaline, causing raised blood pressure, headache, palpitations and blurred vision.

Phantasy A psychoanalytic concept referring to the imagination or visionary notions of a patient. British psychoanalytic writers, particularly Kleinian writers, prefer to use the term 'phantasy' to 'fantasy' (Rycroft, 1968; Laplanche and Pontalis, 1973).

Plague An acute febrile infectious disease with a high fatality rate caused by pasteurella pestis.

Pleurisy An inflammation of the membranous sacks (pleura) containing the lung.

Plexus A network or tangle of nerve cells. It may also refer to a network or tangle of veins or lymphatic vessels.

Polycythaemia A blood disease in which there are excessive red blood cells with enlargement of the heart and raised blood pressure.

Pregenital conflicts A psychoanalytic term referring to those psychological conflicts occurring during the oral and anal phases of emotional development.

Primary gain This is a psychoanalytic term referring to the relief from a conflict or anxiety that is gained by developing a neurosis (Rycroft, 1968). This contrasts with the **secondary gain** from the fact of having the neurosis which leads to attention and increased care by others being shown towards the neurotic.

Projective identification This is a psychoanalytic term referring to a defence mechanism described by Klein in which parts of the personality are **split** off and projected into another person who then comes to represent these split-off parts, leaving the original person sometimes feeling deprived of parts of their own personality.

Prostaglandin A naturally occurring substance found in semen and menstrual fluids and causing strong contraction of the smooth (involuntary) muscles and dilatation of the vascular beds.

Proton pump inhibitor A drug which inhibits the gastric parietal cell enzyme called H + /K + ATPase that catalyzes the final step in gastric acid secretion, resulting in inhibition of basal and stimulated gastric acid secretion. This drug produces a more rapid response and promotes peptic ulcer healing faster than the H2 antagonists (see **H2 receptor antagonists**), e.g., omeprazole.

Psychoanalytic psychotherapy This is a form of long-term individual psychotherapy that draws on the theories and practices of psychoanalysis (Freudian) and analytical psychology (Jungian) and that may involve a patient in attending individual treatment from once to five times per week. It is based on an understanding and appreciation of the role of the dynamic unconscious in emotional and mental disorders. It aims to produce deep-seated and lasting changes in the personality and in emotional development (British Psychoanalytic Council, 2005).

Psychodynamic psychotherapy This is a more general term referring to a form of short and long-term individual or group psychotherapy (including psychoanalytic psychotherapy) and that is also based on an understanding and appreciation of the role of the dynamic unconscious mind in emotional disorders and mental illness.

Psychological mindedness An individual's capacity for self-awareness and for self-reflection.

Pustule A small elevation of the cuticle filled with pus (e.g., pimples in acne vulgaris).

Regression This is a psychoanalytic term referring to a return to an earlier mode of functioning or state. It may refer to a defence mechanism by which a person is able to avoid anxiety by a return to an earlier stage of emotional development (Rycroft, 1968).

Renin A protein-dissolving enzyme liberated by ischaemia (lack of blood supply) of the kidney, or by diminished pulse pressure. It causes hypertensinogen to change into hypertensin.

Reninoma   A tumour of the kidney causing release of a protein-attacking (proteolytic) enzyme.

Repressed hostility   A psychoanalytic term referring to hostility in a person that has been **repressed** and which they are not aware of.

Repression   A psychoanalytic term referring to a defence mechanism which allows an unacceptable idea or impulse to become unconscious.

Sacroilitis   An inflammation of the sacroiliac joint between the sacrum and the ileum.

Saline   A salt solution which is non-allergenic.

Scarlet fever   An acute contagious and exanthematous disease with a scarlet rash.

Schizoid personality   Psychoanalytic term that refers to a type of person who is emotionally withdrawn and detached and whose intellect and emotions seem separated from each other (in psychiatry this term refers to a more profound disturbance of the personality).

Scurvy   A condition caused by vitamin C deficiency, characterized by weakness, anaemia and spongy gums and the tendency to cutaneous haemorrhages and a brawny induration of the muscles of the calves.

Secondary gain   This is a psychoanalytic term which refers to the unconscious advantage a neurotic gains from the attention and care given to them because of their symptoms, contributing significantly to the maintenance of their illness. (Also referred to by behavioural psychologists as illness behaviour or the sick role). To be distinguished from the **primary gain** of the symptom.

Seizure   An epileptic fit.

Self-object   A psychoanalytic concept derived from self-psychology referring to one of the earliest types of object relationships established in emotional development. These are **objects** that are poorly differentiated from the self and perform the important function of maintaining psychic stability in the growing child's emotional environment.

Self-psychology   This is a north American school of psycho-analysis, deriving from the work of Kohut which in its way of conceiving of **self-object** relationships emphasizes the importance of empathic attunement and the **self-regulatory** functions provided by relationships in child and adult life. It argues for the importance of the early affective experiences that the child has with **mirroring** and idealized parental **self-objects**: these have a significant influence on the child's capacity to experience and regulate affects and his or her developing sense of self and interpersonal relations (Bagby and Taylor in Taylor, Bagby and Parker, 1997).

Self-regulation   This is a psychoanalytic concept that refers to the capacity of the growing child to acquire the ability to regulate his or her emotions and their behavioural expressions. It is dependent on the provision of adequate affect regulation by the mother through successful emotional attunement to the needs of her child.

Sensory cortex   Part of the parietal lobe of the brain responsible for the perception of sensation. It receives input from the peripheral sensory nerves from all the parts of the body, and sensory nerve fibres which travel up the spinal cord and brain-stem to the thalamus.

Separation-Individuation phase   A psychoanalytic term coined by Mahler to describe the process of separation from the mother and individuation which begins in the latter part of the first year and continues into the second year of life: exuberance and elation are often a feature of the mobile child's affective state and while the child is practising his or her growing ability to separate himself or herself from the mother, she is still needed for support, usually through physical recontact. This allows for discovery of the self (Joyce from Rayner et al., 2005).

Spleen   An organ situated on the left side of the upper abdomen which helps to disintegrate the red blood cells, thus setting free haemoglobin which is converted subsequently by the liver into bilirubin (the main component of bile).

Splitting   A psychoanalytic term describing a defence mechanism in which a mental structure is replaced by two or more part-structures. When an **object** is split, one part of it is experienced as 'good' and the other part is experienced as 'bad'. In multiple personality disorder, there is an experience of possessing and experiencing different personalities as a result of splitting or dissociation (Rycroft, 1968).

Subconsciously fixed ideas Split parts of the personality, endowed with an autonomous life and development, derived from psychologically traumatic past events that result in hysterical symptoms (a theory of the 19th-century psychologist Pierre Janet).

Subdural haematoma A collection of blood in the subdural space, most commonly occurring in the elderly and infants as a result of trauma to the head.

Suggestion A psychological term referring to the method whereby a hypnotist, by proposing an action to his subject, causes that action to occur, either during the hypnotic trance or after recovery from it. In opposition to Charcot, Bernheim argued that the same effects could be obtained by suggestion to his patients in the waking state that Charcot was obtaining with his patients in the hypnotic state, a procedure that Liébault named 'psychotherapeutics' (Ellenberger, 1970).

Stoma An artificial opening of the bowel onto the abdominal wall that allows bowel contents to be excreted. It is produced by an operative procedure, e.g., ileostomy and colostomy.

Symbiotic personality A psychoanalytic term used by Karush et al. (1977) to describe a type of personality susceptible to chronic ulcerative colitis that is less independent and that has a less differentiated sense of self than the other type, referred to as **individuated personalities.**

Symbiotic phase A psychoanalytic term, coined by Mahler, referring to the earliest phase of emotional development when mother and baby experience a sense of oneness and which is full of feelings of synchrony and closeness. It precedes the **phase of separation-individuation.**

Sympathectomy An interruption of the sympathetic nervous system's effects on the body.

Temporal arteritis An acute inflammation of the arteries, especially those of the face and scalp, accompanied by malaise, fever and anorexia. It may lead to damage to the retinal arteries, resulting in blindness.

Thymus A small gland in a region of the anterior part of the chest (the mediastinum) involved in immune functions. **T-lymphocytes** are produced here.

Thyroid gland An endocrine gland situated in the neck and secreting the hormone thyroxine.

Thyroid stimulating hormone A hormone produced by the pituitary gland responsible for stimulating the thyroid gland to secrete the hormone thyroxine.

T-lymphocyte These are produced by the thymus gland and are responsible for cell-mediated immunity.

Transference A psychoanalytic concept referring to the process whereby a patient projects on to his or her analyst feelings belonging to significant figures from the past (e.g., parents, siblings), endowing the analyst with the significance of another important person from the patient's past. The interpretation by the psychoanalyst of these transference phenomena forms an essential part of psychoanalytic technique.

Tricyclic antidepressants A group of antidepressants acting at the nerve junctions (synapses) where nerve impulses are transmitted from cell to cell. These drugs block the nerve cells reuptake of two neurotransmitters, noradrenalin and serotonin. The effect of this is to prolong the affects of these two neurotransmitters: the mode of action of this drug in depression is nevertheless not clear. Amitriptylline and imipramine are two commonly prescribed tricyclic drugs.

Trigonitis An inflammation of the trigonal (triangular) area of the bladder.

Type 1 diabetes mellitus Insulin-dependent diabetes, i.e., requiring insulin for control of the blood sugar; often beginning in childhood.

Type 2 diabetes mellitus Non-insulin dependent diabetes; in this condition blood sugar may initially be regulated by dietary restriction alone but later medication may be required. Also called late-onset diabetes.

Typhoid fever   A specific eruptive communicable fever caused by salmonella typhosa with inflammation and ulceration of Peyer's patches and enlargement of the spleen and mesenteric membranes and intestinal mucous membrane.

Unconscious   A psychoanalytic term referring to that part of the mind in which mental processes are dynamically unconscious, and external reality is replaced by psychical reality. Those memories, phantasies, wishes, fears or conflicts of which a person is unaware and which he or she cannot bring into consciousness unaided are said to be unconscious and may be the result of **repression**. The dynamic unconscious is manifest in dreams and slips of the tongue (called parapraxes). The dynamic unconscious is distinguished from the descriptive unconscious from which memories can be recalled easily (Rycroft, 1968).

Urethritis   An inflammation of the urethra.

Uveitis   Inflammation of the entire uveal tract (i.e. the iris, the ciliary body and the choroid in the eye).

Vasoconstriction   Narrowing of the lumen of a blood vessel.

Viscera   The organs of the body.

Working alliance   A psychoanalytic concept that describes the healthy adult aspects of the therapeutic relationship between patient and psychoanalyst: it involves the patient's capacity to form a trusting relationship with the analyst. Also referred to as the therapeutic alliance.

References

Abraham, K. (1927) *Selected Papers on Psychoanalysis* (London: Hogarth Press).

Abramson, H. A. and Peshkin, M. M. (1961) 'Group psychotherapy of the parents of intractably asthmatic children', *Journal of Children's Asthma Research Institute and Hospital*, 1: 77–91.

Ackerknecht, E. H. (1982) 'The history of psychosomatic medicine', *Psychological Medicine*, 12: 17–24.

Ader, R. and Cohen, N. (1975) 'Behaviourally conditioned immuno-suppression', *Psychosomatic Medicine*, 37: 333–40.

Akagi, H. and House, A. (2001) 'The epidemiology of hysterical conversion', in *Contemporary Approaches to the Study of Hysteria*, ed. P. W. Halligan, C. Bass and J. C. Marshall (Oxford: Oxford University Press), pp. 73–88.

Alexander, F. (1950) *Psychosomatic Medicine: Its Principles and Application* (New York: W. W. Norton).

Alexander, F., French, T. M. and Pollock, G. H. (1968) *Psychosomatic Specificity*, vol. I: *Experimental Study and Results* (Chicago: University of Chicago Press).

American Psychiatric Association (2004) *Diagnostic and Statistical Manual of Mental Disorders* (DSM-IV-TR), 4th edn (Washington, DC: American Psychiatric Association).

Andersen, A. E. and Yager, J. (2005) 'Eating disorders', in *Comprehensive Textbook of Psychiatry*, 8th edn, ed. B.J. Sadock and V. A. Sadock (Philadelphia, PA: Lippincott Williams and Williams) pp. 2002–21.

Anzieu, D. (1989) *The Skin Ego* (New Haven, CT: Yale University Press).

Balint, M. (1964) *The Doctor, his Patient and the Illness*, 2nd edn (London: Pitman Paperbacks).

Balint, M., Ball, D. H. and Hare, M. L. (1969) 'Training medical students in patient-centered medicine', *Comprehensive Psychiatry*, 10: 249–58.

Ball, D. H. and Wolff, H. H. (1963) 'An experiment in the teaching of psychotherapy to medical students', *Lancet*, i: 214–17.

Bammer, K. (1981) *Krebs und Psychosomatik* (Stuttgart: Kohlhammer).

Barlow, W. (1973) *The Alexander Principle* (London: Arrow Books).

Barr Taylor, C. and Fortmann, S. P. (1985) 'Essential hypertension', in *Psychosomatic Illness Review*, ed. W. Dorfman and L. Cristofar (New York: Macmillan), pp. 90–106.

Barsky, A. J., Wool, C., Barnett, M. C. and Cleary, P. D. (1994) 'Histories of childhood trauma in adult hypochondriacal patients', *American Journal of Psychiatry*, **151**: 397–401.

Barthes, R. (1977) *Roland Barthes*, trans. R. Howard (London: Macmillan).

Bass, C. and Murphy, M. (1991) 'Somatisation disorder in a British teaching hospital: The unnatural history of a non-disease', *British Journal of Clinical Practice*, **45**: 237–44.

Bate, W. J. (1968) *Coleridge* (New York: Macmillan).

Bates, D. W., Schmitt, S. Buchwald, D., Ware, N. C., Lee, J., Thoyer, E., Kornish, R. J. and Komaroff, A. L. (1993) 'Prevalence of fatigue and chronic fatigue syndrome in a primary care practice', *Archives of Internal Medicine*, **153**: 2759–65.

Beard, R. W., Belsey, E. M., Lieberman, B. A. and Wilkinson, J. C. M. (1977) 'Pelvic pain in women', *American Journal of Obstetrics and Gynecology*, **128**: 566–70.

Bennett, A. (2005) 'A view of the helplessness and illness contained in chronic fatigue syndrome', *Journal of the British Association of Psychotherapists*, **43**: 16–32.

Bennett, G. (1970) 'Bristol floods, 1968: controlled survey of effects on health of local community disaster', *British Medical Journal*, **3**: 454–8.

Bowlby, J. (1990) *Charles Darwin: A New Biography* (London: Hutchinson).

Boyce, P. M., Talley, N. J., Balaam, B., Koloski, N. A. and Truman, G. A. (2003) 'Randomised controlled trial of cognitive behaviour therapy, relaxation training and routine clinical care for irritable bowel syndrome', *American Journal of Gastroenterology*, **98**: 2209–18.

Brafman, A. (2003) 'Memorising versus understanding', *Psychoanalytic Psychotherapy*, **17**(2): 119–37.

Breuer, J. and Freud, S. ([1895], 1955) 'Studies in hysteria', in *The Standard Edition of the Complete Psychological Works of Sigmund Freud*, vol. 2, ed. James Strachey (London: Hogarth Press).

British Psychoanalytic Council (2005) *What is Psychoanalytic Psychotherapy?* (London: British Psychoanalytic Council).

Broden, A. R. and Myers, W. A. (1981) 'Hypochondriacal symptoms as derivatives of unconscious fantasies of being beaten or tortured', *Journal of the American Psychoanalytic Association*, **29**: 535–57.

Brown, T. M. (2000) 'The rise and fall of American psychosomatic medicine', published on the internet: *http://human-nature.com/free-associations/riseandfall.html*

Brownell, K. D. and Wadden, T. A. (2000) 'Obesity', in *Comprehensive Textbook of Psychiatry*, 7th edn, ed. B. J. Sadock and V. A. Sadock (Philadelphia, PA: Lippincott Williams and Wilkins), pp. 1787–97.

Brownell, K. D., Wadden, T. A. and Phelan, S. (2005) 'Obesity', in *Comprehensive Textbook of Psychiatry*, 8th edn, ed. B. J. Sadock and V. A. Sadock (Philadelphia, PA: Lippincott Williams and Wilkins), pp. 2124–36.

Bruch, H. (1962) 'Perceptual and conceptual disturbances in anorexia nervosa', *Psychosomatic Medicine*, 24: 187–94.

Bruch, H. (1974) *Eating Disorders: Obesity, Anorexia Nervosa and the Person Within* (London: Routledge and Kegan Paul).

Bruch, H. (1979) *The Golden Cage* (New York: Vintage Books).

Bruch, H. (1982/1983) 'Treatment in anorexia nervosa', *International Journal of Psychoanalytic Psychotherapy*, 9: 303–12.

Bruch, H. (1988) *Conversations with Anorexics*, ed. D. Czyzewski and M. A. Suhr (New York: Basic Books).

Brunet, O., and Lezine, I. (1966) *I primi anni del bambino* (Rome: Armando).

Bucci, W. and Miller, N. E. (1993) 'Primary process analogue: the referential activity (RA) measure', in *Psychodynamic Treatment Research: A Handbook for Clinical Practice*, ed. N. E. Miller, L. Luborsky, J. P. Barber and J. P. Docherty (New York: Basic Books), pp. 387–406.

Buchwald, D., Umali, P., Umali, J., Kith, P., Pearlman, T. and Komaroff, A. L. (1995) 'Chronic fatigue and the chronic fatigue syndrome: prevalence in a Pacific Northwest health care system', *Annals of Internal Medicine*, 123: 81–8.

Burns, L. and Greenfield, D. (1991) 'Comprehensive psychosocial history for infertility (CPHI)', in *Clinical Handbook of Health Psychology*, ed. P. Camic and S. Knight (Seattle: Hogrefe and Huber), pp. 374–5.

Burton, R. (1931) *The Anatomy of Melancholy*, ed. F. Dell and P. Jordan Smith (London: Tudor).

Cannon, W. (1939) *The Wisdom of the Body* (New York: W. W. Norton).

Cash, T. F. (1995) *What Do You See When You Look in the Mirror? Helping Yourself to a Positive Body Image* (New York: Bantam).

Castelnuovo-Tedesco, P. (1962) 'Emotional antecedents of perforation of ulcer of the stomach and duodenum', *Psychosomatic Medicine*, 24: 398–415.

Chodoff, P. and Lyons, H. (1958) 'Hysteria, the hysterical personality and "hysterical conversion"', *American Journal of Psychiatry*, 114: 734–40.

Cloninger, C. R., Sigvardsson, S., von Knorring, A.-L. and Bohman, M. (1984) 'An adoption study of somatoform disorders: II. Identification of two discrete somatoform disorders', *Archives of General Psychiatry*, 41: 335–7.

Cobb, S. and Rose, R. M. (1973) 'Hypertension, peptic ulcer and diabetes in air traffic controllers', *Journal of the American Medical Association*, **224**: 489.

Coleridge, S. T. (1966 [1796]) Letter to Charles Lloyd, Sr., 14 November, in *Collected Letters of Samuel Taylor Coleridge*, ed. E. L. Griggs (Oxford: Clarendon Press).

Coleridge, S. T. (1995) *The Collected Works of Samuel Taylor Coleridge: Shorter Works and Fragments*, vol. II, ed. H. J. Jackson and J. R. de Jackson (Princeton, NJ: Princeton University Press).

Connelly, F. H. and Gipson, M. (1978) 'Dysmorphophobia: a long-term study', *British Journal of Psychiatry*, **132**: 568–70.

Cormia, R. E. (1952) 'Experimental histamine pruritus – I: Influence of physical and psychological factors in threshold activity', *Journal of Investigative Dermatology*, **19**: 21.

Craig, T. K. J. (1989) 'Abdominal pain', in *Life Events and Illness*, ed. G. W. Brown and T. O. Harris (New York: Guilford), pp. 233–59.

Craig, T. K. and Brown, G. W. (1984) 'Goal frustration and life events in the aetiology of painful gastrointestinal disorder', *Journal of Psychosomatic Research*, **38**: 837–48.

Craig, T. K. J., Boardman, A. P., Mills, K., Daly-Jones, O. and Drake, H. (1993) 'The South London Somatization Study – I: longitudinal course and the influence of early life experiences', *British Journal of Psychiatry*, **163**: 579–88.

Creed, F. (1999) 'The relationship between psychosocial parameters and outcome in irritable bowel syndrome', *American Journal of Medicine*, **107**: 74S–80S.

Creed, F. H., Craig, T. K. J. and Farmer, R. (1988) 'Functional abdominal pain, psychiatric illness and life events', *Gut*, **29**: 235–42.

Creed, F. and Olden, K. W. (2005) 'Gastrointestinal disorders', in *The American Psychiatric Publishing Textbook of Psychosomatic Medicine*', ed. J. L. Levenson (Washington, DC: American Psychiatric Publishing), pp. 465–81.

Crick, F. H. C. (1994) *The Astonishing Hypothesis* (London: Simon and Schuster).

Crimlisk, H. L., Bhatia, K., Cope, H., David, A., Marsden, C. D. and Ron, M. A. (1998) 'Slater revisited: 6-year follow-up study of patients with medically unexplained motor symptoms', *British Medical Journal*, **316**: 582–6.

Crisp, A. H. (1980) *Anorexia Nervosa: Let Me Be* (London: Academic Press).

Crown, S., Crown, J. M. and Fleming, A. (1975) 'Aspects of the psychology and epidemiology of rheumatic disease', *Psychological Medicine*, **5**: 291–9.

Cule, J. H. (1980) *A Doctor for the People* (London: Update Books).

Dare, C., Eisler, I., Colahan, M., Crowther, C., Senior, R. and Asen, E. (1995) 'The listening heart and the chi square: clinical and empirical perceptions in the family therapy of anorexia nervosa', *Journal of Family Therapy*, **17**: 31–57.

Dare, C., Eisler, I., Russell, G., Treasure, J. and Dodge, L. (2001) 'Psychological therapies for adult patients with anorexia nervosa: a randomised controlled trial of outpatient treatments', *British Journal of Psychiatry*, **178**: 216–21.

Davis, R. A., Wetzel, R. D. and Kashiwaga, M. D. (1976) 'Personality, depression and headache type', *Headache*, **16**: 246–51.

De Mandeville, B. [1711] *A Treatise of the Hypochondriack and Hysterick Passions Vulgarly Called the Hypo in Men and Vapours in Women*, 1st edn (London: Dryden Leach).

Deutsch, F. (1953) 'Basic psychoanalytic principles in psychosomatic medicine', *Acta Psychotherapeutica, Psychosomatica et Orthopaedagogica*, **1**: 102–11.

Deutsch, F. (1959) *On the Mysterious Leap from the Mind to the Body* (New York: International Universities Press).

Deutsch, F. (1965) 'Psychoanalysis and internal medicine', in *Evolution of Psychosomatic Concepts: Anorexia Nervosa: A Paradigm* (London: Hogarth Press).

Diamond, S. and Baltes, B. J. (1971) 'Chronic tension headache treated with amitriptyline – a double-blind study', *Headache*, **11**: 110–16.

Dickens, C., Levenson, J. L. and Cohen, W. (2005) 'Rheumatology' in *The American Psychiatric Publishing Textbook of Psychosomatic Medicine*, ed. J. L. Levenson (Washington, DC: American Psychiatric Publishing), pp. 542–7.

Dorfman, W. (1968) 'Hypochondriasis as a defense against depression', *Psychosomatics*, **9**: 248–51.

Drossman, D. A., Li, Z., Andruzzi, E., Temple, R. D., Talley, N. J., Thompson, W. G., Whitehead, W. E., Janssens, J., Funch-Jensen, P., Corazziari, E., Richter, J. E. and Koch, G. G. (1993) 'US householder survey of functional gastrointestinal disorders: Prevalence, sociodemography and health impact', *Digestive Diseases and Sciences*, **38**: 1569–80.

Drossman, D. A., Camilleri, M., Mayer, E. A. et al. (2002) 'AGA technical review of irritable bowel syndrome', *Gastroenterology*, **123**: 2108–31.

Drossman, D. A., Creed, F. H. Olden, K. W., Svedlund, J., Toner, B. B. and Whitehead, W. E. (2000) 'Psychosocial aspects of the functional gastrointestinal disorders', in *Rome II: The Functional Gastrointestinal Disorders*, ed. D. A. Drossman, E. Corazziari, N. J. Talley, W. G. Thompson and W. E. Whitehead (Maclean, VA: Degnon Associates), pp. 157–65.

Drossman, D. A., Toner, B. B., Whitehead, W. E. et al. (2003) 'Cognitive-behavioral therapy versus education and desipramine versus placebo for moderate to severe functional bowel disorders', *Gastroenterology*, **125**: 19–31.

Dunbar, F. (1943) *Psychosomatic Diagnosis* (New York: Hoeber).

Dunbar, F. (1947) *Emotions and Bodily Change*, 3rd edn (New York: Columbia University Press).

Dworkin, S. F., Huggins, K. H., LeResche, L., VonKorff, M., Howard, J., Truelove, E. and Sommers, E. (1990) 'Epidemiology of signs and symptoms in temporomandibular disorders: clinical signs in cases and controls', *Journal of the American Dental Association*, **120**: 273–81.

Dworkin, S. F., Turner, J. A., Wilson, L., Massoth, D., Whitney, C., Huggins, K. H., Sommers, E. and Truelove, E. (1994) 'Brief group cognitive-behavioural intervention for temporomandibular disorder', *Pain*, **59**: 175–87.

Edwards, L. (2003) 'New concepts in vulvodynia', *American Journal of Obstetrics and Gynecology*, **189**: 524–30.

Eide, I., Campese, V., Stein, D., Eide, K. and DeQuattro, V. (1978). 'Clinical assessment of sympathetic tone: Orthostatic blood pressure responses in borderline primary hypertension', *Clinical and Experimental Hypotension*, **1**: 51–65.

Ellard, K., Beaurepaire, J., Jones, M. et al. (1990) 'Acute stress in duodenal ulcer disease', *Gastroenterology*, **96**: 1628–32.

Ellenberger, H. (1970) Chapters 2, 3 and 4, in *The Discovery of the Unconscious* (New York: Basic Books), pp. 53–253.

Engel, G. L. (1952) 'Psychological aspects of the management of ulcerative colitis', *New York State Journal of Medicine*, **22**: 2255–61.

Engel, G. L. (1955) 'Studies of ulcerative colitis: III. The nature of the psychological processes', *American Journal of Medicine*, **19**: 231–56.

Engel, G. L. (1958) 'Studies of ulcerative colitis – V: Psychological aspects and their implications for treatment', *American Journal of Digestive Diseases*, **33**: 315–37.

Engel, G. L. (1959) '"Psychogenic" pain and the pain-prone patient', *American Journal of Medicine*, **26**: 899–18.

Engel, G. L. (1967) 'Intestinal disorders', in *Comprehensive Textbook of Psychiatry*, 1st edn, ed. A. M. Freedman, H. I. Kaplan and H. S. Kaplan (Baltimore: Williams and Wilkins), pp. 1054–9.

Engel, G. L. (1968) 'A reconsideration of the role of conversion in somatic disease', *Comprehensive Psychiatry*, **9**: 316–26.

Engel, G. L. (1975) 'The death of a twin: mourning and anniversary reactions: Fragments of 10 years of self-analysis', *International Journal of Psycho-Analysis*, **56**: 23–40.

Engel, G. L. and Reichsman, F. (1956) 'Spontaneous and experimentally induced depressions in an infant with a gastric fistula: A contribution to the problem of depression', *Journal of the American Psychoanalytic Association*, 4: 428–52.

Engel, G. L., Reichsman, F. and Segal, H. L. (1956) 'A study of an infant with a gastric fistula: I. Behaviour and the rate of hydrochloric acid secretion', *Psychosomatic Medicine*, 18: 374–98.

Engel, G. L. and Schmale, A. H. (1967) 'Psychoanalytic theory of somatic disorder: conversion, specificity and the disease onset situation', *Journal of the American Psychoanalytic Association*, 15: 344–65.

Engel, G. L. and Schmale, A. H. (1972) 'Conservation-withdrawal: a primary regulatory process for organismic homeostasis', in *Physiology, Emotion and Psychosomatic Illness*, Ciba Foundation Symposium 8 (Amsterdam: Elsevier).

Engels, W. D. (1985) 'Dermatologic disorders', in *Psychosomatic Illness Review*, ed. W. Dorfman and L. Christofar (Toronto: Macmillan), pp. 146–61.

Enoch, M. D. and Trethowan, W. H. (1979) *Uncommon Psychiatric Syndromes*, 2nd edn (Bristol: Wright).

The ENRICHD Investigators (2000) 'Enhancing recovery in coronary heart disease patients (ENRICHD): Study design and methods', *American Heart Journal*, 139: 1–9.

Escobar, J. I., Burnan, M. A., Karno, M. et al. (1987) 'Somatization in the community', *Archives of General Psychiatry*, 44: 713–18.

Fairburn, C. G. (1985) 'Cognitive-behavioural treatment for bulimia', in *Handbook of Psychotherapy for Anorexia Nervosa and Bulimia*, ed. D. M. Garner and P. E. Garfinkel (New York: Guilford Press), pp. 160–93.

Fairburn, C. G., Cooper, Z. and Shafran, R. (2003) 'Cognitive behaviour therapy for eating disorders: a "transdiagnostic" theory and treatment', *Behaviour Research and Therapy*, 41: 509–28.

Falconer, W. (1788) *The Influence of Passions upon the Disorders of the Body* (London: Dilly).

Farquar, C. M., Rogers, V., Franks, S., Pearce, S., Wadsworth, J. and Beard, R. W. (1990), 'A randomised controlled trial of medroxyprogesterone and psychotherapy for the treatment of pelvic congestion', *British Journal of Obstetrics and Gynaecology*, 6: 1152–62.

Farrell, E. M. (1995) *Lost for Words* (London: Process Press).

Farthing, M. J. G. (2005) 'The treatment of irritable bowel syndrome', *British Medical Journal*, 330: 429–30.

Fava, G. A. and Pavan, L. (1976–7) 'Large bowel disorders – II: Psychopathology and alexithymia', *Psychotherapy and Psychosomatics*, 27: 100–5.

Fava, G. A. and Pavan, L. (1976–7) 'Illness configuration and life events', *Psychotherapy and Psychosomatics*, **27**: 93–9.

Fawzy, F. I., Fawzy, N. W., Hyun, C., Elashoff, R., Guthrie, D., Fahey, J. L. and Morton, D. L. (1993) 'Malignant melanoma: Effects of an early structured psychiatric intervention, coping and affective state on recurrence and survival 6 years later', *Archives of General Psychiatry*, **50** (9): 681–9.

Feinmann, C., Harris, M. and Cawley, R. (1984) 'Psychogenic facial pain: presentation and treatment', *British Medical Journal*, **288**: 436–8.

Feldman, F., Cantor, D., Soll, S. and Bachrach, W. (1967a) 'Psychiatric study of a consecutive series of 34 patients with ulcerative colitis', *British Medical Journal*, **3**: 14–17.

Feldman, F., Cantor, D., Soll, S. and Bachrach, W. (1967b) 'Psychiatric study of a consecutive series of 19 patients with regional ileitis', *British Medical Journal*, **4**: 711–14.

Fenichel, O. (1945) 'Nature and classification of the so-called psychosomatic phenomena', *Psychoanalytic Quarterly*, **14**: 287–312.

Fenichel, O. (1953) 'Respiratory introjection', in *Collected Papers* (New York: W. W. Norton).

Ferenczi, S. (1955) *Final Contributions to the Problems and Methods of Psychoanalysis* (New York: Basic Books).

Fernel, J. (1592) *Universa Medicina*, 5th edn (Frankfurt: A. Wechel).

Ferstl, R., Niemann, T., Biehl, G. et al. (1992) 'Neuropsychological impairment in autoimmune disease', *European Journal of Clinical Investigation*, **20** (suppl. 1): 16–20.

Fischer-Homberger, E. (1983) 'Hypochondriasis', in *Handbook of Psychiatry*, vol 1: *General Psychopathology*, ed. M. Shepherd and O. L. Zangwill (Cambridge: Cambridge University Press), pp. 46–8.

Ford, M. J., Miller, P. and Eastwood, M. A. (1987) 'Life events, psychiatric illness and irritable bowel syndrome', *Gut*, **28**: 160–5.

Foucault, M. (1973) *The Birth of the Clinic* (London: Tavistock Publications).

Frank, R. (1931) 'The hormonal causes of premenstrual tension', *Archives of Neurology and Psychiatry*, **26**: 1053–7.

Freud, S. (1962 [1894]) 'The neuro-psychoses of defence', in *The Standard Edition of the Complete Psychological Works of Sigmund Freud*, vol. 3, ed. James Strachey (London: Hogarth Press).

Freud, S. (1962 [1894]) 'On the grounds for detaching a particular syndrome from neurasthenia under the description "anxiety neurosis"', in *The Standard Edition of the Complete Psychological Works of Sigmund Freud*, vol. 3, ed. James Strachey (London: Hogarth Press).

Freud, S. (1962 [1898]) 'Sexuality in the aetiology of the neuroses', in *The Standard Edition of the Complete Psychological Works of Sigmund Freud*, vol. 3, ed. James Strachey (London: Hogarth Press).

Freud, S. (1962 [1910]) 'The psychoanalytic view of a disturbance of vision', in *The Standard Edition of the Complete Works of Sigmund Freud*, vol. 11, ed. James Strachey (London: Hogarth Press).

Freud, S. (1962 [1914]) 'On narcissism: an introduction. Part II. Narcissism in organic disease, hypochondria, and erotic life', in *The Standard Edition of the Complete Works of Sigmund Freud*, vol. 14, ed. James Strachey (London Hogarth Press).

Freud, S. (1962 [1915]) 'Mourning and melancholia', in *The Standard Edition of the Complete Psychological Works of Sigmund Freud*, vol. 14, ed. James Strachey (London: Hogarth Press).

Friedman, M. and Rosenman, R. (1974) *Type A Behaviour and Your Heart* (New York: Alfred A. Knopf).

Friedman, R., Schwartz, J. E., Schnall, P. L. et al. (2001) 'Psychological variables in hypertension: relationship to causal or ambulatory blood pressure in men', *Psychosomatic Medicine*, 63: 19–31.

Fulcher, K. Y. and White, P. D. (1998) 'Chronic fatigue syndrome: a description of graded exercise treatment', *Physiotherapy*, 84: 223–6.

Galen (1821) *Opera*, ed. L. S. Kuehn, vol. I: *Ars Medica*; vol. II *De sanitate tuenda*.

Garma, A. (1953) 'The internalized mother as harmful food in peptic ulcer patients', *International Journal of Psychoanalysis*, 34: 102–10.

Garralda, M. E. (1992) 'A selective review of child psychiatric syndromes with a somatic presentation', *British Journal of Psychiatry*, 161: 759–73.

Gath, D., Osborn, M., Bungay, G., Iles, S., Day, A., Bond, A. and Passingham, C. (1987) 'Psychiatric disorder and gynaecological symptoms in middle-aged women: A community survey', *British Medical Journal*, 294: 213–18.

Georg, D. de Saussure, C. and Guillun, J. (1999) 'Objectives for undergraduate teaching of psychiatry: survey of doctors and students', *Medical Education*, 33: 639–47.

Gershon, M. D. (1998) *The Second Brain* (New York: HarperCollins).

Gidron, Y., Davidson, K. and Bata, I. (1999) 'The short-term effects of a hostility-reduction intervention in CHD patients', *Health Psychology*, 18: 416–20.

Glover, E. (1939) 'Psychosomatic and allied disorders', in *Psychoanalysis* (London: Staples Press).

Godfrey, S. and Silverman, M. (1973) 'Demonstration of placebo response in asthma by means of exercise testing', *Journal of Psychosomatic Research*, 17: 293–7.

Goldie, L. and Desmarais, I. (2005) *Psychotherapy and the Treatment of Cancer Patients* (London: Routledge).

Goodsitt, A. (1977) 'Narcissistic disturbances in anorexia nervosa', in *Adolescent Psychiatry*, vol. 5, ed. S. C. Feinstein and P. Giovacchini (New York: Jason Aronson), pp. 304–12.

Goodsitt, A. (1982) Book review of J. A. Sours, 'Starving to death in a sea of objects', *International Journal of Eating Disorders*, 1: 70–6.

Goodsitt, A. (1983) 'Self-regulatory disturbances in eating disorders', *International Journal of Eating Disorders*, 2: 51–60.

Goodsitt, A. (1986) 'Self-psychology and the treatment of anorexia nervosa', in *Handbook of Psychotherapy for Anorexia Nervosa and Bulimia*, ed. D. M. Garner and P. E. Garfinkel (New York: Guilford Press), pp. 55–82.

Gowers, W. R. (1904) 'Lumbago: its lessons and analogues', *British Medical Journal*, 1: 117–24.

Graham-Brown, R. and Burns, T. (1996) *Lecture Notes on Dermatology*, 7th edn (Oxford: Blackwell Science).

Groddeck, G. W. (1977 [1925]) 'The meaning of illness', in *The Meaning of Illness: Selected Psychoanalytic Writings*, ed. L. Schacht (London: Hogarth), pp. 197–202.

Groddeck, G. W. (1977) *The Meaning of Illness: Selected Psychoanalytic Writings*, ed. L. Schacht (London: Hogarth).

Gull, W. W. (1873) 'Apepsia hysterica: anorexia hysterica', *Transcripts of the Clinical Society of London*, 7: 22–8.

Guex, P. (1994) *An Introduction to Psycho-Oncology*, trans. H. Goodare (London: Routledge).

Guex, P. and MacDonald, S. (1984) 'Le rôle d'une groupe de relaxation – eutonie dans l'amélioration de la qualité de vie de patients cancéreux', *Médecine et Hygiène*, 42: 2898–902.

Gunn, T. (1969) 'Considering the Snail', in *Poems 1950–1966: A Selection* (London: Faber and Faber).

Guthrie, E. (1991) 'Brief psychotherapy with patients with refractory irritable bowel syndrome', *British Journal of Psychotherapy*, 8: 175–88.

Guthrie, E. and Creed, F. (1996) 'Treatment methods and their effectiveness', in *Liaison Psychiatry*, ed. E. Guthrie and F. Creed (Glasgow: The Royal College of Psychiatrists), pp. 238–73.

Halliday, J. L. (1941) 'The concept of psychosomatic medicine', *Annals of Internal Medicine*, 15: 666–77.

Halmi, K. A. (2000) 'Eating Disorders', in *Comprehensive Textbook of Psychiatry*, 7th edn, ed. B. J. Sadock and V. A. Sadock (Philadelphia: Lippincott, Williams and Wilkins), pp. 1663–76.

Hamilton, M., Pickering, G. W., Roberts, J. A. F. and Sowry, G. S. C. (1954) 'The etiology of essential hypertension', *Clinical Science and Molecular Medicine*, **13**: 273.

Harris, E. C. and Barraclough, B. (1998) 'Excess mortality in mental disorder', *British Journal of Psychiatry*, **173**: 11–53.

Harburg, E., Blakelock, E. and Roeper, P. (1979) 'Resentful and reflective coping with arbitrary authority and blood pressure', *Psychosomatic Medicine*, **41**: 189–202.

Harvey, W. (1976) *An Anatomical Disputation Concerning the Movement of the Heart and Blood in Living Creatures*, trans. G. Whitteridge (Oxford: Blackwell Scientific).

Hayman, R. (1990) *Proust* (London: Minerva).

Heinroth, J. C. A. (1818) *Lehrbuch der Storingen des Seelenlebens oder der Seelenstorungen und ihrer Behandlung* (Leipzig: F. C. W. Vogel), Part 2.

Henderson, J. G. (1966) 'Denial and repression as factors in the delay of patients with cancer presenting themselves to the physicians', *New York Academy of Sciences Annals*, **125**: 856–64.

Hickie, I., Lloyd, A., Hadzi-Pavlovic, D., Parker, G., Bird, K. and Wakefield, D. (1995) 'Can the chronic fatigue syndrome be defined by distinct clinical features?', *Psychological Medicine*, **25**: 925–35.

Hinkle, L. E. and Wolf, S. (1952) 'A summary of experimental evidence relating life stress to diabetes mellitus', *Mount Sinai Journal of Medicine*, **19**: 537–70.

Hinkle, L. E. and Wolff, H. G. (1958) 'Ecologic investigations of the relationship between illness, life experiences and the social environment', *Annals of Internal Medicine*, **49**: 1373–88.

Hinrichsen, H., Barth, J., Ferstl, R. et al. (1989) 'Changes of immunoregulatory cells induced by acoustic stress in patients with systemic lupus erythematosus, sarcoidosis and in healthy controls', *European Journal of Clinical Investigation*, **19**: 372–77.

Hippocrates (1839) *Oeuvres* (ed. E. Littré) vol. 4, pp. 575, 611, 641. (Paris: Baillieàre Oeuvree Complètes d'Hippocrate).

Hobson, R. (1985) *Forms of Feeling* (London: Tavistock).

Hofer, M. A. (1996) 'On the nature and consequences of early loss', *Psychosomatic Medicine*', **58**: 570–81.

Hogan, C. C. (1995) *Psychosomatics, Psychoanalysis, and Inflammatory Disease of the Colon* (Madison: International Universities Press).

Hollifield, M. A. (2005) 'Somatoform disorders', in *Comprehensive Textbook of Psychiatry*, 8th edn, ed. B. J. Sadock and V. A. Sadock (Philadelphia: Lippincott Williams and Wilkins), pp. 1800–28.

Holmes, G. P., Kaplan, J. E., Schonberger, L. B., Straus, S. E., Zegans, L. S., Gantz, N. M., Brus, I., Komaroff, A., Jones, J. F., Dubois, R. E., Cunningham-Rundles, C., Tosato, G., Brown, N. A., Pahwa, S. and Schooley, R. T. (1988) 'Definition of the chronic fatigue syndrome', *Annals of Internal Medicine*, **109**: 512.

Holmes, T. H. and Rahe, R. H. (1967) 'The social adjustment rating scale', *Journal of Psychosomatic Research*, **11**: 213–18.

Hunter, R. C. A. (1979) 'Psychoanalysis, somatization and psychosomatic disease', *Canadian Journal of Psychiatry*, **24**: 383–90.

Jamison, K. R., Wellisch, D. K. and Pasnau, R. O. (1978) 'Psychosocial aspects of mastectomy I: The woman's perspective', *American Journal of Psychiatry*, **135**: 432–6.

Janet, P. (1903) *Les Obsessions et la Psychaesthenie* (Paris: Felix Alcan).

Jessner, L., Lamont, J., Long, R., Rollins, N., Whipple, B. and Prentice, N. (1955) 'Emotional impact of nearness and separation for the asthmatic child and his mother', *The Psychoanalytic Study of the Child*, **10**: 353–75.

Jessup, B. A., Neufeld, R. W. J. and Merskey, H. (1979) 'Biofeedback therapy for headache and other pain: An evaluative review', *Pain*, **7**: 225–70.

Jones, J., Bennett, S., Olmsted, M. P., Lawson, M. L. and Rodin, G. (2001) 'Disordered eating attitudes and behaviours in teenage girls: a school based study', *Canadian Medical Association Journal*, **165**(5): 547–52.

Kafka, F. (1919) 'A country doctor', in *The Dedalus Book of Austrian Fantasy, 1890–2003*, ed. and trans. M. Mitchell (Sawtry, Cambs: Dedalus), pp. 145–52.

Karasek, R., Baker, D., Marxer, F., Ahlbom, A. and Theorell, T. (1981) 'Job decision latitude, job demands and cardiovascular disease: a prospective study of Swedish men', *American Journal of Public Health*, **71**: 694–705.

Karush, A., Daniels, G. E., Flood, C. and O'Connor, J. F. (1977) *Psychotherapy in Chronic Ulcerative Colitis* (Philadelphia: Saunders).

Katon, W., Lin, E., Von Korff, M., Russo, J., Lipscomb, P. and Bush, T. (1991) 'Somatization: a spectrum of severity', *American Journal of Psychiatry*, **148**: 34–40.

Kellner, R. (1985) 'Functional somatic symptoms and hypochondriasis: A survey of empirical studies', *Archives of General Psychiatry*, **42**: 821–33.

Kellner, R. (1986) *Hypochondriasis and Somatization* (New York: Praeger).

Kellner, R. (1987) 'Hypochondriasis and somatization', *Journal of the American Medical Association*, **258**: 2718–22.

Kellner, R. (1990) 'Somatization: theories and research', *Journal of Nervous and Mental Disease*, **178**: 150–60.

Kennedy, T., Jones, R., Darnley, S., Seed, P, Wessely, S., and Chalder, T. (2005) 'Cognitive behaviour therapy in addition to antispasmodic treatment for irritable bowel syndrome in primary care: randomised controlled trial', *British Medical Journal*, **331**: 435–8.

Kirmayer, L. J., Groleau, D., Looper, K. J. and Dominice, M. (2004) 'Explaining medically unexplained symptoms', *The Canadian Journal of Psychiatry*, **49**: 663–72.

Kirsner, H. B. and Shorter, R. G. (1982) 'Recent developments in "nonspecific" bowel diseases', *New England Journal of Medicine*, **306**: 775–8, 837–98.

Kleiger, J. H. and Jones, N. F. (1980) 'Characteristics of alexithymic patients in chronic respiratory illness population', *Journal of Nervous and Mental Diseases*, **168**(8): 465–70.

Klock, S. (1998) 'Obstetric and Gynecological Conditions', in *Clinical Handbook of Health Psychology*, ed. P. Camic, S. Knight (Seattle: Hogrefe and Huber), pp. 349–88.

Knapp, P. H. (1989) 'Psychosomatic Aspects of Bronchial Asthma', in *Psychosomatic Medicine*, vol. 2, ed. S. Cheren (Madison: International Universities Press), pp. 503–64.

Knapp, P. H., Mushatt, C. and Nemetz, S. J. (1970) 'The context of reported asthma during psychoanalysis', *Psychosomatic Medicine*, **32**(2): 167–88.

Knauss, W. and Senf, W. (1983) 'Follow-up results of the Student Psychotherapy Project in Heidelberg', in *First Steps in Psychotherapy*, ed. H. H. Wolff, W. Knauss and W. Brautigam (Berlin: Springer-Verlag), pp. 79–90.

Krystal, H. (1978) 'Trauma and affects', *The Psychoanalytic Study of the Child*, **33**: 81–115.

Krystal, H. (1988) *Integration and Self-healing: Affect, Trauma and Alexithymia* (Hillsdale, New Jersey: Analytic Press).

Krystal, H. (1997) 'Somatization and the consequence of infantile psychic trauma', *Psychoanalytic Inquiry*, **17**: 126–51.

Lake, A. E. III and Saper, J. R. (2002) 'Chronic headache: new advances in treatment strategies', *Neurology*, **59** (suppl. 2): S8–S13.

Lane, D. J. and Storr, A. (1981) *Asthma: The Facts* (Oxford: Oxford University Press).

Laplanche, J. and Pontalis, J.-B. (1973) *The Language of Psycho-Analysis* (London: Hogarth Press).

Lasègue, C. (1964 [1873]) 'De l'anorexie hysterique', *Archives Genérales de Medicine*, ed. R. M. Kaufman and M. Heiman, pp. 141–55.

Laufer, M. and Laufer, E. (1984) *Adolescence and Developmental Breakdown* (New Haven: Yale University Press).

Lawrence, D. H. (1974 [1923]) *Fantasia of the Unconscious and Psychoanalysis and the Unconscious* (London: Penguin Books).

Leboyer (1974) *A Child is Born* (film).

Le Doux, J. (1996) *The Emotional Brain: The Mysterious Underpinnings of Emotional Life* (New York: Simon and Schuster).

Levenstein, S. (1980) 'An undergraduate Balint group in Cape Town', *South African Medical Journal*, **62**(3): 89–90.

Levenstein, S., Prantera, C., Varvo, V., Scribano, M. L., Andreoli, A., Luzi, C., Arcà, M., Berto, E., Milite, G. and Marcheggiano, A. (2000) 'Stress and exacerbation in ulcerative colitis: A prospective study of patients enrolled in remission', *American Journal of Gastroenterology*, **95**: 5, 1213–20.

Leviton, A. (1978) 'Epidemiology of headache', *Advances in Neurology*, **19**: 341–53.

Lewin, J., and Lewis, S. (1995) 'Organic and psychosocial risk factors for duodenal ulcer', *Psychosomatic Research*, **39**: 531–48.

Liebman, R., Minuchin, S. and Baker, L. (1974) 'The use of structural family therapy in the treatment of intractable asthma', *American Journal of Psychiatry*, **131**(5): 535–40.

Lindemann, E. (1950) 'Modifications in the course of ulcerative colitis in relationship to changes in life situations and reaction patterns', *Research Publication of the Association for Research in Nervous and Mental Disease*, **29**: 706–23.

Lipowski, Z. J. (1977) 'Psychosomatic medicine in the seventies: An overview', *American Journal of Psychiatry*, **134**: 233–44.

Lipowski, Z. J., Lipsitt, D. R. and Whybrow, P. C. (ed.) (1977) *Psychosomatic Medicine: Current Trends and Clinical Application* (New York: Oxford University Press).

Lipsitt, D. R. (2001) 'Consultation–liaison psychiatry and psychosomatic medicine: the company they keep', *Psychosomatic Medicine*, **63**: 896–909.

Lipton, R. B., Stewart, W. F. and von Korff, M. (1997) 'Burden of Migraine: societal costs and therapeutic opportunities', *Neurology*, **48**, S4.

Lishman, W. A. (1978) *Organic Psychiatry* (Oxford: Blackwell).

Little, W., Fowler, H. W. and Coulson, J. (1984) *The Shorter Oxford English Dictionary* (Oxford: Clarendon Press).

Loewenstein, R. J. (1990) 'Somatoform disorders in victims of incest and child abuse', in *Incest-related Syndromes of Adult Psychopathology*, ed. R. P. Kluft (Washington, DC: American Psychiatric Press).

Loudon, I. (1986) *Medical Care and the General Practitioner: 1750–1850* (Oxford: Clarendon Press).

Luban-Plozza, B. (1989) 'A new training method: 20 years of student Balint groups', *Schweizerische Rundschau für Medizin – Praxis*, 78: 1192–96.

Luban-Plozza, B., Pöldinger, W. and Kröger, F. (1992) 'Historical introduction', in *Psychosomatic Disorders in General Practice*, 3rd edn (Basel: editiones Roche), pp. 1–24.

Lum, L. C. (1976) 'The syndrome of habitual chronic hyperventilation', in *Modern Trends in Psychosomatic Medicine*, vol. 3, ed. O. W. Hill (London: Butterworths).

Luparello, T. J., Lyons, H. A., Bleecker, E. R. and McFadden, E. R. Jr (1968) 'Influence of suggestion on airway reactivity in asthmatic subjects', *Psychosomatic Medicine*, 30: 819–25.

Mace, C. O. J. (1992) 'Hysterical conversion I: A history', *Britiish Journal of Psychiatry*, 161: 369–78.

Mackenzie, J. N. (1886) 'The production of "rose asthma" by an artificial rose', *American Journal of Medical Science*, 91: 45–58.

Magarey, C. J., Todd, P. B. and Blizard, P. J. (1977) 'Psychosocial factors influencing delay and breast self-examination in women with symptoms of breast cancer', *Social Science and Medicine*, 11: 229–39.

Maharaj, S., Connolly, J., Daneman, D., Olmsted, M. and Rodin, G. (2001) 'An observational study of mother–daughter interactions in young women with diabetes and eating disorders', *Journal of Clinical and Consulting Psychology*, 69: 950–8.

Mai, F. (2004) 'Somatization disorder: A practical review', *The Canadian Journal of Psychiatry*, 49: 652–62.

Mai, F. M. and Merskey, H. (1980) 'Briquet's treatise on hysteria', *Archives of General Psychiatry*, 37: 1401–5.

Maimonides (1963) *Treatise on Asthma*, ed. S. Muntner (Philadelphia: Lippincott).

Manu, P. and Mathews, D. A. (1998) 'Chronic fatigue syndrome', in *Functional Somatic Syndromes*, ed. P. Manu (Cambridge: Cambridge University Press), pp. 8–31.

Margetts, E. L. (1950) 'The early history of the word psycho-somatic', *Canadian Medical Association Journal*, 63: 402–04.

Margo, K., Goldberg, A., Salloway, K. and Thiedke, C. (2004 January) 'Medical student Balint groups: lessons learned from three programs', paper presented at the Society of Teachers of Family Medicine Predoctoral Education Conference, New Orleans, LA.

Marmot, M. and Bartley, M. (2002) 'Social class and coronary heart disease', in *Stress and the Heart*, ed. S. A. Stansfield and M. G. Marmot (London: BMJ Books), pp. 5–19.

Marmot, M. G., Smith, G. D., Stansfield, S. A., Patel, C., North, F., Head, J., White, I., Brunner, E. and Feeney, A. (1991) 'Health inequalities among British civil servants: The Whitehall II Study', *Lancet*, **337**: 1387–93.

Martin, M. J. (1985) 'Muscle-contraction (tension) headache', in *Psychosomatic Illness Review*, ed. W. Dorfman and L. Christofar (New York: Macmillan), pp. 1–10.

Marty, P. and DeBray, R. (1989) 'The current concepts of character disturbance', in *Psychosomatic Medicine: Theory, Physiology and Practice*, vol. I, ed. S. Cheren (Madison: International Universities Press), pp. 159–88.

Marty, P. and de M'Uzan M. (1963) 'La "pensée operatoire"', *Revue Française de Psychoanalyse*, **27** (Suppl.): 1345–56.

Matsushima, Y., Aoyama, N., Fukuda, H., et al. (1999) 'Gastric ulcer formation after the Hanshin-Awaji earthquake: a case study of *Helicobacter pylori* infection and stress-induced gastric ulcers', *Helicobacter*, **4**: 94–9.

Maudsley, H. (1868) *The Physiology and Pathology of the Mind*, 2nd edn (London: Macmillan).

Maunder, R. (2000) 'Mediators of stress effects in inflammatory bowel disease: Not the usual suspects', *Journal of Psychosomatic Research*, **48**: 569–77.

McDougall, J. (1989) *Theatres of the Body*. London: Free Association Books.

McDougall, J. (1980) 'A child is being beaten', *Contemporary Psychoanalysis*, **16**: 417–59.

Mehlman, R. D. and Griesemer, R. D. (1968) 'Alopecia areata in the very young', *American Journal of Psychiatry*, **125**: 605–14.

Mei-Tal, V., Meyerowitz, S. and Engel, G. L. (1970) 'The role of psychological process in a somatic disorder: multiple sclerosis – I: The emotional setting of illness onset and exacerbation', *Psychosomatic Medicine*, **32**: 67–86.

Melzack, R. and Wall, P. D. (1996) *The Challenge of Pain* (London: Penguin Books).

Meng, H. (1934) 'Das problem der organ psychose', *Internatzional Zeitschrift für Psychoanalyse*, **20**: 439–58.

Miller, T. W. (1989) *Stressful Life Events* (Madison: International Universities Press).

Mintz, I. L. (1989) 'Treatment of a case of anorexia and severe asthma', in *Psychosomatic Symptoms: Psychodynamic Treatment of the Underlying Personality Disorder*, ed. C. P. Wilson and I. L. Mintz (Northvale, NJ: Jason Aronson), pp. 251–307.

Minuchin, S., Baker, L. Rosman, B. L., Liebman R., Milman, L. and Told, T. C. (1975) 'A conceptual model of psychosomatic illness in children', *Archives of General Psychiatry*, **32**: 1031–8.

Mirsky, I. A. (1958) 'Physiologic, psychologic and social determinants of psychosomatic disorders in the etiology of duodenal ulcers', *American Journal of Digestive Diseases*, 3: 285.

Moldofsky, H., Scarisbrick, P., England, R. and Smythe, H. (1975) 'Musculoskeletal symptoms and non-REM sleep disturbance in patients with "fibrositis syndrome" and healthy subjects', *Psychosomatic Medicine*, 37: 160–72.

Morgagni, G. B. (1761) *De sedibus et causis morborum (On the Sites and Causes of Disease)* (Venetis Remondiniaria).

Morris, T. (1980) 'A "type" for cancer? Low trait anxiety in pathogenesis of breast cancer', *Cancer Detection and Prevention*, 3: 102.

Morrison, J. (1989) 'Childhood sexual histories of women with somatization disorder', *American Journal of Psychiatry*, 146: 239–41.

Morselli, E. (1886) 'Sulla dismorphophobia e sulla tafephobia (On dysmorphophobia and phobias)', *Bolletino della Accedemia di Genova*, VI: 110–19.

Murray, C. D. (1930a) 'Psychogenic factors in the etiology of coliti and bloody diarrhoea', *American Journal of Medical Science*, 180: 239–48.

Murray, C. D. (1930b) 'A brief psychological analysis of a patient with ulcerative colitis', *Journal of Nervous and Mental Diseases*, 72: 617–27.

Musaph, H. (1964) *Itching and Scratching: Psychodynamics in Dermatology* (Philadelphia: Davis).

Mushatt, C. (1954) 'Psychological aspects of non-specific ulcerative colitis', in *Recent Developments in Psychosomatic Medicine*, ed. E. D. Wittkower and B. A. Cleghorn (Philadelphia: Lippincott), pp. 345–63.

Mushatt, C. (1975) 'Mind–body environment: Toward understanding the impact of loss on psyche and soma', *Psychoanalytic Quarterly* 44: 81–106.

Mushatt, R. C. (1992) 'Anorexia nervosa as an expression of ego-defective development', in *Psychodynamic Techniques in the Treatment of Eating Disorders*, ed. C. P. Wilson (New York: Jason Aronson), pp. 301–11.

M'Uzan de, M. and Bonfils, S. (1961) 'Analyse et classification des aspects psychosomatique de l'ulcère gastroduodenale en milieu hospitalier', *Revue Française Clin. Biol.*, 6: 46–57.

Nemiah, J. C. and Sifneos, P. E. (1970) 'Affect and fantasy in patients with psychosomatic disorders', in *Modern Trends in Psychosomatic Medicine*, vol. 2, ed. O. Hill (London: Butterworths), pp. 26–34.

Nemiah, J. C. (1973) 'Psychology and psychosomatic illness: Reflections on psychosomatic theory and research methodology', *Psychotherapy and Psychosomatics*, 22: 106–11.

Nemiah, J. C. (1987) Foreword, *Psychosomatic Medicine and Contemporary Psychoanalysis*, ed. G. J. Taylor (Madison: International Universities Press), pp. xi–xiii.

Nemiah, J. C. (1991) 'Dissociation, conversion and somatization', in *American Psychiatric Press Review of Psychiatry*, vol. 10, ed. A. Tasman and S. M. Goldfinger (Washington, DC: American Psychiatric Press), pp. 248–60.

Nemiah, J. (1967) 'Conversion reaction', in *Comprehensive Textbook of Psychiatry*, 2nd edn, ed. A. M. Freedman, H. I. Kaplan and H. S. Kaplan (Baltimore: Williams and Wilkins), pp. 870–85.

North, C. S., Alpers, D. H., Helzer, J. E., Spitznagel, E. L. and Clouse, R. E. (1991) 'Do life events or depression exacerbate inflammatory bowel disease? A prospective study', *Annals of Internal Medicine*, **114**: 381–86.

Olmsted, M., Daneman, D., Rydall, A. C., Lawson, M. and Rodin, G. (2002) 'The effects of psychoeducation on disturbed eating attitudes and behaviour in young women with Type 1 diabetes mellitus', *International Journal of Eating Disorders*, **32**: 230–9.

Orbach, S. (1985) 'Accepting the symptom: A feminist psychoanalytic treatment of anorexia nervosa', in *Handbook of Psychotherapy for Anorexia Nervosa and Bulimia*, ed. D. M. Garner and P. E. Garfinkel (New York: Guilford Press), pp. 83–104.

Orgel, S. (1958) 'Effects of psychoanalysis on the course of peptic ulcer', *Psychosomatic Medicine*, **20**: 117–25.

Osler, W. (1910) 'The Lumleian Lectures on angina pectoris', *Lancet*, Lecture I: pp. 697–702. Lecture II: pp. 839–44.

Palazolli, M. S. (1978) *Self-starvation: From Individual to Family Therapy in the Treatment of Anorexia Nervosa* (New York: Jason Aronson).

Palmer, H. (1945) 'Military psychiatric casualties – experience with 12,000 cases', *The Lancet*, 13 October: 45–7.

Paré, A. (1628) *Les oevres de Ambroise Paré*, 8th edn (Paris: J.-B. Baillère, 1840–41).

Parsonnet, J. (1995) 'The incidence of *Helicobacter pylori* infection', *Aliment. Pharmacol. Ther.* **9** (suppl 2): 45–51.

Pascal (1962) *Pensées IV* (Livre de Vie: Éditions du Seuil).

Paull, A. and Hislop, I. G. (1974) 'Etiologic factors in ulcerative colitis: Birth, death and symbolic equivalents', *International Journal of Psychiatric Medicine*, **5**: 57–64.

Paulley, J. W. and Haskell, D. A. L. (1975) 'The treatment of migraine without drugs', *Journal of Psychosomatic Research*, **19**: 367–74.

Pearce, S. (1983) 'A review of cognitive-behavioural methods for the treatment of chronic pain', *Journal of Psychosomatic Research*, **27**: 431–40.

Pickering, G. W. (1955) *High Blood Pressure* (London: Churchill).

Pilowsky, I. (1970) 'Primary and Secondary Hypochondriasis', *Acta Psychiatrica Scandinavica*, 46: 273–85.

Pilowsky, I. and Barrow, C. G. (1990) 'A controlled study of psychotherapy and amitryptiline used individually and in combination in the treatment of chronic intractable "psychogenic" pain', *Pain*, 40: 3–19.

Pilowsky, I., Spalding, D., Shaw, J. and Korner, P. I. (1973) 'Hypertension and personality', *Psychosomatic Medicine*, 35: 50–6.

Pines, D. (1980) 'Skin communication', *International Journal of Psycho-Analysis*, 61: 312–22.

Pines, D. (1993) 'The menopause', in *A Woman's Unconscious Use of Her Body* (London: Virago), pp. 151–66.

Plato (1919) '*Charmenides*', in *Dialogs*, ed. C. F. Hermann, vol. 9, Lipsiae.

Pollak, K. (1963) *The Healers* (London: Nelson).

Pontalis, J.-B. (1981) 'Between Freud and Charcot: From one scene to the other', in *Frontiers in Psychoanalysis* (London: Hogarth Press), pp. 17–22.

Porter, R. (1997) *The Greatest Benefit to Mankind* (London: Harper Collins).

Purcell, K., Brady, K., Chai, H., Muser, J., Molk, L., Gordon, N. and Means, J. (1969) 'The effect on asthma in children of experimental separation from the family', *Psychosomatic Medicine*, 31: 144–64.

Rangell, L. (1959) 'The nature of conversion', *Journal of the American Psychoanalytic Association*, 7: 632–62.

Rapkin, A. J., Kames, L. O., Darke, L. L., Stampler, F. M. and Naliboff, B. D. (1990) 'History of physical and sexual abuse in women with chronic pain', *Obstetrics and Gynecology*, 76: 92–6.

Raskin, N. H. (1985) 'Migraine', in *Psychosomatic Illness Review*, ed. W. Dorfman and L. Christofar (New York: Macmillan), pp. 11–22.

Rayner, E., Joyce, A., Rose, J., Twyman, M. and Clulow, C. (2005) *Human Development* (Hove: Routledge).

Reiser, M. F. (1975) 'Changing theoretical concepts in psychosomatic medicine', in *American Handbook of Psychiatry*, 2nd edn, vol. 4, ed. S. Arieti (New York: Basic Books).

Reiser, M. F. (1978) 'Psychoanalysis in patients with psychosomatic disorders', in *Psychotherapeutics in Medicine*, ed. T. B. Karasu and R. I. Steinmuller (New York: Grune and Stratton).

Ridsdale, L., Godfrey, E., Chalder, T., Seed, T., King, M., Wallace, T. and Wessely, S. (2001) 'Chronic fatigue syndrome in general practice: Is counselling as good as cognitive behaviour therapy? A UK randomised trial', *British Journal of General Practice*, 51: 19–24.

Rimón, R. H. (1969) 'Psychosomatic approach to rheumatoid arthritis', *Acta Rheumatologica Scandinavica*, **13**: (Suppl.) 1–154.

Rimón, R. (1974) 'Depression in rheumatoid arthritis', *Annals of Clinical Research*, **6**: 171.

Rimón, R. H. (1989) 'Connective tissue diseases', in *Psychosomatic Medicine*, vol. 2, ed. S. Cheren (Madison: International Universities Press), pp. 565–609.

Rimón, R. and Laakso, R.-L. (1984) 'Overt psychopathology in rheumatoid arthritis: a fifteen-year follow-up study', *Scandinavian Journal of Rheumatology*, **13**: 324–8.

Ritvo, S. (1984) 'The image and uses of the body in psychic conflict: With special reference to eating disorders in adolescence', in *The Psychoanalytic Study of the Child*, **39**: 449–70.

Robertson, J. and Bowlby, J. (1952) 'Observations of the sequence of response of children aged 18–24 months during the course of separation', *Courier*, **2**: 131–42.

Rodin, G. (1991) 'Somatization: a perspective from self-psychology', *Journal of the American Academy of Psychoanalysis*, **19**: 367–84.

Rodin, G. M., Nolan, R. P. and Katz, M. R. (2005) 'Depression', in *The American Psychiatric Publishing Textbook of Psychosomatic Medicine*, ed. J. L. Levensen (Washington, DC: American Psychiatric Publishing), pp. 193–217.

Rosenfeld, H. (1965) 'The psychopathology of hypochondriachal states', in *Psychotic States: A Psychoanalytical Approach* (New York: International Universities Press), pp. 180–99.

Rycroft, C. (1968) *A Critical Dictionary of Psychoanalysis* (London: Nelson).

Rydall, A. C., Rodin, G. M., Olmsted, M. P., Devenyi, R. G. and Daneman, D. (1997) 'Disordered eating behaviour and microvascular complications in young women with insulin-dependent diabetes mellitus', *New England Journal of Medicine*, **336**: 1847–54.

Sacks, O. (1981) *Migraine: The Natural History of a Disorder* (London: Pan Books).

Sapira, J. D., Scheib, E. T., Moriarty, R. and Shapio, A. P. (1971) 'Differences in perception between hypertensive and normotensive populations', *Psychosomatic Medicine*, **33**: 239–50.

Sapolsky, R. (2003) 'Taming stress', in *The Scientific American* (September 2003).

Sargent J., Liebman, R. and Silver, M. (1985) 'Family therapy for anorexia nervosa', in *Handbook of Psychotherapy for Anorexia Nervosa and Bulimia*, ed. D. M. Garner and P. E. Garfinkel (New York: Guilford Press), pp. 257–79.

Saunders, D. C. (1982) 'Principles of symptom control in terminal care', *Medical Clinics of North America*, **66**: 1169–83.

Saxe, G. N., Chinman, G., Berkowitz, R., Hall, K., Lieberg, G., Schwartz, J. and van der Kolk, B. A. (1994) 'Somatization in patients with dissociative disorder', *American Journal of Psychiatry*, 151:1329–34.

Schmale, A. H. (1958) 'Relationship of separation and depression to disease', *Psychosomatic Medicine*, 20: 259–77.

Schneider, D. (1964) *Psychosomatik in der Pariser Klinik von Pinel bis Trousseau* (Zürich: Juris).

Schur, M. (1955) 'Comments on the metapsychology of somatization', in *The Psychoanalytic Study of the Child*, 10: 119–64.

Selye, H. (1936) 'A syndrome produced by diverse nocuous agents', *Nature*, 138: 32.

Sharpe, M., Hawton, K., Simkin, S., Surawy, C., Hacjman, A. Klimes, I., Peto, T., Warrell, D. and Seagroatt, V. (1996) 'Cognitive behaviour therapy for chronic fatigue syndrome: a randomised controlled trial', *British Medical Journal*, 312: 22–6.

Sharpe, M. C. and O'Malley, P. G. (2005) 'Chronic fatigue and fibromyalgia syndromes', in *The American Psychiatric Publishing Textbook of Psychosomatic Medicine*, ed. J. L. Levenson (Washington, DC: American Psychiatric Publishing), pp. 555–75.

Shekelle, R. B., Hulley, S., Neaton, J., Billings, J. H., Nemato, O. Borhani, Gerace, T. A., Jacobs, D. R., Lasser, N. L., Mittlemark, M. B., Stamler, J.: For the Multiple Risk Factor Intervention Trial (1975) 'The MRFIT Behavioural Pattern Study: II. Types A Behaviour and the Incidence of Coronary Heart Disease', *American Journal of Epidemiology*, 122: 559–70.

Shoenberg, P. J. (1975) 'The symptom as stigma or communication in hysteria', *International Journal of Psychoanalytic Psychotherapy*, 4: 507–18.

Shoenberg, P. J. (1990) 'Psychological aspects of ulcerative colitis', in *Ulcerative Colitis*, ed. O'Morain (Boca Raton: CRC Press), pp. 125–9.

Shoenberg, P. (1992) 'The student psychotherapy scheme at University College and Middlesex School of Medicine: its role in helping medical students to learn about the doctor/patient relationship', *The Journal of the Balint Society*, 20: 10–14.

Shoenberg, P. (1999) 'Aspects du probleme de la toute puissance du therapeute', *Bulletin de la Societé Française de Psycho-Oncologie*, 21: 8–9.

Shoenberg, P. J. (2001) 'Winnicott and the Psyche-Soma', in *Squiggles and Spaces*, vol. 2, ed. M. Bertolini, A. Giannakoulas and M. Hernandez in collaboration with A. Molino (London: Whurr), pp. 147–54.

Shoenberg, P. J. (2002) 'Psychosomatic incidents in psychotherapy', in *Dilemmas in the Consulting Room*, ed. H. Alfillé and J. Cooper (London: Karnac), pp. 101–16.

Sicuteri, F., Anselmi, B. and Fanciullacci, M. (1974) 'The serotonin theory of migraine', in *Advances in Neurology*, vol. 4, ed. J. J. Bonica (New York: Raven Press), pp. 383–94.

Siegrist, J. (1996) 'Adverse health effects of high-effort/low-reward conditions', *Journal of Occupational Health Psychology*, 1: 27–41.

Sikora, K. (1994) 'Foreword', *An Introduction to Psycho-Oncology* (London: Routledge).

Simpson, F. O. (1979) 'Principles of drug treatment for hypertension: Indication for treatment and for selection of drugs', *Pharmacology and Therapeutics*, 7: 153–72.

Smadja, C. (2005) *The Psychosomatic Paradox*, trans. A. M. Brewer (London: Free Association Books).

Smith, G. R., Monson, R. A. and Ray, D. C. (1986) 'Patients with multiple unexplained symptoms: Their characteristics, functional health, and health care utilisation', *Archives of Internal Medicine*, 146: 69–72.

Sneddon, I. B. and Church, R. E. (1971) *Practical Dermatology*, 2nd edn (London: Edward Arnold).

Sours, J. A. (1980) *Starving to Death in a Sea of Objects* (New York: Jason Aronson).

Sperling, M. (1963) 'A psychoanalytic study of bronchial asthma in children', in *The Asthmatic Child*, ed. H. Schneer (New York: Harper and Row).

Sperling, M. (1973) 'Conversion hysteria and conversion symptoms', *Journal of the American Psychoanalytic Association*, 21: 745–71.

Sperling, M. (1978) *Psychosomatic Disorders in Childhood* (New York: Aronson).

Spiegel, D., Bloom, J. R., Kraemer, H. C. and Gottheil, E. (1989) 'Effect of psychosocial treatment on survival of patients with metastatic breast cancer', *Lancet*, 2(8668): 888–91.

Spiegel, D. and Classen, C. (2000) *Group Therapy for Cancer Patients* (New York: Basic Books).

Spitz, R. A. (1945) 'Hospitalism: An inquiry into the genesis of psychiatric conditions in early childhood', *The Psychoanalytic Study of the Child*, 1: 53–74.

Spitz, R. A. (1946) 'Hospitalism: A follow-up report', *The Psychoanalytic Study of the Child*, 2: 113–17.

Sprince, M. (1984) 'Early psychic disturbances in anorexic and bulimic patients as reflected in the analytic process', *Journal of Child Psychotherapy*, 10: 199–216.

Stansfield, S. and Fuhrer, R. (2002) 'Depression and coronary heart disease', in *Stress and the Heart*, ed. S. A. Stansfield and M. G. Marmot (London: BMJ Books), 101–24.

Starobinski, J. (1980) 'Le passé de la passion', *Nouvelle Revue de Psychoanalyse*, **21**: 52–76.

Stein, M., Schleiffer, S. J. and Keller, S. E. (1985) 'Immune disorders', in *Comprehensive Textbook of Psychiatry IV*, vol. 2, ed. H. I. Kaplan and B. J. Sadock (Baltimore: Williams and Wilkins), pp. 1206–12.

Stekel, W. (1925) *Peculiarities of Behaviour*, vols I–II (London: Williams and Norgate).

Stephanos, S. (1989) 'Analytical psychosomatic treatment of inpatients in internal medicine', in *Psychosomatic Medicine*, vol. 2, ed. S. Cheren (Madison: International Universities Press), pp. 899–926.

Stewart, D. E., Reicher, A. E., Gerulath, A. H. and Boychell, K. M. (1994) 'Vulvodynia and psychological distress', *Obstetrics and Gynecology*, **84**: 587–90.

Stewart, D. E. and Stotland, N. L. (1993) *Psychological Aspects of Women's Health Care* (Washington, DC: American Psychiatric Press).

Stockman (1904) 'The causes, pathology and treatment of chronic rheumatism', *Edinburgh Medical Journal*, **15**: 107–16, 223–35.

Stotland, N. L., Stewart, D. E., Munce, S. E. and Rolfe, D. E. (2005) 'Obstetrics and Gynecology', in *The American Psychiatric Publishing Textbook of Psychosomatic Medicine*, ed. J. L. Levenson (Washington, DC: American Psychiatric Publishing), pp. 733–59.

Strang, J. P. (1989) 'Gastrointestinal disorders', in *Psychosomatic Medicine*, vol. 2, ed. S. Cheren (Madison: International Universities Press), pp. 427–501.

Sucheki, D., Nelson, D. Y., Van Oers, H. and Levine, S. (1995) 'Activation and inhibition of the hypothalamic–pituary–adrenal axis of the neonatal rat: Effects of maternal deprivation', *Psychoneuroendocrinology*, **20**: 169–82.

Svedlund, J. (1983) 'Psychotherapy in irritable bowel syndrome: A controlled outcome study', *Acta Psychiatrica Scandinavica*, 67(suppl. 306): 1–86.

Szasz, T. (1962) *The Myth of Mental Illness* (London: Secker and Warburg).

Taerk, G. and Gnam, W. (1994) 'A psychodynamic view of the chronic fatigue syndrome', *General Hospital Psychiatry*, **16**: 319–25.

Tan, A., Zimmermann, C. and Rodin, G. (2005) 'Attachment style and interpersonal processes in palliative care', *Palliative Medicine*, **19**: 143–50.

Taylor, C. B. (1980) 'Behavioural approaches to hypertension', in *Comprehensive Handbook of Behavioural Medicine*, vol. 1, ed. J. L. Ferguson and C. B. Taylor (New York: Spectrum), pp. 55–88.

Taylor, G. J. (1987) *Psychosomatic Medicine and Contemporary Psychoanalysis* (Madison: International Universities Press).

Taylor, G. J. and Bagby, R. M. (1988) 'Measurement of alexithymia', *Psychiatric Clinics of North America*, 11: 351–66.

Taylor, G. J., Bagby, R. M. and Parker, J. D. A. (1992) 'The Revised Toronto Alexithymia Scale: some reliability, validity, and normative data', *Psychotherapy and Psychosomatics*, 57: 34–41.

Taylor, G. J. (1993) 'Clinical application of a dysregulation model of illness and disease: a case of spasmodic torticollis', *International Journal of Psychoanalysis*, 74: 581–95.

Taylor, G. J. (1997) 'Somatoform disorders', in *Disorders of Affect Regulation*, ed. G. J. Taylor, M. R. Bagby and J. D. A. Parker (Cambridge: Cambridge University Press), pp. 114–37.

Taylor, G. J., Bagby, R.M. and Lumet, O. (2000) 'Assessment of alexithymia: Self-report and observer rated measures', in *The Handbook of Emotional Intelligence*, ed. R. Bar-On and J. D. A. Parker (San Francisco: Jossey-Bass), pp. 301–19.

Taylor, G. J (2003) 'Somatization and conversion: distinct or overlapping constructs?' *Journal of the American Academy of Psychoanalysis and Dynamic Psychiatry*, 31(3): 485–506.

Temoshok, L. (1987) 'Personality, coping style, emotion and cancer: Towards an integrative model', *Cancer Surveys*, 6: 545–67.

Temoshok, L. and Dreher, H. (1992) *The Type C Connection: The Behavioral Links to Cancer and Your Health* (New York, NY: Random House).

Thomas, C. B. and Greenstreet, R. L. (1973) 'Psychological characteristics in youth as predictors of five disease states: suicide, mental illness, hypertension, coronary artery disease and tumours', *Johns Hopkins Medical Journal*, 132: 16–43.

Thubron, C. (2000) *In Siberia* (London: Penguin Books).

Tourette, G. Gilles de la (1895) *Traité Clinique et Thérapeutique de l'Hystérie*, 3rd edn (Paris: Plor Nourit).

Trousseau, A. (1861) *Clinique Medicale*, vol. 1 (Paris: Baillière).

Tuke, D. H. (1872) *On the Influence of the Mind on the Body* (London: Churchill).

Tuke, D. H. and Buckhill, J. C. (1858) *Manual of Psychological Medicine* (London: Churchill).

Turner, A. L. (2005) 'Making space for the doctor–patient relationship through Balint training in the first year of medical school', *Proceedings of the 14th International Balint Congress Stockholm*.

Tyrer, P. (1973) 'Relevance of bodily feelings in emotion', *The Lancet*, i: 915–16.

Valko, R. J. (1976) 'Group therapy for patients with hysteria (Briquet's disorder)', *Diseases of the Nervous System*, 484–7.

Verrier, R. L. and Mittleman, M. A. (1996) 'Life-threatening cardio-vascular consequences of anger in patients with coronary artery disease', *Cardiology Clinics*, **14**: 289–307.

Wahl, C. W. (1963) 'Unconscious factors in the psychodynamics of the hypochondriacal patient', *Psychosomatics*, **4**: 9–14.

Waller, J. V., Kaufman, M. R. and Deutsch, F. (1940, 1964) 'Anorexia nervosa: A psychosomatic entity', in *Evolution of Psychosomatic Concepts. Anorexia Nervosa: A Paradigm*, ed. M. B. Kaufman and M. Heiman (New York: International Universities Press), pp. 145–276.

Weaver, S., Clifford, E., Hay, D. et al. (1997) 'Psychosocial adjustment to unsuccessful IVF and GFT treatment', *Patient Education and Counselling*, **31**: 7–18

Weiner, H., Thaler, M., Reiser, M. F. and Mirsky, I. A. (1957) 'Etiology of duodenal ulcer, I: relation of specific psychological characteristics to rate of gastric secretion (serum pepsinogen)', *Psychosomatic Medicine*, **19**: 1–10.

Weiner, H. (1977) *Psychobiology and Human Disease* (New York: Elsevier), pp. 103–217 and 414–94.

Weiner, H. (1982) 'Contributions of psychoanalysis to psychosomatic medicine', *Journal of the American Academy of Psychoanalysis*, **10**: 27–46.

Weiner, H. (1985) 'Respiratory disorders', in *Comprehensive Textbook of Psychiatry/IV*, ed. H. I. Kaplan and B. J. Sadock (Baltimore: Williams and Wilkins).

Weinstock, H. I. (1962) 'Successful treatment of ulcerative colitis by psychoanalysis: A survey of 28 cases with follow up', *Journal of Psychosomatic Research*, **6**: 243–9.

Weiss, E. (1922) 'Psychoanalyse einer fallses von nervosen asthma', *Internatzional Zeitschrift für Psychoanalyse*, **8**: 440–5.

Wessely, S., Butler, D. A. and Chalder, T. (1989) 'Management of chronic (post-viral) fatigue syndrome', *Journal of the Royal College of General Practitioners*, **39**: 26–9.

White, P. D. and Naish, N. A. (2001) 'Graded movement therapy for chronic fatigue syndrome', *Physiotherapy*, **87**/11: 614–16.

Whiting, P., Bagnall, A., Sowden, A. et al. (2001) 'Interventions for the treatment and management of chronic fatigue syndrome: a systematic review', *Journal of the American Medical Association*, **286**: 1360–8.

Wilding, J. (1997) 'Obesity treatment: A clinical review', *British Medical Journal*, **315**: 997–1000.

Wilfley, D. E., Welch, R. R., Stein, R. I. et al. (2002) 'A random-ised comparison of gross cognitive-behavioural therapy and group interpersonal psychotherapy for the treatment of overweight individuals with binge eating disorder', *Archives of General Psychiatry*, 59(8): 713–21.

Williams, D. A., Lewis-Faning, E., Rees, L., Jacobs, J. and Thomas, A. (1958) 'Assessment of the relative importance of the allergic, infective and psychological factors in asthma', *Acta Allergol.* 12: 376–95.

Williams, R. B., Haney, T. L., Lee, K. L., Blumenthal, J. A. and Kong, Y. (1980) 'Type A behaviour, hostility, and coronary atherosclerosis', *Psychosomatic Medicine*, 42: 539–49.

Wilson, C. P. (1992) 'Ego functioning and technique', in *Psychodynamic Technique in the Treatment of Eating Disorders*, ed. C. P. Wilson (New York: Jason Aronson).

Winnicott, D. W. (1975 [1941])) 'The observation of infants in a set situation', in *Through Paediatrics to Psycho-Analysis* (London: Hogarth Press), pp. 52–69.

Winnicott, D. W. (1975 [1945]) 'Primitive emotional development', in *Through Paediatrics to Psychoanalysis* (London: Hogarth Press), pp. 145–57.

Winnicott, D. W. (1975 [1949]) 'The Mind and its Relation to the Psyche-Soma', in *Through Paediatrics to Psychoanalysis* (London: Hogarth Press), pp. 243–55.

Winnicott, D. W. (1965) 'Ego distortion in terms of the true and false self', in *The Maturational Processes and the Facilitating Environment* (London: Hogarth Press), pp. 140–52.

Winnicott, D. W. (1989) 'Fear of breakdown', in *Psycho-Analytic Explorations*, ed. C. Winnicott, R. Shepherd and M. Davis (London: Karnac), pp. 87–96.

Winnicott, D. W. (1989) 'Psycho-somatic illness in its positive and negative aspects', in *Psycho-Analytic Explorations*, ed. C. Winnicott, R. Shepherd and M. Davies (London: Karnac), pp. 103–15.

Winnicott, D. W. (1989) 'Physiotherapy and human relations', in *Psycho-Analytic Explorations*, ed. C. Winnicott, R. Shepherd and M. Davis (London: Karnac), pp. 561–9.

Winnicott, D. W. (1989) 'On the basis for self in the body', in *Psycho-Analytic Explorations*, ed. C. Winnicott, R. Shepherd and M. Davis (Cambridge, Mass.: Harvard University Press), pp. 261–83.

Wittkower, E. D. and Russell B. (1953) *Emotional Factors in Skin Disease* (New York: Hoeber).

Wittkower, E. (1938) 'Ulcerative colitis: personality studies', *British Medical Journal*, 2: 1356–60.

Wolfe, F., Cathey, A., Kleinheksel, S., Amos, S. P., Hoffman, R. G., Young, D. Y. and Hawley, D. J. (1984) 'Psychological status in primary fibrositis and fibrositis associated with rheumatoid arthritis', *Journal of Rheumatology*, 11: 500–6.

Wolfe, F., Ross, K., Anderson, J., Russell, I., and Herbert, L. T. (1995) 'Prevalence and characteristics of fibromyalgia in the general population', *Arthritis and Rheumatism*, 38: 19–28.

Wolff, H. G. (1937) 'Personality features and reactions of subjects with migraine', *Archives of Neurology and Psychiatry*, 37: 895–921.

Wolff, H. G. (1950) 'Life stress and bodily disease: A formulation', in *Life Stress and Bodily Disease*, ed. H. G. Wolff, S. Wolf, Jr. and C. E. Hare (Baltimore: Williams and Wilkins).

Wolff, H. and Shoenberg, P. (1990) 'Psychosomatic aspects of individual disorders', in *UCH Textbook of Psychiatry*, ed. H. Wolff, A. Bateman and D. Sturgeon (London: Duckworth), pp. 440–8.

Wolf, S. and Wolff, M. G. (1947) *Human Gastric Function* (New York: Oxford University Press).

Wordsworth, W. (1936) 'Perfect Woman', in *The Poetical Works of Wordsworth*, ed. T. Hutchinson (Oxford: Oxford University Press).

World Health Organization Programme of Maternal and Child Health and Family Planning Unit (1991) 'Infertility: A tabulation of available data on prevalence of primary and secondary infertility' (WHO/MCM/91.9). Available at: *http://www.who.int.reproductive-health/publications/Abstracts/infertility.html*

Yakeley, J., Shoenberg, P. and Heady, A. (2004) 'Who wants to do psychiatry?', *Psychiatric Bulletin*, 28: 208–12.

Young, M., Benjamin, B. and Wallis, G. (1963) 'The mortality of widowers', *Lancet*, 2: 454–6.

Zalidis, S. (2001) 'Obesity is a multifactorial issue', in *A General Practitioner, his Patients and their Feelings* (London: Free Association Books), pp. 164–74.

Zalidis, S. (2001) 'Breathing and feeling', in *A General Practitioner, his Patients and their Feelings* (London: Free Association Books), pp. 66–87.

Zilboorg, G. (1967) *A History of Medical Psychology* (New York: W. W. Norton).

Zondervan, K., Yudkin, P., Vessey, M. et al. (1999) 'Patterns of diagnosis and referral in women consulting for chronic pelvic pain in UK primary care', *British Journal of Obstetrics and Gynaecology*, 106: 1149–55.

Index

Page numbers in **bold** denote glossary reference